iOS and OS X Network Programming Cookbook

Over 50 recipes to develop network applications in both
the iOS and OS X environment

Jon Hoffman

BIRMINGHAM - MUMBAI

iOS and OS X Network Programming Cookbook

First published: January 2014

Production Reference: 1150114

Published by Packt Publishing Ltd.
Livery Place
35 Livery Street
Birmingham B3 2PB, UK.

ISBN 978-1-84969-808-5

www.packtpub.com

Cover Image by Jarosław Blaminsky (milak6@wp.pl)

Credits

Author
Jon Hoffman

Reviewers
Chady Kassouf
Shahin Katebi
Josh Rufer

Acquisition Editor
Vinay Argekar

Lead Technical Editor
Ritika Dewani

Technical Editors
Pratik More
Shweta Pant
Ritika Singh
Nachiket Vartak

Copy Editors
Dipti Kapadia
Kirti Pai
Shambhavi Pai

Project Coordinator
Joel Goveya

Proofreader
Joanna McMahon

Indexer
Monica Ajmera Mehta

Graphics
Yuvraj Mannari
Abhinash Sahu

Production Coordinator
Adonia Jones

Cover Work
Adonia Jones

About the Author

Jon Hoffman has close to 20 years of experience in the field of Information Technology. Over these 20 years, Jon has worked in the areas of system administration, network administration, network security, development and architecture. Currently, he works as a software engineer at Syn-Tech Systems. He has started a network development blog at `http://network-development.blogspot.com` that will enhance and expand on the material covered in this book.

Over the past five years, he has developed numerous applications for the iOS platform. These include several apps that he has published in the App Store, apps that he has written for third parties, and numerous enterprise applications.

What really drives Jon are the challenges in Information Technology; there is nothing more exhilarating for him than overcoming a challenge. Some of Jon's other interests are watching baseball (Go Sox!) and basketball (Go Celtics!). Jon also really enjoys Taekwondo; he and his eldest daughter Kailey are on pace to get their black belts together in the spring of 2014.

I would like to thank my wonderful wife Kim, without whose support, encouragement, patience, and understanding, this book would have never been written. I would also like to thank my two wonderful daughters Kailey and Kara, who have both been my inspiration and driving force since they were born. To my dog, Buddy, maybe one day I will be the person who he thinks I am.

I would like to give special thanks to all of the wonderful people at Packt Publishing who have helped me along the way.

About the Reviewers

Chady Kassouf is an independent iOS and web development expert. He started programming 21 years ago and hasn't stopped since.

Five years ago, he decided to leave his job as a team leader in one of the leading digital agencies, and started his own business.

His interests outside of computers include arts, music, and fitness. He can be found online at http://chady.net/.

Shahin Katebi is a software architect and developer with 10 years of experience in creating apps for various platforms (Mac, iOS, Windows, and the Web). He works as a mobile solutions consultant with different companies, and also works with some startup teams worldwide. He teaches iOS/Mac OS development, and as a mentor at Startup Weekend events, helps startup teams make their own business. He is the founder and team leader at Seeb Co. (http://seeb.co/), a creative mobile app development organization creating apps for customers around the world.

Josh Rufer attended university and majored in graphic arts. As passionate as he was for his traditional artwork, he found far more enjoyment in the art of human interaction. His first position was as the junior interface designer for a small XP programming group. Without enough work to keep him busy, he quickly outpaced his job title and was promoted to senior user experience engineer. On enhancing his programming skills in Java and C++, he was promoted to the position of junior programmer and again promoted as a senior software engineer.

Always looking for more challenges, he formed a one-man design and software engineering firm called Guy Writes Code. This allowed him to focus his free time on the things that most interested him: designing and development for the iPhone and iPad. He has created several public applications for companies such as Metabahn and Camdilleo Media. He is currently working on iPad-based training and simulation applications, including augmented reality training on the iPad.

When possible, Josh has helped with fact checking and technical editing for books such as *Deploying with JRuby* by *Joe Kutner*.

www.PacktPub.com

Support files, eBooks, discount offers and more

You might want to visit www.PacktPub.com for support files and downloads related to your book.

Did you know that Packt offers eBook versions of every book published, with PDF and ePub files available? You can upgrade to the eBook version at www.PacktPub.com and as a print book customer, you are entitled to a discount on the eBook copy. Get in touch with us at service@packtpub.com for more details.

At www.PacktPub.com, you can also read a collection of free technical articles, sign up for a range of free newsletters and receive exclusive discounts and offers on Packt books and eBooks.

http://PacktLib.PacktPub.com

Do you need instant solutions to your IT questions? PacktLib is Packt's online digital book library. Here, you can access, read and search across Packt's entire library of books.

Why Subscribe?

- ▶ Fully searchable across every book published by Packt
- ▶ Copy and paste, print and bookmark content
- ▶ On demand and accessible via web browser

Free Access for Packt account holders

If you have an account with Packt at www.PacktPub.com, you can use this to access PacktLib today and view nine entirely free books. Simply use your login credentials for immediate access.

Table of Contents

Preface

Darwin forms the core set of components for OS X and iOS, and is compatible with **Single UNIX Specification Version 3** and **POSIX UNIX**. Therefore, OS X and iOS are considered to be Unix operating systems. This means that OS X and iOS use the same basic networking stack that all Unix operating systems use.

Apple has added several frameworks on top of the basic Unix networking stack. This includes frameworks such as CFNetworking and Bonjour, as well as classes such as NSURLConnection. There are also several outstanding third-party frameworks written specifically for OS X and/or iOS.

There are numerous books written to teach network development in a Unix environment. However, it is hard to find books dedicated to teaching network development, specifically in an Apple environment that discusses Apple-specific libraries and frameworks. Using and understanding these frameworks can greatly reduce the time needed to add network components to our applications.

This book will begin by discussing the lower-level frameworks, such as BSD Sockets and CFNetworking. Higher-level frameworks and third-party libraries are based on these frameworks, so understanding how they work is essential for understanding how the higher-level libraries work.

We will then look at two libraries, one to construct and inject network packets, and another to capture incoming packets. These libraries are specific to OS X development. We will then look at Apple's higher-level frameworks followed by two outstanding third-party frameworks.

What this book covers

Chapter 1, BSD Socket Library, shows the reader how they can use the BSD Socket Library in their iOS and OS X applications. While this chapter will show them how to obtain network address information and also how to check the network status, the primary focus will be on creating client/server applications for both iOS and OS X devices. We will be creating server applications for iOS devices. This is a very important chapter for the reader because every other API is directly or indirectly based on the BSD Socket Library.

Chapter 2, Apple Low-level Networking, will show the reader how to obtain network address information but the primary focus will be on creating client/server applications for iOS and OS X devices. CFNetworking is Apple's wrapper around the BSD Socket Library. These APIs are designed for easier usage, to integrate better with run loops, and they contain a number of classes to help implement various protocols without having to know the details of those protocols.

Chapter 3, Using Libnet, shows the reader how to use libnet to retrieve network address information, perform network address resolution, and also to manually construct network packets. The chapter is written specifically for OS X. Libnet is a packet construction library that allows the developer to manually create and send out individual packets.

Chapter 4, Using Libpcap, shows how to use libpcap with an OS X application and will end by building a utility to capture packets. This chapter is written specifically for OS X. Libpcap is a packet-capture library that has been complied for virtually every Unix/Linux distribution, and this includes the OS X environment, but unfortunately it does not include iOS.

Chapter 5, Apple High-level Networking, covers some of Apple's higher-level APIs that can be used for specific purposes. This includes Synchronous and Asynchronous HTTP connections for retrieving XML feeds and also the Bluetooth connectivity between two devices.

Chapter 6, Bonjour, shows the reader how they can implement Bonjour network services in their applications. By the end of the chapter, the reader will be able to implement Bonjour services in their application.

Chapter 7, AFNetworking 2.0 Library, shows the reader how to retrieve and send text as well as data to and from remote servers by using the AFNetworking library. AFNetworking is an amazing network library for iOS and OS X. It is built on top of Apple's foundation framework and is incredibly easy to use.

Chapter 8, MKNetworkKit, shows the reader how to retrieve and send text as well as data to and from remote servers by using the MKNetworkKit library. MKNetworkKit is an awesome networking framework written in Objective-C. The framework is based on blocks and is ARC ready.

What you need for this book

To follow the examples in this book, the reader should have a good understanding of iOS and OS X development techniques, as well as a good understanding of Objective-C and the Xcode development environment. It is also recommended that the reader have at least a basic understanding of TCP networks and how they work.

Readers should have an Apple computer with OS X 10.8 or higher installed. They also need to install Xcode Version 4.3.2 or higher.

Who this book is for

This book is written for both Enterprise and App Store developers who are interested in adding networking components to their applications. The examples in this book, with the exception of *Chapter 2*, *Apple Low-level Networking*, and *Chapter 3*, *Using Libnet*, can be applied to both OS X and iOS developers.

Enterprise developers will find the examples in the book extremely helpful while connecting their applications with the backend servers. Whether these connections are custom socket connections or web APIs, the examples in this book will be invaluable resources to an Enterprise developer.

iOS and OS X App Store developers will find the examples extremely helpful while adding network components to their applications. The examples in this book cover both peer-to-peer and client/server applications.

Conventions

In this book, you will find a number of styles of text that distinguish between different kinds of information. Here are some examples of these styles, and an explanation of their meaning.

Code words in text are shown as follows: "This recipe will introduce `libnet_init()` and `libnet_destroy()` functions."

A block of code is set as follows:

```
libnet_t *lnet;
 u_int32_t target, source;
 u_int16_t id,seq;
 char payload[] = "Hello from libnet";
 char errbuf[LIBNET_ERRBUF_SIZE];
```

When we wish to draw your attention to a particular part of a code block, the relevant lines or items are set in bold:

```
#import <Foundation/Foundation.h>

#define LISTENQ 1024
#define MAXLINE 4096

typedef NS_ENUM(NSUInteger, BSDServerErrorCode) {
    NOERROR,
    SOCKETERROR,
    BINDERROR,
    LISTENERROR,
    ACCEPTINGERROR
};
```

```
@interface BSDSocketServer : NSObject

@property int errorCode, listenfd;

-(id)initOnPort:(int)port;
-(void)echoServerListenWithDescriptor:(int)lfd;
-(void)dataServerListenWithDescriptor:(int)lfd;

@end
```

Any command-line input or output is written as follows:

```
cd ~/Downloads
tar xopf libnet-1.2-rc2.tar
cd libnet-1.2-rc2
```

New terms and important words are shown in bold. Words that you see on the screen, in menus or dialog boxes for example, appear in the text like this: "To run your project as root, from the top menu navigate to **Project | Scheme | Edit Scheme** as shown in the following screenshot:"

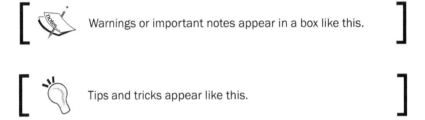

Warnings or important notes appear in a box like this.

Tips and tricks appear like this.

Reader feedback

Feedback from our readers is always welcome. Let us know what you think about this book—what you liked or may have disliked. Reader feedback is important for us to develop titles that you really get the most out of.

To send us general feedback, simply send an e-mail to feedback@packtpub.com, and mention the book title via the subject of your message. If there is a topic that you have expertise in and you are interested in either writing or contributing to a book, see our author guide on www.packtpub.com/authors.

Customer support

Now that you are the proud owner of a Packt book, we have a number of things to help you to get the most from your purchase.

Downloading the example code

You can download the example code files for all Packt books you have purchased from your account at http://www.packtpub.com. If you purchased this book elsewhere, you can visit http://www.packtpub.com/support and register to have the files e-mailed directly to you.

Errata

Although we have taken every care to ensure the accuracy of our content, mistakes do happen. If you find a mistake in one of our books—maybe a mistake in the text or the code—we would be grateful if you would report this to us. By doing so, you can save other readers from frustration and help us improve subsequent versions of this book. If you find any errata, please report them by visiting http://www.packtpub.com/support, selecting your book, clicking on the **errata submission form** link, and entering the details of your errata. Once your errata are verified, your submission will be accepted and the errata will be uploaded to our website, or added to any list of existing errata, under the Errata section of that title.

Piracy

Piracy of copyright material on the Internet is an ongoing problem across all media. At Packt, we take the protection of our copyright and licenses very seriously. If you come across any illegal copies of our works, in any form, on the Internet, please provide us with the location address or website name immediately so that we can pursue a remedy.

Please contact us at copyright@packtpub.com with a link to the suspected pirated material.

We appreciate your help in protecting our authors, and our ability to bring you valuable content.

Questions

You can contact us at questions@packtpub.com if you are having a problem with any aspect of the book, and we will do our best to address it.

1
BSD Socket Library

In this chapter, we will cover:

- ▶ Finding the byte order of your device
- ▶ Retrieving network address information
- ▶ Performing network address resolution
- ▶ Creating an echo server
- ▶ Creating an echo client
- ▶ Creating a data server
- ▶ Creating a data client

Introduction

The **Berkeley Socket API** (where API stands for **Application Programming Interface**) is a set of standard functions used for inter-process network communications. Other socket APIs also exist; however, the Berkeley socket is generally regarded as the standard.

The Berkeley Socket API was originally introduced in 1983 when 4.2 BSD was released. The API has evolved with very few modifications into a part of the **Portable Operating System Interface for Unix** (**POSIX**) specification. All modern operating systems have some implementation of the Berkeley Socket Interface for connecting devices to the Internet. Even Winsock, which is MS Window's socket implementation, closely follows the Berkeley standards.

BSD sockets generally rely on client/server architecture when they establish their connections. Client/server architecture is a networking approach where a device is assigned one of the two following roles:

- ▶ **Server**: A server is a device that selectively shares resources with other devices on the network

▶ **Client**: A client is a device that connects to a server to make use of the shared resources

Great examples of the client/server architecture are web pages. When you open a web page in your favorite browser, for example `https://www.packtpub.com`, your browser (and therefore your computer) becomes the client and Packt Publishing's web servers become the servers.

One very important concept to keep in mind is that any device can be a server, a client, or both. For example, you may be visiting the Packt Publishing website, which makes you a client, and at the same time you have file sharing enabled, which also makes your device a server.

The Socket API generally uses one of the following two core protocols:

▶ **Transmission Control Protocol (TCP)**: TCP provides a reliable, ordered, and error-checked delivery of a stream of data between two devices on the same network. TCP is generally used when you need to ensure that all packets are correctly received and are in the correct order (for example, web pages).

▶ **User Datagram Protocol** (**UDP**): UDP does not provide any of the error-checking or reliability features of TCP, but offers much less overhead. UDP is generally used when providing information to the client quickly is more important than missing packets (for example, a streaming video).

Darwin, which is an open source POSIX compliant operating system, forms the core set of components upon which Mac OS X and iOS are based. This means that both OS X and iOS contain the BSD Socket Library.

> The last paragraph is very important to understand when you begin thinking about creating network applications for the iOS platform, because almost any code example that uses the BSD Socket Library will work on the iOS platform. The biggest difference between using the BSD Socket API on any standard Unix platform and the iOS platform is that the iOS platform does not support forking of processes. You will need to use multiple threads rather than multiple processes.

The BSD Socket API can be used to build both client and server applications; in this chapter, we will be building both types of applications. In the downloadable code, you will find server/client applications for both the iOS and OS X platforms. Before we begin with our recipes, there are a few networking concepts that you should understand:

▶ **IP address**: Any device on an **Internet Protocol** (**IP**) network, whether it is a client or server, has a unique identifier known as an IP address. The IP address serves two basic purposes: host identification and location identification.

There are currently two IP address formats:

- ❑ **IPv4**: This is currently the standard for the Internet and most internal intranets. This is an example of an IPv4 address: `83.166.169.231`.

- ❑ **IPv6**: This is the latest revision of the Internet Protocol (IP). It was developed to eventually replace IPv4 and to address the long-anticipated problem of running out of IPv4 addresses. This is an example of an IPv6 address: `2001:0db8:0000:0000:0000:ff00:0042:8329`. An IPv6 can be shortened by replacing all the consecutive zero fields with two colons. The previous address could be rewritten as `2001:0db8::ff00:0042:8329`.

▸ **Ports**: A port is an application or process-specific software construct serving as a communications endpoint on a device connected to an IP network, where the IP address identifies the device to connect to, and the port number identifies the application to connect to.

The best way to think of network addressing is to think about how you mail a letter. For a letter to reach its destination, you must put the complete address on the envelope. For example, if you were going to send a letter to friend who lived at the following address:

Your Friend

123 Main St

Apt. 223

San Francisco CA, 94123

If I were to translate that into network addressing, the IP address would be equal to the street address, city, state, and zip code (123 Main St, San Francisco CA, 94123), and the apartment number would be equal to the port number (`223`). So the IP address gets you to the exact location, and the port number will tell you which door to knock on.

A device has 65,536 available ports with the first 1024 being reserved for common protocols such as HTTP, HTTPS, SSH, and SMTP.

▸ **Fully Qualified Domain Name (FQDN)**: As humans, we are not very good at remembering numbers; for example, if your friend tells you that he found a really excellent website for books and the address was `83.166.169.231`, you probably would not remember that two minutes from now. However, if he tells you that the address was `www.packtpub.com`, you would probably remember it. FQDN is the name that can be used to refer to a device on an IP network.

So now you may be asking yourself, how does the name get translated to the IP address? The **Domain Name Server** (**DNS**) would do that.

▶ **Domain Name System Servers**: A Domain Name System Server translates a fully qualified domain name to an IP address. When you use an FQDN of `www.packtpub.com`, your computer must get the IP address of the device from the DNS configured in your system. To find out what the primary DNS is for your machine, open a terminal window and type the following command:

```
cat /etc/resolv.conf
```

▶ **Byte order**: As humans, when we look at a number, we put the most significant number first and the least significant number last; for example, in number 123, 1 represents 100, so it is the most significant number, while 3 is the least significant number. For computers, the byte order refers to the order in which data (not only integers) is stored into memory. Some computers store the most significant bytes first (at the lowest byte address), while others store the most significant bytes last.

If a device stores the most significant bytes first, it is known as big-endian, while a device that stores the most significant bytes last is known as little-endian.

The order of how data is stored in memory is of great importance when developing network applications, where you may have two devices that use different byte-ordering communication. You will need to account for this by using the Network-to-Host and Host-to-Network functions to convert between the byte order of your device and the byte order of the network.

> The byte order of the device is commonly referred to as the host byte order, and the byte order of the network is commonly referred to as the network byte order.

The discussion on byte order does lead us directly to the first recipe of this chapter, *Finding the byte order of your device*.

Finding the byte order of your device

In the *Introduction* section of this chapter, one of the concepts that was briefly discussed was how devices store information in memory (byte order). After that discussion, you may be wondering what the byte order of your device is.

> The byte order of a device depends on the Microprocessor architecture being used by the device. You can pretty easily go on to the Internet and search for "Mac OS X i386 byte order" and find out what the byte order is, but where is the fun in that? We are developers, so let's see if we can figure it out with code.

We can determine the byte order of our devices with a few lines of C code; however, like most of the code in this book, we will put the C code within an Objective-C wrapper to make it easy to port to your projects. The downloadable code for this chapter contains the Objective-C classes within an application to test your system.

Getting ready

This recipe is compatible with both iOS and OS X. No extra frameworks or libraries are required.

How to do it...

Let's get started by defining an ENUM in our header file:

1. We create an ENUM that will be used to identify the byte order of the system as shown in the following code:

```
typedef NS_ENUM(NSUInteger, EndianType) {
    ENDIAN_UNKNOWN,
    ENDIAN_LITTLE,
    ENDIAN_BIG
};
```

2. To determine the byte order of the device, we will use the byteOrder method as shown in the following code:

```
-( EndianType)byteOrder {
    union {
        short sNum;
        char cNum[sizeof(short)];
    } un;
    un.sNum = 0x0102;
    if (sizeof(short) == 2) {
        if(un.cNum[0] == 1 && un.cNum[1] == 2)
            return ENDIAN_BIG;
        else if (un.cNum[0] == 2 && un.cNum[1] == 1)
            return ENDIAN_LITTLE;
        else
            return ENDIAN_UNKNOWN;
    } else
        return ENDIAN_UNKNOWN;
}
```

Downloading the example code

You can download the example code files for all Packt Publishing books you have purchased from your account at `http://www.packtpub.com`. If you purchased this book elsewhere, you can visit `http://www.packtpub.com/support` and register to have the files e-mailed directly to you.

How it works...

In the `ByteOrder` header file, we defined an `ENUM` with three constants. The constants are as follows:

- `ENDIAN_UNKNOWN`: We are unable to determine the byte order of the device
- `ENDIAN_LITTLE`: This specifies that the most significant bytes are last (little-endian)
- `ENDIAN_BIG`: This specifies that the most significant bytes are first (big-endian)

The `byteOrder` method determines the byte order of our device and returns an integer that can be translated using the constants defined in the header file. To determine the byte order of our device, we begin by creating a union of `short int` and `char[]`. We then store the value `0x0102` in the union. Finally, we look at the character array to determine the order in which the integer was stored in the character array. If the number one was stored first, it means that the device uses big-endian; if the number two was stored first, it means that the device uses little-endian.

The downloadable code contains projects for both the Mac OS X and iOS devices, so you can see how to use this class and also test the byte order of your devices.

Retrieving network address information

Many programs will need to know the network information about the available interfaces on the device they are running on. This recipe will show you how to retrieve the network information for all the active network interfaces on your device. The information that we will be retrieving is the interface name, IP version, IP address, netmask, and default gateway.

We will start off by creating a `NetworkAddressStore` class that can be used to store the information for a given network interface. We will then get a list of active network interfaces and create an instance of the `NetworkAddressStore` class for each interface. These objects will then be stored in `NSMutableArray`.

This recipe will also introduce several new functions and two new structures, including the very important `sockaddr` family of structures. We will discuss these new functions and structures as we describe the code.

Getting ready

This recipe is compatible with both iOS and OS X. No extra frameworks or libraries are required.

How to do it...

Let's retrieve the network address information for our device as follows:

1. To retrieve the network address information, we will use the `getifaddrs()` function. This function will store a reference to a linked list of `ifaddrs` structures. Each `ifaddrs` structure will represent a physical or virtual network interface. The `getifaddrs()` function will return 0 if it was successful, or -1 if there was a problem.

   The `getifaddrs(struct ifaddrs **ifad)` function is not a part of the POSIX standard, but it is a part of most BSD systems; therefore, it is on both OS X and iOS. Refer to the following code:

   ```
   struct ifaddrs *interfaces = NULL;
   int success = 0;
   success = getifaddrs(&interfaces);
   ```

2. Once we have the linked list of `ifaddrs`, we will need to loop through the list and retrieve the information about each network interface as shown in the following code:

   ```
   struct ifaddrs *temp_addr = interfaces;
   for (temp_addr = interfaces; temp_addr != NULL; temp_addr =
     temp_addr->ifa_next) {

           int ipversion;
           NSLog(@"***********************");
           if(temp_addr->ifa_addr->sa_family == AF_INET) {
               NSLog(@"IPv4");
               ipversion = AF_INET;
           } else if(temp_addr->ifa_addr->sa_family == AF_INET6) {
               NSLog(@"IPv6");
               ipversion = AF_INET6;
           } else {
               NSLog(@"Unknown IP version");
               ipversion = 0;
           }
   ```

   The `temp_addr` `ifaddrs` structure is a temporary structure that will be used as we loop through the linked list. We will need to keep a pointer pointing to the first `ifaddrs` structure so we can properly release the structure using the `freeifaddrs()` function when we are done with it.

We then create a `for` loop to loop through our `ifaddrs` linked list.

We check the IP address version being used by checking `sa_family`; if it is IPv4, we set `ipversion` to `AF_INET`; if it is IPv6, we set `ipversion` to `AF_INET6`. We will use this variable later in our `inet_ntop()` functions.

If the IP address version is neither IPv4 nor IPv6, we set `ipversion` to `0`.

3. We need to define three character arrays to hold our network address, netmask, and gateway information for the network interfaces. In the following code snippet, three character arrays are defined:

```
char naddr[INET6_ADDRSTRLEN];
char nmask[INET6_ADDRSTRLEN];
char ngate[INET6_ADDRSTRLEN];
```

We set the size of the array to `INET6_ADDRSTRLEN` because it is larger than `INET_ADDRSTRLEN`, so it will hold either IPv4 or IPv6 addresses. `INET6_ADDRSTRLEN` is defined as `46`, and `INET_ADDRSTRLEN` as `16`.

4. Now we need to show the result, for which we will use the following code:

```
NSLog(@"Name:    %@", [NSString stringWithUTF8String:temp_addr->ifa_name]);
inet_ntop(ipversion,&((struct sockaddr_in *)temp_addr->ifa_addr)->sin_addr,naddr,INET_ADDRSTRLEN);
NSLog(@"Address:    %@", [NSString stringWithUTF8String:naddr]);
if ((struct sockaddr_in6 *)temp_addr->ifa_netmask != NULL) {
    inet_ntop(ipversion,&((struct sockaddr_in *)temp_addr->ifa_netmask)->sin_addr,nmask,INET_ADDRSTRLEN);
    NSLog(@"Netmask:    %@", [NSString stringWithUTF8String:nmask]);
}
if ((struct sockaddr_in6 *)temp_addr->ifa_dstaddr != NULL) {
    inet_ntop(ipversion,&((struct sockaddr_in *)temp_addr->ifa_dstaddr)->sin_addr,ngate,INET_ADDRSTRLEN);
    NSLog(@"Gateway:    ", [NSString stringWithUTF8String:ngate]);
}
}
freeifaddrs(interfaces);
```

The `ifa_name` character array of the `ifaddr` structure contains the name of the interface; therefore, we convert `ifa_name` to `NSString` and log it.

We then use the `inet_ntop` function to populate the `naddr`, `nmask`, and `ngate` character arrays, convert them to `NSStrings`, and log them.

The data returned from the get ifaddrs() function is dynamically allocated and should be released using the freeifaddrs() function when it is no longer needed to avoid any memory leaks.

How it works...

The getifaddrs() function will store a reference to a linked list of ifaddrs structures. The ifaddrs structure looks like the following:

```
struct ifaddrs  {  *ifa_next;      /* Pointer to next struct */
    char              *ifa_name;     /*Interface name */
    u_int              ifa_flags;    /*Interface flags */
    struct sockaddr  *ifa_addr;     /*Interface address */
    struct sockaddr  *ifa_netmask;  /*Interface netmask */
    struct sockaddr  *ifa_dstaddr;  /*P2P interface destination or
Broadcast address */
    void              *ifa_data;     /*Address specific data */
}
```

We use ifa_next in our for loop because it points to the next element in our linked list. If ifa_next equals NULL, we have reached the end of our linked list.

If you look closely, you will notice that the ifaddrs structure contains three sockaddr structures. The sockaddr structure is a generic structure that pointers are cast to. The sockaddr structure looks like the following code snippet:

```
struct sockaddr {
  uint8_t sa_len;
  sa_family_t sa_family;
  char sa_data[14];
}
```

Depending on the value of sa_family, we can cast the sockaddr structure as sockaddr_in (for IPv4 addresses) or sockaddr_in6 (for IPv6 addresses) before retrieving the address information. We use sa_family to determine the IP address version of the structure. The sa_family values contain one of the following listed values:

▶ AF_UNIX: Local to host (pipes)
▶ AF_INET: The IPv4 address family
▶ AF_INET6: The IPv6 address family
▶ AF_NS: Xerox NS protocols
▶ AF_CCITT: CCITT protocols, X.25
▶ AF_HYLINK: NSC Hyperchannel
▶ AF_ISO: ISO protocols

We use ifa_name of the ifaddrs structure to determine the name of the interface.

We used the inet_ntop function to convert the binary representation of the network address that is stored in the sockaddr structure to a character array. If you look at the ntop part of the function name, n stands for network and p stands for the presentation, so you can read the function name as the "inet network to presentation" function. There is a corresponding inet_pton function that converts an ASCII string to binary, which you can think of as inet presentation to network.

The downloadable code contains projects for both the Mac OS X and iOS devices. Sample projects use a NetworkAddressStore class to store the information returned by the getifaddrs() functions. This will make it easier to integrate this recipe with your project.

Performing a network address resolution

Most applications will eventually need to convert host/service names to sockaddr structures and sockaddr structures to host/service names. The BSD Socket Library has two functions to assist with these conversions:

- ▶ Getaddrinfo(): This is a function that will return information about a given host/service name. The results are returned in an addrinfo structure.

- ▶ Getnameinfo(): This is a function that will return the host and service names, given a sockaddr structure.

The getaddrinfo() and getnameinfo() functions make the gethostbyname(), gethostbyaddr(), and getservbyport() functions obsolete. One of the main advantages that the getaddrinfo() and getnameinfo() functions has over the obsolete functions is that they are compatible with both IPv4 and IPv6 addresses.

In this recipe, we will encapsulate getaddrinfo() and getnameinfo() into an Objective-C class. This class will not hide most of the complexity of the two functions; however, it will save you from having to worry about NSString to character array conversions and will also handle the memory management of the addrinfo structures for you.

Getting ready

This recipe is compatible with both iOS and OS X. No extra frameworks or libraries are required.

How to do it...

Let's get started with the AddrInfo class.

Creating the AddrInfo header file

The header file for the `AddrInfo` class looks like the following:

```
#import <Foundation/Foundation.h>

@interface AddrInfo : NSObject

@property (nonatomic, strong) NSString *hostname, *service;
@property (nonatomic) struct addrinfo *results;
@property (nonatomic) struct sockaddr *sa;
@property (nonatomic, readonly) int errorCode;

  -(void)addrWithHostname:(NSString*)lHostname Service:(NSString *)
lService andHints:(struct addrinfo*)lHints;
  -(void)nameWithSockaddr:(struct sockaddr *)saddr;

  -(NSString *)errorString;

@end
```

The `addrinfo` header file defines four properties. The `hostname`, `service`, and `results` properties will contain the results of the address resolution queries, and the `errorCode` property will contain any error code that is returned.

We are also defining three methods in our header file. The `addrWithHostname:Service: andHints:` method, which takes supplied `hostname`, `service`, and `hints` (we will discuss the `hints` structure when we discuss how to use the `AddrInfo` class) and populates the `results` property using the `getaddrinfo()` function. The `nameWithSockaddr:` method, which takes supplied `sockaddr` and populates the `hostname` and `service` properties using the `getnameinfo()` function. If there is an error with either of the methods, the `errorCode` property is set to the returned error code.

The `errorString` method takes the error code from the `errorCode` property and returns a string that tells what the error code is.

Creating the AddrInfo implementation file

To create the `AddrInfo` implementation file, we use the following code:

```
#import "AddrInfo.h"
#import <netdb.h>
#import <netinet/in.h>
#import <netinet6/in6.h>

@implementation AddrInfo
```

```objc
- (instancetype) init {
    self = [super init];
    if (self) {
        [self setVars];
    }
    return self;
}
```

We begin the implementation file by importing the headers that are needed. We also define an `init` constructor for our class that uses the `setVars` method to reset our properties to default values. Let's look at the `addrWithHostname:Service:andHints:` method:

```objc
- (void) addrWithHostname: (NSString*) lHostname Service: (NSString *)
lService andHints: (struct addrinfo*) lHints {

    [self setVars];
    self.hostname = lHostname;
    self.service = lService;

    struct addrinfo *res;

    _errorCode = getaddrinfo([_hostname UTF8String], [_service
UTF8String], lHints, &res);
    self.results = res;


}
```

The `addrWithHostname:Service:andHints:` method will retrieve the addresses for a given hostname. We start off by resetting the properties to default values using the `setVars` method. We then set the `hostname` and `service` properties with the values passed to the method.

Since the `getaddrinfo()` function expects character arrays for `hostname` and `service`, we need to convert our `NSString` values to character arrays. This is done by using the `UTF8String` method of the `NSString` class. We also pass the `addrinfo hints` structure and the address of the `res addrinfo` structure. The results of the `getaddrinfo()` function are put into the `errorCode` property. If the `getaddrinfo()` function call was successful, `errorCode` will be equal to 0.

When the `getaddrinfo()` function returns, the `res` structure contains the results that we use to set the `results` property:

```objc
- (void) nameWithSockaddr: (struct sockaddr *) saddr {

    [self setVars];
    char host[1024];
    char serv[20];
```

```
    _errorCode = getnameinfo(saddr, sizeof saddr, host, sizeof host,
serv, sizeof serv, 0);

    self.hostname = [NSString stringWithUTF8String:host];
    self.service = [NSString stringWithUTF8String:serv];


}
```

The `nameWithSockaddr:` method will retrieve the names associated with a given IP address. We start this method by calling the `setVars` method to initialize the object's properties. We then define the two character arrays that will contain the results of the `getnameinfo()` function call.

The `getnameinfo()` function will take the address information from the `saddr` `sockaddr` structure, perform a lookup for the host/service name, and put the results into the `host` and `serv` character arrays. If the `getnameinfo()` function was successful, it will return `0`, otherwise it will return `-1`.

Finally, we convert the `host` and `serv` character arrays to `NSStrings` and put the values into the `hostname` and `service` properties:

```
-(void)setVars {
    self.hostname = @"";
    self.service = @"";
    self.results = @"";
    _errorCode = 0;
}
```

The `setVars` method simply sets all the method's `NSString` properties to empty strings and the `errorcode` property to `0`. This gives us a well-defined starting point for the method properties to make sure they do not contain stale information. Let's look at the `errorString:` method:

```
-(NSString *)errorString {
    return [NSString stringWithCString:gai_strerror(_errorCode) encodi
ng:NSASCIIStringEncoding];
}
```

The `errorStiring` method uses the `gai_strerror()` function to convert the error code from either the `getnameinfo()` or `getaddrinfo()` function calls to an actual error method that can tell us what went wrong; let's look at the `setResults:` method:

```
-(void)setResults:(struct addrinfo *)lResults {
    freeaddrinfo(self.results);
    _results = lResults;
}
```

We create the `setResults:` method because we need to call the `freeaddrinfo()` function to release the results before setting the new results. This will avoid memory leaks in our application.

Using the AddrInfo class to perform the address/hostname resolution

In the following sample code, we will show how to get the hostname `www.packtpub.com` to list the IP addresses and then convert those IP addresses back to the hostnames:

```
struct addrinfo *res;
struct addrinfo hints;

memset(&hints, 0, sizeof hints);
hints.ai_family = AF_UNSPEC;
hints.ai_socktype = SOCK_STREAM;
```

We begin our address/hostname resolution code by setting up two `addrinfo` structures. The `res` structure will be used as a temporary store when we loop though the linked list of results that are returned to us from the `addrWithHostname:Service:andHints:` method. The `hints` structure will store the hints that we are going to pass to the `addrWithHostname:Service:andHints:` method to let the method know what type of addresses we are looking for.

Whenever you create a new structure that you plan on setting the values for, you should always use the `memset()` function to clear the memory of the structure. This will ensure that there is nothing in the memory that will corrupt the structure.

We set `ai_family` to `AF_UNSPEC` and `ai_socktype` to `SOCK_STREAM`. This tells the `getaddrinfo()` function that we are looking for any IP version (IPv4 or IPv6) but limiting our socket type to socket streams (these settings are used when we want to make a TCP connection). We could set the `ai_family` to `AF_INET4` to limit the results to only IPv4 results, or set it to `AF_INET6` for only IPv6 results. Let's look at how we would initiate the AddrInfo object:

```
AddrInfo *ai = [[AddrInfo alloc] init];
[ai addrWithHostname:@"www.packtpub.com" Service:@"443"
  andHints:&hints];
if (ai.errorCode != 0) {
    NSLog(@"Error in getaddrinfo():  %@",[ai getErrorString]);
    return -1;
}
```

We now initiate our `AddrInfo` object and call the `addrWithHostname:Service:andHints:` method. For our example, we are requesting an address lookup for the `www.packtpub.com` hostname. The service we are requesting is port `443`, which is HTTPS, and we are also supplying our `hints` structure, which specifies the type of addresses we are looking for.

The code then checks to see if we have any errors; if so, it logs them and exits. Depending on what your application does, you will probably want to catch the error and display a message to the user. Let's loop though the addresses and display the results:

```
struct addrinfo *results = ai.results;
for (res = results; res!= NULL; res = res->ai_next) {
    void *addr;
    NSString *ipver = @"";
    char ipstr[INET6_ADDRSTRLEN];

    if (res->ai_family == AF_INET) {
        struct sockaddr_in *ipv4 = (struct sockaddr_in *)res->ai_
addr;
        addr = &(ipv4->sin_addr);
        ipver = @"IPv4";
    } else if (res->ai_family == AF_INET6){
        struct sockaddr_in6 *ipv6 = (struct sockaddr_in6 *)res->ai_
addr;
        addr = &(ipv6->sin6_addr);
        ipver = @"IPv6";
    } else {
        continue;
    }
    inet_ntop(res->ai_family, addr, ipstr,sizeof ipstr);
    NSLog(@"    %@  %s", ipver, ipstr);
    AddrInfo *ai2 = [[AddrInfo alloc] init];
    [ai2 getNameWithSockaddr:res->ai_addr];
    if (ai2.errorCode ==0)
        NSLog(@"--%@ %@",ai2.hostname, ai2.service);
}
freeaddrinfo(results);
```

If there are no errors, we loop though the results. After we initialize the variables, we check to see if the address family is AF_INET (IPv4 address). If so, we create a sockaddr_in structure, retrieve the address from the sin_addr variable, and set ipver to IPv4.

If the address family was not AF_INET, we check to see if the address family is AF_INET6 (IPv6 address). If so, we create a sockaddr_in6 structure, retrieve the address from the sin_addr6 variable, and set ipver to IPv6.

If the address family is neither AF_INET nor AF_INET6, we continue the for loop without logging the address.

The inet_ntop() function converts the address from binary to text form so that we can display it. The NSLog line will display the IP version followed by the IP address.

Now that we have retrieved the IP address, we will need to send it back to the hostname. For this, we take the `sockaddr` from our `results` structure and send it to the `nameWithSockaddr:` method of the `AddrInfo` class. When the `nameWithSockaddr:` method completes, it will populate the `hostname` and `service` properties of the `AddrInfo` object.

Finally, we use the `freeaddrinfo()` function to release the results in order to prevent any memory leaks.

How it works...

In this recipe, we used the `getaddrinfo()` and `getnameinfo()` functions to get the IP address and hostname. These functions are provided as part of the standard POSIX API.

While these functions are black-box functions, there is really nothing magical about them. Internally, these functions call lower-level functions to send our requests to the appropriate DNS server to perform the resolution.

Creating an echo server

In this recipe, we will be creating an echo server that will listen on port `2004`. Once the connection is established, the server will echo the text received back to the client.

As we did in the earlier recipes, we will encapsulate the socket, bind, and listen steps into an Objective-C class, complete with error checking to make it easy for you to add this code to your project.

Getting ready

This recipe is compatible with both iOS and OS X. No extra frameworks or libraries are required.

How to do it....

Let's get started by creating a `BSDSocketServer` class that will greatly simplify the creation of a BSD socket server. While this recipe is focused on setting up an echo server, in the *Creating a data server* recipe of this chapter, you will see that the code can be modified very easily to create other types of servers.

Creating the BSDSocketServer header file

The BSDSocketServer header file looks like the following code:

```
#import <Foundation/Foundation.h>

#define LISTENQ 1024
#define MAXLINE 4096

typedef NS_ENUM(NSUInteger, BSDServerErrorCode) {
    NOERROR,
    SOCKETERROR,
    BINDERROR,
    LISTENERROR,
    ACCEPTINGERROR
};

@interface BSDSocketServer : NSObject

@property (nonatomic) int errorCode, listenfd;
-(id)initOnPort:(int)port;
-(void)echoServerListenWithDescriptor:(int)lfd;

@end
```

The header file of the BSDSocketServer class starts off by defining the LISTENQ constant as 1024. This constant will be the maximum number of pending connections that can be queued up at any given time before the sockets stop accepting new connection requests.

We also define the maximum length of the inbound string for the echo server, which we will set as 4096 characters.

We then define an ENUM with our five error conditions:

- ▶ NOERROR: This determines that no errors occurred while performing the socket, bind, and listen steps
- ▶ SOCKETERROR: This determines that the error occurred while creating the socket
- ▶ BINDERROR: This determines that the error occurred while binding the sockaddr family of structures with the socket
- ▶ LISTENERROR: This determines that the error occurred while preparing to listen on the socket
- ▶ ACCEPTINGERROR: This determines that the error occurred while accepting a connection

The `BSDSocketServer` has two properties. The `errorCode` property will contain the error code if any of the functions fails, while the `listenfd` property will contain the socket descriptor. This descriptor can be used outside the `BSDSocketServer` object to create your server if you want to have your server code outside the `BSDSocketServer` class.

The header defines one constructor called `initWithPort:`, which has one parameter to define the port number to listen on. The header file also defines one method that sets up the echo server once we initialize the server within the `initWithPort:` constructor. As you build your own servers, you will want to add separate methods such as the `echoServerListenWithDescriptor:` method, to handle them while using the `initWithPort:` constructor to initialize the server.

Creating the BSDSocketServer implementation file

Now let's look at the `BSDSocketServer` implementation file. The code for this implementation file is as follows:

```
#import "BSDSocketServer.h"
#import <sys/types.h>
#import <arpa/inet.h>
@implementation BSDSocketServer
```

We begin the implementation file by importing the header files needed to implement our echo server. Let's look at the `initOnPort:` constructor:

```
-(instancetype)initOnPort:(int)port {
    self = [super init];
    if (self) {
        struct sockaddr_in servaddr;

        self.errorCode = NOERRROR;
        if ( (self.listenfd = socket(AF_INET, SOCK_STREAM, 0)) < 0)
            self.errorCode = SOCKETERROR;
        else {
memset(&servaddr, 0, sizeof(servaddr));
servaddr.sin_family = AF_INET;
            servaddr.sin_addr.s_addr = htonl(INADDR_ANY);
            servaddr.sin_port = htons(port);

            if (bind(self.listenfd, (struct sockaddr *)&servaddr,
sizeof(servaddr)) <0) {
                self.errorCode = BINDERROR;
            } else {
```

```
                if ((listen (self.listenfd, LISTENQ)) <0) {
                    self.errorCode = LISTENERROR;
                }
            }
        }
    }
    return self;
}
```

The `BSDSocketSever.m` class has a single constructor called `initWithPort:`. This constructor will take a single parameter named `port` of type `int`. This `port` parameter is the port number that we want our server to bind to. This number can range from 0-65535; however, you will need to have the root access to bind to ports below `1024`, so I recommend you to use port numbers greater than `1024`.

We define a `sockaddr_in` structure (remember, `sockaddr_in` is for IPv4 and `sockaddr_in6` is for IPv6) named `servaddr`. To begin with, we set the `errorCode` variable to `NOERROR`.

To set up a socket, we will need to call the `socket()`, `bind()`, and `listen()` functions. If any of these functions fail, we will want to set the `errorCode` variable and skip the rest of the initialization.

We use the `socket()` function to create our socket using the `AF_INET` (IPv4) and `SOCK_STREAM` (TCP) parameters. If you would like to use IPv6, you would change `AF_INET` to `AF_INET6`. If you would like to use UDP instead of TCP, you would change `SOCK_STREAM` to `SOCK_DGRAM`.

Prior to calling the `bind()` function, we need to set up a `sockaddr` structure that contains the IP version, interface, and port number that we will be binding the socket to. Before populating the `sockaddr` structure with the information, we would want to clear the memory to make sure there is no stale information that may cause our `bind` function to fail. We do this using the `memset()` function.

After we clear the memory of the `sockaddr` structure, we set the values. The `sin_family` address family is set to `AF_INET`, which sets the IP version to IPv4. The `sin_addr.s_addr` address is set using `htonl(INADDR_ANY)` to let the socket bind to any interface on the device. The `sin_port` number is set to the port number using the `htons(port)` function.

The `htonl()` and `htons()` functions convert the byte order of the values passed in from the host byte order to the network byte order, so the values can be properly interpreted when making network calls. If you are unsure what byte order is, you can refer to the *Finding the byte order of your device* recipe of this chapter.

After we have our `sockaddr` structure set, we use it to bind the socket to the address specified in the `servaddr` structure.

If our `bind()` function call is successful, we attempt to listen to the socket for new connections. We set the maximum number of backlog connection attempts to the `LISTENQ` constant, which is defined as `1024`.

After we initiate the `BSDSocketServer` object using the `initOnPort:` constructor, we will have a server that is actively listening for new connections on the port, but now we need to do something when the connection comes in. That is where the `echoServerListenWithDescriptor:` method comes in. The `echoServerListenWithDescriptor:` method will listen for new connections and when one comes in, it will start a new thread to handle the connection, as shown in the following code:

```objc
- (void)echoServerListenWithDescriptor:(int)lfd {
    int connfd;
    socklen_t clilen;
    struct sockaddr_in cliaddr;
    char buf[MAXLINE];

    for (;;) {
        clilen = sizeof(cliaddr);
        if ((connfd = accept(lfd, (struct sockaddr *)&cliaddr,
&clilen))<0) {
            if (errno != EINTR) {
                self.errorCode = ACCEPTINGERROR;
                NSLog(@"Error accepting connection");
            }
        } else {
            self.errorCode = NOERRROR;
            NSString *connStr = [NSString
stringWithFormat:@"Connection from %s, port %d", inet_ntop(AF_INET,
&cliaddr.sin_addr,buf, sizeof(buf)),ntohs(cliaddr.sin_port)];
            NSLog(@"%@", connStr);

            //Multi-threaded
            dispatch_async(dispatch_get_global_queue(DISPATCH_
QUEUE_PRIORITY_HIGH, 0), ^{
                [self strEchoServer:@(connfd)];
            });
        }
    }
}
```

The `echoServerListenWithDescriptor:` method will use the `accept()` function to accept incoming connections on the supplied socket descriptor.

Within the `echoServerListenWithDescriptor:` method, we create a `for` loop that will loop forever because each time a new connection is accepted, we will want to pass the control of that connection to a separate thread and then come back and wait for the next connection.

The `accept()` function detects and initializes incoming connections on the listening socket. When a new connection is made, it will return a new socket descriptor. If there is a problem initializing the connection, the `accept()` function will return `-1`. If the connection is successfully initialized, we determine the IP address and port number from where the client is connecting and log it.

Finally, we use `dispatch_async()` to add our `strEchoServer()` method to the dispatch queue. If we simply called the method directly without `dispatch_async()`, the server would only be able to handle one incoming connection at a time. With `dispatch_async()`, each time a new connection comes in, the `strEchoServer()` method gets passed to the queue and then the server can go back to listening for new connections. The `strEchoServer()` method listens to establish connections for incoming text and then echoes that text back to the client. Refer to the following code:

```
- (void) strEchoServer: (NSNumber *) sockfdNum {
    ssize_t n;
    char buf [MAXLINE] ;

    int sockfd = [sockfdNum intValue];
    while ((n=recv(sockfd, buf, MAXLINE -1,0)) > 0) {
        [self written:sockfd char:buf size:n] ;
        buf [n] ='\0' ;
        NSLog (@"%s",buf) ;
        [[NSNotificationCenter defaultCenter] postNotificationName:
@"posttext" object:[NSString stringWithCString:buf encoding:NSUTF8Str
ingEncoding]] ;

    }
    NSLog (@"Closing Socket") ;
    close (sockfdNum) ;
}
```

The `strEchoServer:` method has one parameter that is a socket descriptor to read from. We set up the `while` loop that will loop each time data comes in on the socket. When the data is received, the `recv()` function will put the incoming bytes into the buffer pointed to by `buf`. The `recv()` function will then return the number of bytes that are read. If the number of bytes is zero, the client is disconnected; if it is less than zero, there is an error. For the purpose of this recipe, we will close the socket if the number of bytes returned is zero or less.

As soon as the data is read from the socket, we call the `written:char:size:` function to write the data back to the client. This essentially is our echo server; however, we want to perform some additional steps so we can see when the data is received.

We will want to terminate the `buf` character array with a `NULL` terminator prior to converting it to `NSString`, so we do not get any additional garbage in our string. After we terminate the character array, we post a notification named `posttext` with the text from the socket. This will allow us to set an observer within our program that will receive all incoming text from the socket. In our example code, this notification will be used to display the incoming text to the screen, but it can also be used for logging or anything else we think of. If you do not want to do anything with the text that is sent, you can safely ignore the notification.

Once the client closes the connection, we will want to close the socket on our end. The `close()` function at the end of the `strEchoServer:` method does this for us if the number of bytes returned from the `recv()` function is zero or less:

```
-(ssize_t) written:(int)sockfdNum char:(const void *)vptr
size:(size_t)n {

    size_t    nleft;
    ssize_t   nwritten;
    const char *ptr;

    ptr = vptr;
    nleft = n;
    while (nleft > 0) {
      if ( (nwritten = write(sockfdNum, ptr, nleft)) <= 0) {
        if (nwritten < 0 && errno == EINTR)
          nwritten = 0;    /* and call write() again */
        else
          return -1;    /* error */
      }

      nleft -= nwritten;
      ptr   += nwritten;
    }
    return(n);
}

@end
```

The `written:char:size:` method is used to write the text back to the client and has three parameters. These parameters are: `sockfdNum`, which is the socket descriptor to write to; the `vptr` pointer, which points to the text to be written; and `n`, which is the length of the text to be written.

The `written:char:size:` method uses the `write()` function to write the text back to the client. This method returns the number of bytes written, which may be less than the total number of bytes you told it to write. When that happens, we will need to make multiple write calls until everything is written back to the client.

We set `ptr` to point to the beginning of the text to send back and then set `nleft` to the size of the text to write. If the `write` function does not send all the text to the client, `ptr` will be moved to point to where we will begin the next write from and `nleft` will be set to the number of remaining bytes to write. The `while` loop will continue to loop until all text is written back to the client. If the `write` function returns a number less than 0, it means that there was a problem writing to the socket, so we return `-1`.

Using the BSDSocketServer class to start the echo server

The following code will start our server and can be used on both the iOS and OS X platforms:

```
BSDSocketServer *bsdServ = [[BSDSocketServer alloc] initOnPort:2004];
if (bsdServ.errorCode == NOERRROR) {
    [bsdServ echoServerListenWithDescriptor:bsdServ.listenfd];

} else {
    NSLog(@"%@",NSString stringWithFormat:@"Error code %d recieved.
Server was not started", bsdServ.errorCode]);
}
```

We begin by initializing our `BSDSocketServer` object by setting the port number for our server. In this example, we use port `2004`. We then verify that we did not have any issues initializing our server and if everything was good, we call the echo server listener method.

When you create your own server, you will want to keep the `initWithPort:` constructor to establish the connection and then create your protocol in a separate method such as the `echoServerListenWithDescriptor:` method shown in this recipe. You will see an example of this in the *Creating a data server* recipe of this chapter.

The downloadable code contains sample projects for both iOS and OS X.

Once you download the code, you can start the server and test it using the following `telnet` command:

`telnet localhost 2004`

Once telnet makes the connection, type any text and press the *Enter* key. Once you press the *Enter* key, the text you typed in will be echoed back to you.

The following screenshot shows how the telnet session will work with our echo server:

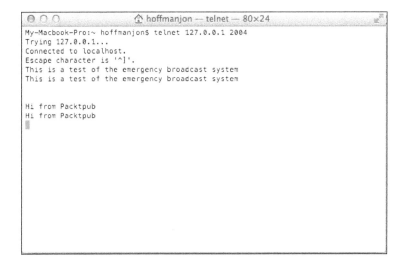

```
● ○ ○                 ⌂ hoffmanjon — telnet — 80×24
My-Macbook-Pro:~ hoffmanjon$ telnet 127.0.0.1 2004
Trying 127.0.0.1...
Connected to localhost.
Escape character is '^]'.
This is a test of the emergency broadcast system
This is a test of the emergency broadcast system

Hi from Packtpub
Hi from Packtpub
```

How it works...

When you create a server using BSD sockets, you need to call the `socket()`, `bind()`, and `listen()` methods in that order:

> ▸ `int socket(int domain, int type, int protocol)`: This function returns an integer descriptor that can be used to identify the socket in all future function calls.

> ▸ `int bind(int sockfd, const struct sockaddr *my_addr, socklen_t addrlen)`: This function will bind the network interface and port combination to the socket. We will need to create a `sockaddr` structure with the IP version, network interfaces, and the port number to bind the socket prior to calling the `bind()` function.

> ▸ `int listen(int sockfd, int backlog)`: This function begins listening to the socket for any incoming connections.

The socket, bind, and listen steps described are the normal steps needed to prepare a TCP server and to create a listening descriptor. The listening descriptor will be used to accept incoming connections. Once we have the listening descriptor, we can then wait for incoming connections and respond to them.

When you create your own servers, you will want to use the `initOnPort:` constructor to initiate the server, but write separate functions to handle the incoming requests. You will see this in the *Creating a data server* recipe when we create a data server to receive images from a client.

Once we have our socket created, we can call the method that will listen on the socket (the `echoServerListenWithDescriptor:` method). This method uses the `accept()` function to listen for incoming connections. The `accept()` function will create a new socket for each incoming connection and then remove the connection from the listen queue. If you recall, we defined that the listen queue can contain up to 1024 connections before it stops accepting new ones.

The `strEchoServer:` function is where we actually implement our echo server. This method uses the `recv()` function to receive the incoming data (in our case, incoming text) from an open socket. Once the text is received, we call the `written:char:size:` method to write the data back to the client.

Creating an echo client

In the *Creating an echo server* recipe of this chapter, we created an echo server and then tested it using telnet. Creating the server was pretty fun, but testing with telnet was a kind of anti-climax; so in this recipe, we will be creating a client that we can use to connect to our echo server.

When we created the echo server, we created a `BSDSocketServer` class to help with the creation of our server applications. In this recipe, we will be creating a `BSDSocketClient` class to help with the creation of our client applications.

Getting ready

This recipe is compatible with both iOS and OS X. No extra frameworks or libraries are required.

How to do it...

Now let's create an echo client that will communicate with our echo server:

Creating the BSDSocketClient header file

We will begin by creating the `BSDSocketClient` header file, as shown in the following code:

```
#import <Foundation/Foundation.h>
typedef NS_ENUM(NSUInteger, BSDClientErrorCode) {
    NOERRROR,
    SOCKETERROR,
    CONNECTERROR,
    READERROR,
    WRITEERROR
};
```

```
#define MAXLINE 4096

@interface BSDSocketClient : NSObject

@property (nonatomic) int errorCode, sockfd;

-(instancetype)initWithAddress:(NSString *)addr andPort:(int)port;
-(ssize_t) writtenToSocket:(int)sockfdNum withChar:(NSString *)vptr;
-(NSString *) recvFromSocket:(int)lsockfd withMaxChar:(int)max;
```

We begin the header file by defining the five error conditions that may occur while we are connecting to the server. If an error occurs, we will set the errorCode property with the appropriate code.

We then define the maximum size of the text that we can send to our server. This is really used strictly for this example; on production servers, you will not want to put a limit such as this.

The BSDSocketClient header defines two properties, errorCode and sockfd. We expose the errorCode property, so classes that use the BSDSocketClient class can check for errors, and we expose the sockfd socket descriptor in case we want to create the client protocol outside the BSDSocketClient class.

The header file also defines one constructor and two methods, which we will be exposing in the BSDSocketClient class.

The initWithAddress:andPort: constructor creates the BSDSocketClient object with the IP address and port combination for connection. The writtenToSocket:withChar: method will write data to the socket that we are connected to, and the recvFromSocket:withMaxChar: method will receive characters from the socket.

Creating the BSDSocketClient implementation file

Now we need to create the BSDSocketClient implementation file, as shown in the following code:

```
#import "BSDSocketClient.h"
#import <sys/types.h>
#import <arpa/inet.h>

@implementation BSDSocketClient
```

We begin the `BSDSocketClient` implementation file by importing the headers needed to create our client. Let's look at the `initWithAddress:andPort:` constructor:

```
-(id)initWithAddress:(NSString *)addr andPort:(int)port {
    self = [super init];
    if (self) {
        struct sockaddr_in   servaddr;

        self.errorCode = NOERRROR;
        if ( (self.sockfd = socket(AF_INET, SOCK_STREAM, 0)) < 0)
            self.errorCode = SOCKETERROR;
        else {
            memset(&servaddr,0, sizeof(servaddr));
            servaddr.sin_family = AF_INET;
            servaddr.sin_port = htons(port);
            inet_pton(AF_INET, [addr cStringUsingEncoding:NSUTF8Strin
gEncoding], &servaddr.sin_addr);

            if (connect(self.sockfd, (struct sockaddr *)&servaddr,
sizeof(servaddr)) < 0) {
                self.errorCode = CONNECTERROR;
            }
        }
    }
    return self;
}
```

The `initWithAddress:andPort:` constructor is used to set up the connection with the server. We define a `sockaddr_in` structure named `servaddr`. This structure will be used to define the address, port, and IP version of our connection.

If you recall, we initialized the server for the echo server by making the `socket()`, `bind()`, and `listen()` function calls. To initialize a client, you only need to make two function calls. These are the same `socket()` call you made for the server followed by a new function called `connect()`.

We make the `socket()` function call using the `AF_INET` (IPv4) and `SOCK_STREAM` (TCP) parameters. If you would like to use IPv6, you would change `AF_INET` to `AF_INET6`. If you would like to use UDP instead of TCP, you would change `SOCK_STREAM` to `SOCK_DGRAM`. If there is an issue creating the socket, we will set the `errorCode` variable to `SOCKETERROR` and skip the rest of the code.

Prior to calling the `connect` function, we need to set up a `sockaddr` structure that contains the IP version, address, and port number we will be connecting to. Before populating the `sockaddr` structure with the information, we will want to clear the memory to make sure that there is no stale information that may cause our `bind` function to fail. We do this using the `memset()` function.

After we clear the memory for the `sockaddr` structure, we set the values. We set the IP version to IPv4 by setting the `sin_family` address to `AF_INET`. The `sin_port` number is set to the port number by using the `htons()` function. We convert the IP address that we are connecting to from `NSString` to `cString` and use the `inet_pton()` function to convert the address to a network address structure that is put into `servaddr.sin_addr`.

After we have our `sockaddr` structure set, we attempt to connect to the server using the `connect()` function. If the connection fails, the `connect()` function returns `-1`. Let's look at the `writtenToSocket:withChar:` method:

```
-(ssize_t) writtenToSocket:(int)sockfdNum withChar:(NSString *)vptr {

    size_t    nleft;
    ssize_t   nwritten;
    const char  *ptr = [vptr cStringUsingEncoding:NSUTF8StringEncodi
ng];

    nleft = sizeof(ptr);
    size_t n=nleft;
    while (nleft > 0) {
      if ( (nwritten = write(sockfdNum, ptr, nleft)) <= 0) {
        if (nwritten < 0 && errno == EINTR)
          nwritten = 0;
        else {
                self.errorCode = WRITEERROR;
          return(-1);
              }
      }

      nleft -= nwritten;
    ptr   += nwritten;
    }
    return(n);
}
```

The `writtenToSocket:withChar:` method is used to write the text to the server. This method has two parameters: `sockfdNum`, which is the socket descriptor to write to, and `vptr` `NSString`, which contains the text to send to the server.

The `writtenToSocket:withChar:` method uses the `write()` function to write the text to the client. This method returns the number of bytes written, which may be less than the total number of bytes you told it to write. When that happens, we will need to make multiple write calls until everything is written back to the client.

We convert `vptr` to `cString` pointed to by the `ptr` pointer using the `cStringUsingEncoding:` method.

If the `write()` function does not send all the text to the client, the `ptr` pointer will be moved to point where we will begin the next write from, and `nleft` will be set to the number of remaining bytes to write. The `while` loop will continue to loop until all the text is written. If the `write` function returns `0` or less, we check for errorsLet's look at the `recvFromSocket:withMaxChar:` method:

```
-(NSString *) recvFromSocket:(int)lsockfd withMaxChar:(int)max {
    char recvline[max];
    ssize_t n;

    if ((n=recv(lsockfd, recvline, max -1,0)) > 0) {
        recvline[n]='\0';
        return [NSString stringWithCString:recvline
encoding:NSUTF8StringEncoding];
    } else {
        self.errorCode = READERROR;
        return @"Server Terminated Prematurely";
    }
}

@end
```

The `recvFromSocket:withMaxChar:` method is used to receive characters from the server and returns an `NSString` representing the characters received.

When the data comes in, the `recv()` function will put the incoming text into the buffer pointed to by the `recvline` pointer. The `recv()` function will return the number of bytes read. If the number of bytes is zero, the client is disconnected; if it is less than zero, it means there was an error.

If we successfully received text from the client, we put a `NULL` terminator at the end of the text, convert it to `NSString`, and return it.

Using the BSDSocketClient to connect to our echo server

The downloadable code contains examples for both iOS and OS X. If you run the iOS example in the iPhone simulator, the app looks like the following screenshot:

You will type the text you wish to send in the `UITextField` and then click on the **Send** button. The text that is received back from the server, in our case **Hello from Packt**, is displayed below the **Text Received:** label.

We will look at the `sendPressed:` method in the iOS sample code as an example of how to use the `BSDSocketClient` method. This method is called when you click on the **Send** button. Refer to the following code:

```
- (IBAction)sendPressed:(id)sender {
    NSString *str = textField.text;
    BSDSocketClient *bsdCli = [[BSDSocketClient alloc]
initWithAddress:@"127.0.0.1" andPort:2004];
    if (bsdCli.errorCode == NOERRROR) {
        [bsdCli writtenToSocket:bsdCli.sockfd withChar:str];

        NSString *recv = [bsdCli recvFromSocket:bsdCli.sockfd
withMaxChar:MAXLINE];
        textRecvLabel.text = recv;
        textField.text = @"";
```

```
    } else {
        NSLog(@"%@", [NSString stringWithFormat:@"Error code %d
recieved.  Server was not started", bsdCli.errorCode]);
    }
}
```

We begin by retrieving the text that was entered in the `UITextField`. This is the text that we will be sending to the echo server.

We then initialize the `BSDSocketClient` object with an IP address of `127.0.0.1`, which is the local loopback adapter, and a port number of `2004` (this needs to be the same port that your server is listening on). If you run this on an iPhone, you will need to set the IP address to the address of the computer that is running the echo server.

Once the connection with the server is established, we call the `writtenToSocket:withChar:` method to write the text entered in the `UITextField` to the server.

Now that we have sent the text, we need to retrieve what comes back. This is done by calling the `recvFromSocket:withMaxChar:` method to listen to the socket and retrieve any text that comes back.

Finally, we display the text that was received from the server to the screen and clear the `UITextField` so that we can enter in the next text.

How it works...

When we created the BSD echo server in the *Creating an echo server* recipe of this chapter, we went through a three-step process to prepare the TCP server. These were the socket (create a socket), bind (bind the socket to the interface), and listen (listen for incoming connections) steps.

When we create the BSD echo client, we make the connection in a two-step process. These are the socket (create a socket just like the echo server) and connect (this connects to the server) steps. The client calls the `connect()` function to establish a connection with the server. If no errors occur, it means we have successfully created a connection between the server and the client.

When you create your own clients, you will want to use the `initWithAddress:andPort:` constructor to initiate the connection and then write your own code to handle your protocol. You can see the *Create a data client* recipe of this chapter when we create a data client to send an image to the server.

Creating a data server

In the *Creating an echo server* recipe, we created a server that accepted incoming text and echoed it back to the client. That recipe demonstrated how to send and receive text through a socket connection. Now you may be asking yourself, how do I send and receive datafiles, such as images or PDF files, through a socket connection?

Sending and receiving data over a socket connection is really not that different from sending and receiving text. You go through all the same steps to set up your sockets for sending or receiving, but at the end you get `NSData` instead of a character array.

For this recipe, we will be using the same `BSDSocketServer` class that we used in the *Creating an echo server* recipe of this chapter, since we can reuse the `initOnPort:` constructor and just add the methods to implement the protocol.

Getting ready

This recipe is compatible with both iOS and OS X. No extra frameworks or libraries are required.

How to do it...

Let's start creating our data server.

Updating the BSDSocketServer header file

We will be updating the `BSDSocketServer` header file that we created in the *Creating an echo server* recipe of this chapter. The new header file looks like the following code:

```
#import <Foundation/Foundation.h>

#define LISTENQ 1024
#define MAXLINE 4096

typedef NS_ENUM(NSUInteger, BSDServerErrorCode) {
    NOERROR,
    SOCKETERROR,
    BINDERROR,
    LISTENERROR,
    ACCEPTINGERROR
};
@interface BSDSocketServer : NSObject

@property int errorCode, listenfd;
```

```
    -(id)initOnPort:(int)port;
    -(void)echoServerListenWithDescriptor:(int)lfd;
    -(void)dataServerListenWithDescriptor:(int)lfd;

@end
```

The only addition to the header file is where we added the new method that will be used to listen and process new requests for our data server. As we create new types of servers, we can reuse the `initOnPort:` constructor since all the sockets are set up the same way. How each type of server handles the incoming request will vary; therefore, you will need a separate method to handle each of the protocols.

Updating the BSDSocketServer implementation file

Even though we only define one new method in our header file, we really need two new methods in our implementation file. The first one is the `dataServerListenWithDescriptor:` method we defined in the header file; refer to the following code:

```
    -(void)dataServerListenWithDescriptor:(int)lfd {
        int connfd;
        socklen_t clilen;
        struct sockaddr_in cliaddr;
        char buf[MAXLINE];

        for (;;) {
            clilen = sizeof(cliaddr);
            if ((connfd = accept(lfd, (struct sockaddr *)&cliaddr,
&clilen))<0) {
                if (errno != EINTR) {
                    self.errorCode = ACCEPTINGERROR;
                    NSLog(@"Error accepting connection");
                }
            } else {
                self.errorCode = NOERRROR;
                NSString *connStr = [NSString
stringWithFormat:@"Connection from %s, port %d", inet_ntop(AF_INET,
&cliaddr.sin_addr,buf, sizeof(buf)),ntohs(cliaddr.sin_port)];
                NSLog(@"%@", connStr);

                //Multi-threaded
                dispatch_async(dispatch_get_global_queue(DISPATCH_
QUEUE_PRIORITY_HIGH, 0), ^{
                    [self getData:@(connfd)];
                });
            }
        }
    }
```

The `dataServerListenWithDescriptor:` method is almost an exact duplicate of the `echoServerListenWithDescriptor:` method. The `dataServerListenWithDescriptor:` method uses the `accept()` function to accept incoming connections on the supplied socket descriptor.

Within the `dataServerListenWithDescriptor:` method, we create a forever loop because each time a new connection is accepted, we will want to pass control of that connection to a separate thread and then come back and wait for the next connection.

The `accept()` function detects and initializes incoming connections on the listening socket. When a new connection is made, the `accept()` function will return a new socket descriptor. If there is a problem in initializing the connection, the `accept` function will return `-1`. If the connection is successfully initialized, we determine the IP address and port number that the client is connecting from and log them to the screen.

Finally, we use `dispatch_async` to add our `getData()` method to the queue. If we simply called the method directly without `dispatch_async`, the server would only be able to handle one incoming connection at a time. With `dispatch_async`, each time a new connection is established, the `getData()` method gets passed to the queue and the server can go back to listening for new connections.

The `getData()` method listens to establish connections for incoming data:

```
-(void)getData:(NSNumber *) sockfdNum {
    ssize_t n;
    UInt8 buf[MAXLINE];
    NSMutableData *data = [[NSMutableData alloc] init];

    int sockfd = [sockfdNum intValue];
    while ((n=recv(sockfd, buf, MAXLINE -1,0)) > 0) {

        [data appendBytes:buf length:n];
    }
    close(sockfd);

    [[NSNotificationCenter defaultCenter] postNotificationName:@"pos
tdata" object:data];

    NSLog(@"Done");
}
```

In the `strEchoServer:` method that was used to retrieve text for our echo server, we used a `char buf[MAXLINE]` buffer to store the characters that we received. In the `getData:` method, we will use a `UInt8 buf[MAXLINE]` buffer to store our data as it comes in. We also define a `NSMutableData` object that holds all the data that is received.

Keep in mind that the MAXLINE constant limits the amount of data retrieved at a time and does not limit the total data. Where the MAXLINE constant is defined to be 4096, if we were receiving a file of 8000 bytes, we would receive the first 4096 bytes chunks. These first 4096 bytes would be appended to the NSMutableData object and then we would receive the next 3904 bytes, which would also be appended to the NSMutableData object, thus forming the entire file.

Once we receive all the data, we close the socket and post a notification with the name postdata. This notification can then be captured in our code so that we can do something with the incoming data once all the data is received. The iOS example expects the incoming data to be an image, so it displays the incoming data in a UIImageView.

Using the BSDSocketServer to create our data server

The downloadable code for this chapter contains samples for both iOS and OS X. Let's take a quick look at how we start the server in the iOS sample, by referring to the following code:

```
- (void) startServer {
    [[NSNotificationCenter defaultCenter] addObserver:self
selector:@selector(newDataRecieved:) name:@"postdata" object:nil ] ;

    BSDSocketServer *bsdServ = [[BSDSocketServer alloc]
initOnPort:2006];
    if (bsdServ.errorCode == NOERRROR) {
        [bsdServ dataServerListenWithDescriptor:bsdServ.listenfd];

    } else {
        NSLog(@"%@",[NSString stringWithFormat:@"Error code %d
recieved.  Server was not started", bsdServ.errorCode]);
    }

}

- (void) newDataRecieved:(NSNotification *)notification {
    NSData *data = notification.object;
    imageView.image = [UIImage imageWithData:data];
}
```

In the startSvr method, the first thing we do is set up a notification that will listen for the postdata notification. When the postdata notification is received, the listener will send the data to the newDataReceived: method to update our imageView with the data.

We initialize the BSDSocketServer object and tell it to listen on port 2006. If there are no errors while initializing the server, we call the dataServerListenWithDescriptor: method, which will listen for incoming data and process it.

How it works...

When we created the data server, we used the same `initOnPort:` constructor that we used for the echo server. This is because the same socket, bind, and listen steps are required for both. What we had to change were the methods that listened and processed incoming connections. When you create your own servers, you will also want to use the `initOnPort:` constructor and then write your own methods to handle the incoming connections.

Once we have our socket created, we can call the method that will listen on the socket. This is the `dataServerListenWithDescriptor:` method. This method uses the `accept()` function to listen for incoming connections. The `accept()` function will create a new socket for each incoming connection and then remove the connection from the listen queue. If you recall, we defined that the listen queue can contain up to 1024 connections before it stops accepting new ones.

The `getData:` method is where we actually implement our server. This method uses the `recv()` function to receive the incoming data. As the data comes in, we append it to the `NSMutableData` object until all the data is received.

Creating a data client

In the *Creating a data server* recipe of this chapter, we updated our `BSDSocketServer` class so we could set up a server that could receive data. In this recipe, we will be updating our `BSDSocketClient` class so we can set up a client to upload data to our data server.

Getting ready

This recipe is compatible with both iOS and OS X. No extra frameworks or libraries are required.

How to do it...

Let's update the `BSDSocketClient` class to include our data client.

Updating the BSDSocketClient header file

Since we will be able to use the same constructor (`initWithAddress:andPort:`) that we used when we connected to the echo server, all we need to do is to add a method to send the data itself. This method will be called `sendData:toSocket:`. The following is the new `BSDSocketClient` header file:

```
#import <Foundation/Foundation.h>

typedef NS_ENUM(NSUInteger, BSDClientErrorCode) {
  NOERRROR,
```

```
        SOCKETERROR,
        CONNECTERROR,
        READERROR,
        WRITEERROR
    };
      #define MAXLINE 4096

      @interface BSDSocketClient : NSObject

      @property int errorCode, sockfd;

      -(id)initWithAddress:(NSString *)addr andPort:(int)port;
      -(ssize_t) writtenToSocket:(int)sockfdNum withChar:(NSString *)vptr;
      -(NSString *) recvFromSocket:(int)lsockfd withMaxChar:(int)max;
      -(ssize_t)sendData:(NSData *)data toSocket:(int)lsockfd;

      @end
```

Updating the BSDSocketClient implementation file

We now need to add the `sendData:toSocket:` method to our `BSDSocketClient` class:

```
    -(ssize_t)sendData:(NSData *)data toSocket:(int)lsockfd
    {
        NSLog(@"sending");
        ssize_t n;
        const UInt8 *buf = (const UInt8 *)[data bytes];

        if ((n = send(lsockfd, buf, [data length],0)) <=0) {
            errorCode = WRITEERROR;
            return -1;
        } else {
            errorCode = NOERRROR;
            return n;
        }
    }
```

The `sendData:toSocket:` method accepts two parameters: the data to send to the server and the socket descriptor to which we want to send the data. Since the BSD Socket Library does not recognize the `NSData` objects, we will need to convert the data to bytes and then to a `UInt8` buffer prior to sending it.

Once we have our `UInt8` buffer, we use the `send()` function to send the data to the server. The `send()` function will return the number of bytes sent to the server; if that number is less than 0, it means there is a problem and we return an error.

Using the BSDSocketClient to connect to our data server

Let's take a look at the sample code that uses the `sendData:toSocket` method:

```
    BSDSocketClient *bsdCli = [[BSDSocketClient alloc]
initWithAddress:@"127.0.0.1" andPort:2006];
    if (bsdCli.errorCode == NOERRROR) {
        NSData *data = [NSData dataWithContentsOfFile:@"/Users/
hoffmanjon/Documents/GreenGuyLarge.png"];
        [bsdCli sendData:data toSocket:bsdCli.sockfd];
    } else {
        NSLog(@"%@",[NSString stringWithFormat:@"Error code %d recieved.
", bsdCli.errorCode]);
    }
```

We start off by initializing the `BSDSocketClient` object with the IP address `127.0.0.1` and with a port of `2006`. If you are running the sample server on another device, you will need to change the IP address. If there are no issues initializing the client, we load an image and convert it to an `NSData` object. You will need to change the location of the file to the location on your machine that contains an image.

We then pass the `NSData` object that contains the image to the `sendData:toSocket` method.

How it works...

When we created the BSD data server, we went through a three-step process to prepare the TCP server and to create listen on the socket. These were socket (create a socket), bind (bind the socket to the interface), and listen (listen for incoming connections).

When we create the BSD data client, we make the connection in a two-step process. These steps are `socket` (create a socket just like the echo server) and `connect` (this connects to the server). The client calls the `connect()` function to establish a connection with the server. If no error occurs, we have a connection between the server and the client. This connection process is the same code we used to establish a connection with the echo server.

Once we have the connection established with the server, we need to send our data to the server. In our example, we will be sending an image file over; however, this same code can be used to send any binary file. The client and the server just need to agree on what type of file is to be sent.

The first thing we need to do is to convert the file to an `NSData` object and pass that to the `sendData:toScoket:` method. When the `sendData:toSocket:` method has the `NSData` object, it converts it to a `Uint8` buffer. We then use the `send()` function to send the `Uint8` buffer to the server.

2
Apple Low-level Networking

In this chapter, we will cover:

- ▶ Retrieving network address information
- ▶ Performing network address resolution
- ▶ Creating an echo server
- ▶ Creating an echo client
- ▶ Creating a server to receive data
- ▶ Creating a client to send data
- ▶ Checking the network status

Introduction

The primary API behind Apple's low-level networking is the CFNetwork API.

The simplest way to describe CFNetworking is to say that it is an Apple-specific extension to the BSD socket API. The CFNetworking stack is based on and relies on the BSD socket API that was discussed in *Chapter 1*, *BSD Socket Library*. It is recommended that the reader understands the concepts discussed in *Chapter 1*, *BSD Socket Library*, prior to going through this chapter. While this chapter will focus primarily on CFNetworking for most of the recipes, we will also use NSHost and the system configuration framework for retrieving network address information and checking the network status recipes. The biggest advantage that BSD sockets have over CFNetwork is the compatibility with other forms of Unix. This is a pretty big advantage when you think of all the BSD socket code on the Internet that you can use. However, if your application is Apple-specific, it is recommended that you use CFNetwork wherever you can.

CFNetwork offers numerous advantages over BSD sockets. The biggest advantage is the run-loop integration. So if your application is run-loop-based, you will be able to implement network services without implementing numerous threads.

CFNetwork also contains a number of objects to help you implement specific protocols without having to know the implementation details about the protocols. This includes the CFFTP API to assist in implementing the FTP protocol, and CFHTTP to assist in implementing the HTTP protocol.

To understand CFNetworking, you should be aware of the main building blocks that make up CFNetwork, which are as follows:

 ▶ **CFSocket**: It is an abstraction of the BSD socket covered in *Chapter 1, BSD Socket Library*. One of the main differences between the BSD socket and the CFSocket is that the CFSocket can be integrated with a run loop.

 ▶ **CFStream**: It provides both read and write streams and makes it easy to exchange data not only across networks but also with files and memory objects.

 ▶ **CFSocketStream**: It provides an extension for CFStream to work with network sockets.

 ▶ **CFFTP**: It provides an API for communicating with FTP servers.

 ▶ **CFHTTP**: It provides an API for communicating with HTTP servers.

 ▶ **CFHTTPAuthentication**: It provides an API for responding to HTTP authentication challenges.

Retrieving network address information

Most applications that communicate over a network will eventually need to know the information from the available network interfaces of the device they are running on. This recipe will show you how to retrieve the network addresses for all the active network interfaces on the device.

This recipe will use the NSHost class to retrieve a list of addresses on your local device. While NSHost is available on iOS, it is a private (undocumented) class. It is also noted on a number of forum posts that Apple has rejected iOS apps for using NSHost. If you need to retrieve network address information within an iOS application, it is recommended that you use the *Retrieving network address information* recipe from *Chapter 1, BSD Socket Library*, in this book, and not the NSHost class described in this recipe.

Getting ready

This recipe is compatible with both iOS and OS X, but it is recommended that you do not use NSHost on the iOS platform. No extra frameworks or libraries are required.

How to do it...

We retrieve the network address information in the following manner:

1. Let's retrieve the network address information of our local device:

```
NSHost* myHost =[NSHost currentHost];
if (myHost)
{
  NSArray *addresses = [myHost addresses];

  for (NSString *address in addresses) {
    NSLog(@"%@", address );
  }
}
```

2. To create an NSHost object, you will want to use one of the following three class methods (do not use alloc and init to create the object):

   ❑ currentHost: It returns an NSHost object, which represents the host the process is currently running on.

   ❑ hostWithAddress: It returns an NSHost object representing the host defined by the supplied IP address. You would use this method by supplying the address as an NSString object; for example, [NSHost hostWithAddress:@"83.166.169.231"].

   ❑ hostWithName: It returns an NSHost object representing the host defined by the supplied hostname. You would use this method by supplying the address as an NSString object; for example, [NSHost hostWithName:@"www.packtpub.com"].

For our recipe, we are looking for the network address information of the localhost; therefore, we will use the currentHost method to create our NSHost object.

How it works...

The NSHost class provides various methods that can be used to access the name and address information for a host. An NSHost object will represent an individual host and will contain all the network addresses and names associated with that host.

While NSHost is much easier to use than the *Retrieving network address information* recipe in *Chapter 1, BSD Socket Library,* NSHost is an undocumented (private) class for iOS. It could be changed or removed anytime from the iOS SDK. Apple could also reject your iOS app for using NSHost; therefore, it should only be used in OS X applications.

Performing a network address resolution

Most applications that use the Internet to communicate will eventually need to convert a hostname to an IP address or an IP address to a hostname. This recipe will encapsulate the network address resolution functionality into a standalone Objective-C class. You will notice in this recipe that most of the CFNetworking API calls are made up of C functions, and use a structure similar to the `addrinfo` structure that the BSD API uses.

Getting ready

This recipe is compatible with both iOS and OS X. No extra frameworks or libraries are required.

How to do it...

Let's get started!

Creating the CFNetworkUtilities header file

The following is the code snippet for creating the `CFNetworkUtilities` header file:

```
#import <Foundation/Foundation.h>

typedef NS_ENUM(NSUInteger, CFNetworkingSelf.errorCode) {
  NOERROR,
  HOSTRESOLUTIONERROR,
  ADDRESSRESOLUTIONERROR
};
@interface CFNetworkUtilities : NSObject

@property int (nonatomic) self.errorCode;

-(NSArray *)addressesForHostname:(NSString *)hostname;
-(NSArray *)hostnamesForAddress:(NSString *)address;

@end
```

The `CFNetworkUtilities` header file begins by defining an `enum` datatype that will represent our error conditions. These error conditions will be stored in the `errorCode` property.

We are also defining two methods for our implementation:

> ▶ `addressesForHostname`: This method returns the network addresses for the given hostnames

▸ hostnamesForAddress: This method returns the hostnames for the given network addresses

Creating the CFNetworkUtilities implementation file

The following is the code snippet for creating the CFNetworkUtilities implementation file:

```
#import "CFNetworkUtilities.h"
#if TARGET_OS_IPHONE
#import <CFNetwork/CFNetwork.h>
#else
#import <CoreServices/CoreServices.h>
#endif

#import <sys/types.h>
#import <sys/socket.h>
#import <netdb.h>

@implementation CFNetworkUtilities
```

We begin our CFNetworkUtilities implementation file by importing the header files that we will need for our address resolution. Notice the #if...#else...#endif block; it will import the correct headers based on the platform the code is running on.

Now let's create the addressesForHostname: method. This method is used to obtain a list of IP addresses associated with the hostname.

```
-(NSArray *)addressesForHostname:(NSString *)hostname {
  self.errorCode = NOERROR;
  char ipAddr[INET6_ADDRSTRLEN];
  NSMutableArray *addresses = [[NSMutableArray alloc]
    init];

  CFHostRef hostRef =
    CFHostCreateWithName(kCFAllocatorDefault,
    (CFStringRef)hostname);
```

This method begins by setting the errorCode property to NOERROR. If any error occurs during the execution of this method, we will set errorCode and return nil.

We then define the ipAddr array of type char and set the length to the value defined by the INET6_ADDRSTRLEN constant. We set the char array to INET6_ADDRSTRLEN so it can hold either IPv6 or IPv4 addresses. The INET6_ADDRSTRLEN constant is defined as 46, and the INET_ADDRSTRLEN constant is defined as 16.

We also define the NSMutableArray object that will be used to store and return the list of IP addresses for the hostname.

We create a reference to a CFHost object using the CFHostCreateWithName() function. This function creates a reference to a CFHost object, given a hostname. There is another function that you will see in our hostnamesForAddress: method later in this section, named CFHostCreateWithAddress(), which will return a reference to a CFHost object, given the IP address. The CFHostStartInfoResolution() function begins the address resolution as follows:

```
BOOL success = CFHostStartInfoResolution(hostRef,
  kCFHostAddresses, nil);
if (!success) {
  self.errorCode = HOSTRESOLUTIONERROR;
  return nil;
}

CFArrayRef addressesRef =
  CFHostGetAddressing(hostRef, nil);
if (addressesRef == nil){
  self.errorCode = HOSTRESOLUTIONERROR;
  return nil;
}
```

The type of resolution to perform is defined by the second parameter. In this example, we use kCFHostAddresses, which specifies that we want to retrieve the list of IP addresses. You can also use the kCFHostNames constant to specify that you want to retrieve the list of hostnames, or kCFHostReachability to specify that you would like to retrieve the reachability information.

Next, we call the CFHostGetAddressing() function to retrieve the list of addresses for the host. You must call the CFHostStartInfoResolution() function to perform the address resolution prior to calling the CFHostGetAddressing() function, as CFHostGetAddressing() is the function that performs the actual address resolution.

Now we need to loop though the list of addresses for the host:

```
CFIndex numAddresses = CFArrayGetCount(addressesRef);
for (CFIndex currentIndex = 0; currentIndex <
  numAddresses; currentIndex++) {
  struct sockaddr *address = (struct sockaddr
    *)CFDataGetBytePtr(CFArrayGetValueAtIndex(
      addressesRef, currentIndex));
  if (address == nil){
    self.errorCode = HOSTRESOLUTIONERROR;
    return nil;
  }
```

```
            getnameinfo(address, address->sa_len,
              ipAddr, INET6_ADDRSTRLEN, nil, 0, NI_NUMERICHOST);
            if (ipAddr == nil){
              self.errorCode = HOSTRESOLUTIONERROR;
              return nil;
            }
            [addresses addObject:[
              NSString stringWithCString:ipAddr
              encoding:NSASCIIStringEncoding]];
          }

          return addresses;
        }
```

The `CFArrayGetValueAtIndex()` function retrieves a pointer to the value at the given index in a `CFArray`. The `CFDataGetBytePtr()` function returns a pointer to the `CFData` object's internal bytes, which we cast as a `sockaddr` pointer.

The `getnameinfo()` function then returns the IP address from the `sockaddr` structure and puts the value into the `ipAddr` character array. The `NI_NUMERICHOST` flag defines that we would like to return the address in the numeric form instead of the hostname.

Once all addresses are processed, we return the `addresses` array, which contains the list of the IP addresses associated with the host.

Now let's create the `hostnamesForAddress:` function.

The `hostnamesForAddress:` method is used to provide an IP address to a list of hostnames associated with the address.

```
  - (NSArray *)hostnamesForAddress:(NSString *)address {
    self.errorCode = NOERROR;
    struct addrinfo hints;
    struct addrinfo *result = NULL;
    memset(&hints, 0, sizeof(hints));
    hints.ai_family   = AF_UNSPEC;  // Any Address Version,
      could set to AF_INET or AF_INET6 if we wanted to limit
      the IP version
    hints.ai_socktype = SOCK_STREAM;  // Limit our search to
      Socket Stream, se could also set this to SOCK_DGRAM
    hints.ai_protocol = 0;
```

The `hostnamesForAddress:` method begins by defining the `errorCode` property to `NOERROR`. If any error occurs during the execution of this method, we will set the `errorCode` property and return `nil`.

We then define the `addrinfo` structures, `hints` and `result`. The `addrinfo` structure is the same `addrinfo` structure that was discussed in *Chapter 1, BSD Socket Library*.

The `memset()` function is used to clear the memory needed for the `hints` structure. We clear the `hints` structure prior to using it to ensure that there is nothing in the memory that may corrupt the `getaddrinfo()` function call.

Now we call the `getaddrinfor()` function to convert the IP address into a linked list of `addrinfo` structures:

```
int error = getaddrinfo([address
  cStringUsingEncoding:NSASCIIStringEncoding], NULL,
  &hints, &result);
if (error != 0) {
  self.errorCode = ADDRESSRESOLUTIONERROR;
  return nil;
}
CFDataRef addressRef = CFDataCreate(NULL, (
  UInt8 *)result->ai_addr, result->ai_addrlen);

if (addressRef == nil){
  self.errorCode = ADDRESSRESOLUTIONERROR;
  return nil;
}
freeaddrinfo(result);
```

The `getaddrinfo()` function expects character arrays for the hostname and service, so we need to convert our `NSString` values to character arrays. This is done using the `cStringUsingEncoding:` method of the `NSString` class. We also pass the addresses of the `hints` and `result` structures. The results of the `getaddrinfo()` function are put into the `error` variable. If the `getaddrinfo()` function call was unsuccessful, it will return `0`. If the `getaddrinfo()` function was successful, it will return the `result` structure, which contains the results.

We create a reference to a `CFData` object by calling the `CFDataCreate()` function and passing to it the `ai_addr` structure. Now that we have the address information we are looking for in `addressRef`, we can free our `result` structure by calling the `freeaddrinfo()` function. We use the `CFHostCreateWithAddress()` function to create a reference to the `CFHost` object using the `CFDataRef` we just created as follows:

```
CFHostRef hostRef = CFHostCreateWithAddress(
  kCFAllocatorDefault, addressRef);
if (hostRef == nil) {
  self.errorCode = ADDRESSRESOLUTIONERROR;
  return nil;
}
```

```
CFRelease(addressRef);

BOOL isSuccess = CFHostStartInfoResolution(
  hostRef, kCFHostNames, NULL);
if (!isSuccess) {
  self.errorCode = ADDRESSRESOLUTIONERROR;
  return nil;
}
```

Once we have our reference to the CFHost object, we can release the addressRef by calling the CFRealease() function. Remember, it is very important to release the structures and references once you are done with them; otherwise, your application will contain memory leaks.

The CFHostStartInfoResolution() function begins the address resolution. If you remember from the addressesForHostname: method mentioned earlier, the type of resolution to perform is defined by the second parameter. In this example, we use kCFHostName, which specifies that we are looking for the hostname.

```
CFArrayRef hostnamesRef = CFHostGetNames(hostRef, NULL);
NSMutableArray *hostnames = [NSMutableArray array];
for (int currentIndex = 0; currentIndex < [(NSArray
  *)hostnamesRef count]; currentIndex++) {
  [hostnames addObject:[(NSArray *)hostnamesRef
    objectAtIndex:currentIndex]];
}

return hostnames;
}
```

We now use the CFHostGetNames() function to retrieve a list of hostnames. You must call the CFHostStartInforResolution() function to perform the name resolution prior to calling the CFHostGetNames() function.

Now that we have the list of hostnames for our host, we loop through the list of names, convert them to NSString objects, and put them in a NSMutableArray. This array is then returned.

The downloadable code has sample code for both iOS and OS X platforms. The iOS example looks like the following screenshot:

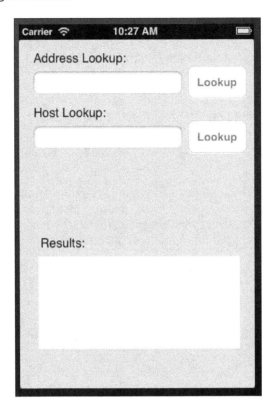

This sample app lets the user put a hostname in the **Address Lookup** field to look up the address information associated with the hostname. The user can also put an IP address in the **Host Lookup** field to look up the hostname information. The results will appear in the **Results** text field at the bottom of the screen.

How it works...

The four steps for the hostname to an IP address resolution are as follows:

1. First, the CFHostCreateWithName() function creates a CFHost reference.
2. Then CFHostStartInfoResolution() begins the address to host resolution.
3. Next, CFHostGetAddressing() gets the addresses for the host. At this point, you have a reference to a CFArray that contains the sockaddr structures, which represent the address information for the host.
4. Finally, Getnameinfo() retrieves the IP address of the host using the sockaddr structure.

The following are the steps for an IP address to hostname resolution:

1. Create an `addrinfo` structure that contains the information about the type of address we are looking for.
2. Using the `Getaddrinfo()` function is used to populate a linked list of the `addrinfo` structures that represent the host.
3. Next, `CFDataCreate()` creates a reference to the `CFData` object for the address from the `addrinfo` structure.
4. Then `CFHostCreateWithAddress()` creates a reference to the `CFHost` object from the `CFData` reference.
5. Next, `CFHostStartInfoResolution()` begins the address to host resolution.
6. Finally, `CFHostGetNames()` gets the hostnames for the host. At this point, you have the reference to a `CFArray` that contains the hostnames for the host.

Creating an echo server

In this recipe, we will be creating an echo server that will listen on a specified port. Once a connection is established, the server will echo any text received back by the client.

There are several ways to create a CFSocket. For this recipe, we will create a BSD socket and then use the `CFSocketCreateWithNative()` method to create the CFSocket from the native BSD socket.

To create a BSD socket, you must first create a socket using the `socket()` function. This function returns an integer descriptor that can be used to identify the socket for all future function calls. Once we have the socket descriptor, we need to bind the network interfaces and port to the socket. We create a `sockaddr` structure with the IP address version, IP address, and the port number to bind the socket. We will then call the `bind()` function to bind the `sockaddr` structure and the socket together. Finally, we will need to listen on the socket for new connections. This can be done with the `listen()` function.

The socket's bind and listen steps are the normal steps needed to prepare a TCP server and to create a listening descriptor with the BSD socket API. The listening descriptor will then be used in the `CFSocketCreateWithNative()` function to create the CFSocket from the native BSD socket. Once the CFSocket is created, we will then add it as the source to our run loop.

In the downloadable code for this recipe, we will encapsulate the creation of the server into an Objective-C class complete with error checking, to make it easy for you to add this code to your project.

This recipe is compatible with both iOS and OS X. No extra frameworks or libraries are required.

How to do it...

Let's get started!

Creating the CFSocketServer header file

The following is the code snippet for creating the `CFSocketServer` header file:

```objc
#import <Foundation/Foundation.h>

typedef NS_ENUM(NSUInteger, BSDServerErrorCode) {
  NOERROR,
  SOCKETERROR,
  BINDERROR,
  LISTENERROR,
  CFSOCKETCREATEERROR,
  ACCEPTINGERROR
};
@interface CFSocketServer : NSObject

@property (nonatomic) CFSocketRef sRef;
@property (nonatomic) int listenfd, self.errorCode;

- (instancetype)initOnPort:(int)port;

@end
```

The `CFSocketServer` header file begins by defining an `enum` datatype that contains the six error conditions that can be returned when attempting to create the socket. The header file also defines two properties (`listenfd` and `errorCode`) and one constructor.

If you have reviewed the recipe from *Chapter 1*, *BSD Socket Library*, where we created an echo server using BSD sockets, you may be wondering where the method to listen on the socket is. Since we are creating the server using CFNetwork and CFSockets, we will be using the run loop to monitor the socket and notify us when a connection comes in. This is the pretty big advantage of using CFNetwork.

Creating the CFSocketServer implementation file

We start off by importing the headers that we need as follows:

```
#import "CFSocketServer.h"
#import <CoreFoundation/CFSocket.h>
#import <sys/socket.h>
#import <netinet/in.h>

#define LISTENQ 1024

@implementation CFSocketServer
```

We start off by importing the headers that are needed for the CFSocketServer implementation. The LISTENQ constant is the maximum number of pending connections that can be queued up at any one time before the sockets stop accepting new connection requests.

Now let's create the initOnPort: constructor.

This constructor will take a single parameter named port of type int. The port parameter is the port number to bind to the server. This number can range from 0 to 65535; however, you will need root access to bind to the ports below 1024, so I recommend you use port numbers greater than 1024.

```
- (instancetype)initOnPort:(int)port {
  struct sockaddr_in servaddr;
  CFRunLoopSourceRef source;
  const CFSocketContext context = {0, NULL, NULL, NULL, NULL};
  self.errorCode = NOERROR;
  if ((self.listenfd = socket(AF_INET, SOCK_STREAM,
    IPPROTO_TCP))<0) {
    self.errorCode = SOCKETERROR;
  } else {
    memset(&servaddr, 0, sizeof(servaddr));
    servaddr.sin_family = AF_INET;
    servaddr.sin_addr.s_addr = htonl(INADDR_ANY);
    servaddr.sin_port = htons(port);
    if (bind(self.listenfd, (struct sockaddr *)&servaddr,
      sizeof(servaddr)) <0) {
      self.errorCode = BINDERROR;
    } else {
      if (listen(self.listenfd, LISTENQ) <0) {
        self.errorCode = LISTENERROR;
      } else {
```

```
      self.sRef = CFSocketCreateWithNative(NULL, self.listenfd,
        kCFSocketAcceptCallBack,
      acceptConnection, &context);
      if (self.sRef == NULL) {
        self.errorCode = CFSOCKETCREATEERROR;
      }else {
        source = CFSocketCreateRunLoopSource
          (kCFAllocatorDefault, self.sRef, 0);
        CFRunLoopAddSource(CFRunLoopGetCurrent(), source,
          kCFRunLoopDefaultMode);
        CFRelease(source);
        CFRunLoopRun();
      }
    }
  }

  }
  return self;
}
```

We start the `initOnPort:` constructor by defining `sockaddr_in`, `CFRunLoopSourceRef`, and `CFSocketContext`. The `sockaddr_in` structure is the same that we saw in *Chapter 1, BSD Socket Library*.

To set up a socket, we will need to call the `socket()`, `bind()`, and `listen()` functions just as in the recipes from *Chapter 1, BSD Socket Library*. If any of these functions fail, we will want to set the `errorCode` property and skip the rest of the initialization.

We use the `socket()` function to create our socket using the `AF_INET` (IPv4) and `SOCK_STREAM` (TCP) parameters. If you would like to use IPv6, you will need to change `AF_INET` to `AF_INET6`. If you would like to use UDP instead of TCP, you will need to change `SOCK_STREAM` to `SOCK_DGRAM`.

Prior to calling the `bind()` function, we need to set up a `sockaddr` structure that contains the IP address version, IP address, and port number that we will be binding the socket to. Before populating the `sockaddr` structure with the information, we will need to clear the memory to make sure there is no stale information that may cause our `bind()` function to fail. We do this using the `memset()` function.

After we clear the memory for the `sockaddr` structure, we will set the values. The `sin_family` field is set to `AF_INET` to set the IP address version to IPv4. The `sin_addr.s_addr` field is set to `INADDR_ANY` to let the socket bind to any interface on the device. The `sin_port` field is set to the `port` number.

The `htonl()` and `htons()` functions convert the byte order of the values from host byte order to network byte order, so the values can be properly interpreted when making the network calls. If you are unsure what byte order is, you can refer to the *Finding the byte order of your device* recipe in *Chapter 1, BSD Socket Library*.

Once we have the `sockaddr` structure set, we use it to bind the socket to the address(es) specified in the `servaddr` structure. If our `bind()` function call was successful, we attempt to listen to the socket for new connections. We set the maximum number of backlog connection attempts to the `LISTENQ` constant, which is defined as `1024`.

At this point, we have our BSD socket listening for incoming connections.

We use the `CFSocketCreateWithNative()` function to create the CFSocket from our native BSD socket. This function will either return a reference to the CFSocket or return `NULL`, if there was an error. The `CFSocketCreateWithNative()` functions accept several parameters in the following order:

- `CFAllocatorRef`: This is the allocator used to allocate memory to the new object. Generally, this is set to `NULL` or `kCFAllocatorDefault` to use the current default.
- `CFSocketNativeHandle`: This is the native BSD socket that we created earlier.
- `CFOptionFlags`: It is a bitwise OR combination of socket activities that should cause a callback to be triggered.. The options are as follows:
  - `kCFSocketNoCallBack`
  - `kCFSocketReadCallBack`
  - `kCFSocketAcceptCallBack`
  - `kCFSocketDataCallBack`
  - `kCFSocketConnectCallBack`
  - `kCFSocketWriteCallBack`
- `CFSocketCallBack`: It is the C function to be called when a callback is triggered.
- `CFSocketContext`: The `CFSocketContext` parameter is created at the beginning of the `initWithPort:` constructor.

If the CFSocket was successfully created, we create a `CFRunLoopSourceRef` by calling the `CFSocketCreateRunLoopSource()` function. The `CFSocketCreateRunLoopSource()` function accepts three parameters in the following order:

- `CFAllocatorRef`: This is the allocator parameter used to allocate memory to the new object. Generally, this is set to `NULL` or `kCFAllocatorDefault` to use the current default.
- `CFSocketRef`: The `CFSocketRef` that was created using the `CFSocketCreateWithNative()` function.

▸ CFIndex: It is a priority index that indicates the order in which the run loop is processed.

We now add our CFRunLoopSourceRef to a run loop. This is done using the CFRunLoopAddSource() function. The CFRunLoopAddSource() function has three parameters in the following order:

▸ CFRunLoopRef: It is the run loop to add our CFRunLoopSourceRef.

▸ CFRunLoopSourceRef: It is the run loop source reference that we created.

▸ CFStringRef: It is the run loop mode to add to the source. The only option at this time is the kCFRunLoopDefaultMode constant.

Once we add the CFRunLoopSourceRef to a run loop, we can clean up the references that are no longer needed. This is done using the CFRelease() function.

The last thing we do is call the CFRunLoopRun() function to run the current thread's CFRunLoop. At this point, our server is listening on the port defined by our port variable, and will call our acceptConnection() function defined in the CFSocketCreateWithNative() function every time a new connection comes in.

Now let's write the acceptConnection() function to accept the incoming connections:

```
void acceptConnection(CFSocketRef sRef, CFSocketCallBackType
  cType, CFDataRef address, const void *data, void *info)
{
  CFSocketNativeHandle csock = *(CFSocketNativeHandle *)data;
  CFSocketRef sn;
  CFRunLoopSourceRef source;

  const CFSocketContext context = {0, NULL, NULL, NULL, NULL};

  sn = CFSocketCreateWithNative(NULL, csock,
    kCFSocketDataCallBack, receiveData, &context);

  source = CFSocketCreateRunLoopSource(NULL, sn, 0);
  CFRunLoopAddSource(CFRunLoopGetCurrent(), source,
    kCFRunLoopDefaultMode);
  CFRelease(source);
  CFRelease(sn);
}
```

The acceptConnection() function accepts the standard parameters of a CFSocket callback. We begin this function by retrieving the native socket handle from the incoming data by typecasting it as CFSocketNativeHandle. The CFSocketNativeHandle is the typedef of an int type.

We use the CFSocketCreateWithNative() function to create a new CFSocketRef from CFSocketNativeHandle (csock). In the CFSocketCreateWithNative() function call, we define a callback of type kCFSocketDataCallBack. This callback will call the receiveData() function every time new data is received.

We then create a CFRunLoopSourceRef using the CFSocketCreateRunLoopSource() function, add the CFRunLoopSourceRef to the current run loop, and release the references.

Now let's write the receiveData() function to receive the text as it comes in. The receiveData() function accepts the standard parameters for a CFSocket callback.

```
void receiveData(CFSocketRef sRef, CFSocketCallBackType
cType,CFDataRef address, const void *data, void *info)
{
  CFDataRef df = (CFDataRef) data;
  long len = CFDataGetLength(df);
  if(len <= 0) return;

  UInt8 buf[len];
  CFRange range = CFRangeMake(0,len);

  CFDataGetBytes(df, range, buf);
  buf[len]='\0';
  NSString *str = [[NSString alloc] initWithData:(NSData*)data
  encoding:NSASCIIStringEncoding];
  NSLog(@"Received:  %@",str);
  [[NSNotificationCenter defaultCenter]
    postNotificationName:@"posttext" object:str];
  CFSocketSendData(sRef, address, df, 0);  // Echo back
}
```

In the receiveData() function, the data parameter contains the incoming data. This is standard for a callback of type kCFSocketDataCallBack. So the first thing we do in the receiveData() function is to convert the data to a CFDataRef reference, and then check the length to verify that it is greater than 0.

We convert the CFDataRef to a UInt8 array, which is then converted to an NSString object. We then post an NSNotification object with the name posttext that contains the incoming text. This notification can be safely ignored if you do not want to do anything with the text.

Finally, we call the `CFSocketSendData()` function to echo the text back to the client that sent it.

Once you have downloaded the code, you can start the server and test it using the following telnet command:

telnet localhost 2004

Once telnet makes the connection, type any text in and press the *Enter* key.

Once you press the *Enter* key, the text you typed in will be echoed back to you.

How it works...

In order to create our socket, we start off by creating a native (BSD) socket. The code to create a native BSD socket is the same code that we used in *Chapter 1, BSD Socket Library*. Once the socket is created, we then use the `CFSocketCreateWithNative()` method to create the CFSocket.

To create a server using BSD sockets, you must first create a socket using the `socket()` function. This function returns an integer descriptor that can be used to identify the socket for all future function calls.

We will need to create a `sockaddr` structure with the IP address version, IP address, and the port number to bind the socket. We then call the `bind()` function to bind the `sockaddr` structure and the socket together.

Finally, we will need to listen on the socket for new connections. This can be done with the `listen()` function.

The socket's bind and listen steps are the normal steps needed to prepare a TCP server, and to create a listening descriptor. The listening descriptor will be used to accept incoming connections.

Once we have created the native socket, we create the CFSocket using the `CFSocketCreateWithNative()` function. The CFSocket is used to create a run loop source with the `CFSocketCreateRunLoopSource()` function, which is then added to the run loop.

When we created the CFSocket using the `CFSocketCreateWithNative()` function, we created a callback that would call the `acceptConnection()` method each time a new connection came in.

The `acceptConnection()` method creates a new socket for each incoming connection, and then removes the connection from the listen queue. If you recall, we set the maximum number of connections in the queue to be 1024 before it stops accepting new connections. When we create the CFSocket, we use the `CFSocketCreateWithNative()` function again, but this time we create a callback that will call the `receiveData()` method whenever data is received on the socket.

The `receiveData()` method uses the `CFSocketSendData()` function to echo the text back to the client.

Creating an echo client

In the *Creating an echo server* recipe of this chapter, we created an echo server using CFNetworking and tested it with the telnet command. In this recipe, we will create an echo client that can be used to test the echo server. Also note that the echo client and server applications created in *Chapter 1, BSD Socket Library,* can be used interchangeably with the echo client and server applications created in this chapter.

Getting ready

This recipe is compatible with both iOS and OS X. No extra frameworks or libraries are required.

How to do it...

Let's begin!

Creating the CFSocketClient header file

The following is the code snippet for creating the `CFSocketClient` header file:

```
#import <Foundation/Foundation.h>

typedef NS_ENUM(NSUInteger, CFNetworkServerErrorCode) {
  NOERROR,
  SOCKETERROR,
  CONNECTERROR,
  READERROR,
  WRITEERROR
};

#define MAXLINE 4096

@interface CFSocketClient : NSObject
```

```
@property (nonatomic) int errorCode;
@property (nonatomic) CFSocketRef sockfd;

-(instancetype)initWithAddress:(NSString *)addr andPort:(int)port;

-(NSString *) writtenToSocket:(CFSocketRef)sockfdNum
withChar:(NSString *)vptr;

@end
```

The `CFSocketClient` header file begins by defining the five error conditions in an `enum` datatype that could occur while our echo client is running. We also define the `errorCode` and `sockfd` properties. The `errorCode` property will contain one of the five error conditions, and the `sockfd` property will contain the socket handle once the connection is made to the server.

The header file also defines the `initWithAddress:onPort:` constructor. This constructor will attempt to make a connection to an echo server on the port defined by the `port` parameter.

The `writtenToSocket:withChar:` method will write the text to the server and also receive the response.

Creating the CFSocketClient implementation file

The following is the code snippet for creating the `CFSocketClient` implementation file:

```
#import "CFSocketClient.h"
#import <CoreFoundation/CFSocket.h>
#import <sys/socket.h>
#import <netinet/in.h>
#import <arpa/inet.h>

@implementation CFSocketClient
```

We begin our `CFSocketClient` implementation file by importing the headers we need to make our CFSocket client.

Let's create the `initOnAddres:withPort:` constructor. This constructor will attempt to make a connection to the server using the IP address and port number combination that is passed to it. You could make another constructor that would take a hostname rather than an IP address, and use the `CFNetworkUtility` class from the *Performing network address resolution* recipe in this chapter to convert the hostname to an IP address:

```
-(instancetype)initWithAddress:(NSString *)addr andPort:(int)port {
```

```
self.sockfd = CFSocketCreate(NULL, AF_INET, SOCK_STREAM,
   IPPROTO_TCP,0, NULL,NULL);
if (self.sockfd == NULL)
self.errorCode = SOCKETERROR;
else {

   struct sockaddr_in servaddr;
   memset(&servaddr, 0, sizeof(servaddr));
   servaddr.sin_len = sizeof(servaddr);
   servaddr.sin_family = AF_INET;
   servaddr.sin_port = htons(port);
   inet_pton(AF_INET, [addr cStringUsingEncoding:
     NSUTF8StringEncoding], &servaddr.sin_addr);
   CFDataRef connectAddr = CFDataCreate(NULL, (unsigned char
     *)&servaddr, sizeof(servaddr));
   if (connectAddr == NULL)
   self.errorCode = CONNECTERROR;
   else {
     if (CFSocketConnectToAddress(self.sockfd, connectAddr, 30)
       != kCFSocketSuccess)
     self.errorCode = CONNECTERROR;
   }
 }
 return self;
}
```

We begin the `initOnAddress:withPort:` constructor by calling the `CFSocketCreate()` function to create a CFSocket. The `CFSocketCreate()` function accepts several parameters in the following order:

- ▸ `CFAllocatorRef`: This is the allocator used to allocate memory for the new object. Generally, this is set to `NULL` or `kCFAllocatorDefault` to use the current default.

- ▸ `SInt32`: This is the protocol family for the socket. In our example, we are using `AF_INET`; however, we could also use `AF_INET6` if we wanted to use IPv6.

- ▸ `SInt32`: This is the socket type for the socket. In our example, we use `SOCK_STREAM` to create a socket stream (TCP). If we wanted to use UDP, we would set it to `SOCK_DGRAM`.

- ▸ `SINT32`: This is the protocol to be used. In our example, we set it to `IPPROTO_TCP`, but it could also be `IPPROTO_UDP`.

- ▸ `CFOptionFlags`: This is the callback type that is a bitwise OR combination of socket activities, which should cause a callback to be triggered. The options are:

    - ❑ `kCFSocketNoCallBack`
    - ❑ `kCFSocketReadCallBack`

- ❑ kCFSocketAcceptCallBack
- ❑ kCFSocketDataCallBack
- ❑ kCFSocketConnectCallBack
- ❑ kCFSocketWriteCallBack

▸ CFSocketCallBack: This is the C function to be called when a callback is triggered.

▸ CFSocketContext: In this example, we are setting it to NULL.

After we create our CFSocket, we need to create a sockaddr structure that contains the server information that we are trying to connect to. Whenever you create a sockaddr structure, you should always clear the memory used by the structure prior to setting the structure's information. In this example, we use the memset() function to do this.

After we clear the memory of our sockaddr structure, we can set the values. The sin_family field is set to AF_INET to set the IP address version to IPv4. The sin_port field is set to the port number passed to the constructor using the htons() function. We then use the inet_pton() function to convert the address to an address structure (in_addr) and put the results into servaddr.sin_addr.

The sockaddr structure, once created, will need to be converted to CFData to be used in the CFSocketConnectToAddress() function. This is done with the CFDataCreate() function, which returns a CFDataRef. The CFSocketConnectToAddress() function is called to open up a connection to the remote server.

Now let's create the writtenToSocket:withChar: method:

```
- (NSString *) writtenToSocket:(CFSocketRef)sockfdNum
  withChar:(NSString *)vptr
{

  char buffer[MAXLINE];

  CFSocketNativeHandle sock = CFSocketGetNative(sockfdnum);
  const char *mess = [vptr
    cStringUsingEncoding:NSUTF8StringEncoding];

  NSLog(@"%s", mess);
  send(sock, mess, strlen(mess)+1, 0);
  recv(sock, buffer, sizeof(buffer), 0);
  NSLog(@"%s", buffer);
  return [NSString stringWithUTF8String:buffer];
}
```

The `writtenToSocket:withChar:` method writes the characters to the socket identifier. This method takes two parameters: `sockfdNum`, which is a `CFSocketRef`, and `vptr`, which is a pointer to the string we wish to send to the server. We use the `CFSocketGetNative()` method to convert the `CFSocketRef` to a native BSD socket handle.

We then convert the `NSString` object to a `char` pointer, and use the BSD `send()` function to send the text to the echo server. After we send the text, we listen on the socket for the returning characters. This is done with the `recv()` function.

Using the CFSocketClient class

The downloadable code contains examples for both iOS and OS X. If you run the iOS example in the iPhone simulator, the app looks like the following screenshot:

Type the text you wish to send in the **Text to send** field, and then click on the **Send** button. The text that is received back from the server, in this case **Hello**, appears directly below the **Text Received** label.

We will look at the `sendPressed:` method in the iOS sample code as an example of how to use the `BSDSocketClient` method. This method is called when you click on the **Send** button.

```
- (IBAction)sendPressed:(id)sender {
    NSString *str = textField.text;
    CFSocketClient *cf = [[[CFSocketClient alloc]
        initWithAddress:@"127.0.0.1" andPort:2004] autorelease];
```

```
    if (cf.self.errorCode == NOERRROR) {
      NSString *recv = [cf writtenToSocket:cf.sockfd withChar:str];
      NSLog(@"%@",recv);
      textRecvLabel.text = recv;
      textField.text = @"";

    } else {
      NSLog(@"%@", [NSString stringWithFormat:@"Error code %d
        recieved.  Server was not started", cf.self.errorCode]);
    }
  }
```

We start executing the method by retrieving the text that was entered in the **Text to send** field. This is the text that we will be sending to the echo server.

We then initiate the BSDSocketClient object with the IP address 127.0.0.1, which is the local loopback adapter, and the port number as 2004. If you run this on an iPhone, you will need to set the IP address to the address of the computer that is running the echo server. You will also need to set the port number to the port that the server is bound to.

Once we have successfully connected the client, we call the writtenToSocket:withChar: method to write the text entered in the **Text to send** field to the server.

Finally, we populate the UITextField with the information received back from the echo server.

How it works...

The following are the steps to create a CFSocket connection to a server:

1. Create a CFSocket reference using the CFSocketCreate() function.
2. Create a sockaddr structure with the IP address version, IP address, and port number.
3. Use the CFDataCreate() function to create a reference to a CFData object that represents the sockaddr structure from step 2.
4. Use the CFSocketConnectToAddress() function to create a connection to the server. At this point, if nothing failed, we will have an open socket connection to the server and you can use any of the BSD or CFNetwork functions to read or write to the socket.

Creating a server to receive data

In the *Creating an echo server* recipe of this chapter, we created an echo server using Apple's CFNetwork API. This server accepted incoming text and echoed it back to the client. That recipe demonstrated how to send and receive text through a socket connection.

This following recipe will demonstrate how to send and receive datafiles such as images through a socket connection. Sending and receiving data over a socket connection with CFNetworking is not that different from sending and receiving text. You basically go through all the same steps to set up the socket, but you finally receive `CFData` rather than a character array.

We will be updating the `CFSocketServer` class from the *Creating an echo server* recipe of this chapter, to handle both our echo and data servers depending on the flag you set.

Getting ready

This recipe is compatible with both iOS and OS X. No extra frameworks or libraries are required.

How to do it...

Let's get started!

Updating the CFSocketServer header file

The following is the code snippet for creating the `CFSocketServer` header file:

```
#import <Foundation/Foundation.h>

typedef NS_ENUM(NSUInteger, CFNetworkServerErrorCode) {
  NOERROR,
  SOCKETERROR,
  BINDERROR,
  LISTENERROR,
  CFSOCKETCREATEERROR,
  ACCEPTINGERROR
};

typedef  NS_ENUM(NSUInteger, CFNetworkServerType) {
  SERVERTYPEECHO,
  SERVERTYPEIMAGE
};

#define NOTIFICATIONTEXT @"posttext"
#define NOTIFICATIONIMAGE @"postimage"

@interface CFSocketServer : NSObject

@property (nonatomic) int errorCode;
@proprtyy (nonatomic) CFSocketRef sRef;
```

```
-(id)initOnPort:(int)port andServerType:(int)sType;

@end
```

The CFSocketServer header file begins by defining the six error conditions that could occur within an `enum` datatype. We also set up another `enum` datatype that is used to define the server type (echo server or image server). You can add additional server types, such as PDF and Word doc, as your need arises, or simply create a generic datatype to accept any data connection. We then define the name of the notifications that are used to post incoming text and image data.

We changed the constructor that was used in the *Creating an echo server* recipe of this chapter to the `initOnPort:andServerType:` constructor. This will allow us to define the server type that we are going to create, which requires us to have separate `CFSocketCreateWithNative()` function calls for each type of server.

Updating the CFSocketServer implementation file

We start off with adding the imports needed for the `CFSocketServer` file implementation as follows:

```
#import "CFSocketServer.h"
#import <CoreFoundation/CFSocket.h>
#import <sys/socket.h>
#import <netinet/in.h>
#import <arpa/inet.h>
#define LISTENQ 1024

@implementation CFSocketServer
```

We begin the implementation file by importing the headers files needed. We also define our `LISTENQ` constant as `1024`. The `LISTENQ` constant represents the number of pending connections that can be queued up before our server stops accepting new connections.

Now let's update the `initOnPort:andServerType:` constructor. The `initOnPort:andServerType:` constructor is the same constructor that we created in the *Creating an echo server* recipe, except for one very important change. This change occurs at the end where we create the CFSocket from the native BSD socket. If you recall from the *Creating an echo server* recipe, we used the `CFSocketCreateWithNative()` function to create the CFSocket. This function defines the callback to call when you receive an incoming connection.

In our example, we will want to call a different function depending on the server type. This requires us to have separate `CFSocketCreateWithNative` calls for each type of server.

```
-(instancetype)initOnPort:(int)port andServerType:(int)sType {
  struct sockaddr_in servaddr;
  CFRunLoopSourceRef source;
```

```
const CFSocketContext context = {0, NULL, NULL, NULL, NULL};
self.errorCode = NOERROR;
int listenfd;
if ((listenfd = socket(AF_INET, SOCK_STREAM, IPPROTO_TCP))<0) {
  self.self.errorCode = SOCKETERROR;
} else {
  memset(&servaddr, 0, sizeof(servaddr));
  servaddr.sin_family = AF_INET;
  servaddr.sin_addr.s_addr = htonl(INADDR_ANY);
  servaddr.sin_port = htons(port);
  if (bind(listenfd, (struct sockaddr *)&servaddr,
    sizeof(servaddr)) <0) {
    self.self.errorCode = BINDERROR;
  } else {
    if (listen(listenfd, LISTENQ) <0) {
      self.errorCode = LISTENERROR;
    } else {
      if (sType == SERVERTYPEECHO)
      self.sRef = CFSocketCreateWithNative(NULL, listenfd,
        kCFSocketAcceptCallBack, acceptConnectionEcho, &context);
      else if (sType == SERVERTYPEIMAGE)
      self.sRef = CFSocketCreateWithNative(NULL, listenfd,
        kCFSocketAcceptCallBack, acceptConnectionData, &context);
      else
      self.sRef = NULL;
      if (self.sRef == NULL) {
        self.errorCode = CFSOCKETCREATEERROR;
      }else {
        NSLog(@"Starting");
        source = CFSocketCreateRunLoopSource(NULL, self.sRef, 0);
        CFRunLoopAddSource(CFRunLoopGetCurrent(), source,
          kCFRunLoopDefaultMode);
        CFRelease(source);
        CFRunLoopRun();
      }
      }
    }
  }

}
return self;
}
```

We start the `initOnPort:andServerTyper:` constructor by defining a `sockaddr_in` structure, `CFRunLoopSourceRef`, and `CFSocketContext`. The `sockaddr_in` structure is the same that is referred to in the BSD socket API.

If you recall from the recipe's introduction, in order to set up a socket, we will need to call the socket(), bind(), and listen() functions. If any of these functions fail, we will want to set the errorCode property and skip the rest of the initialization.

We attempt to create our socket using the AF_INET (IPv4) and SOCK_STREAM (TCP) parameters. If you would like to use IPv6, you will need to change the AF_INET parameter to AF_INET6. If you would like to use UDP instead of TCP, you could change the SOCK_STREAM parameter to SOCK_DGRAM.

Prior to calling the bind() function, we need to set up a sockaddr structure that contains the IP address version, IP address, and port number that we will be binding the socket to. Before populating the sockaddr structure with the information, we need to clear the memory to make sure there is no stale information that may cause our bind() function to fail. We do this using the memset() function.

After we clear the memory for our sockaddr structure, we set the values. The sin_family field is set to AF_INET to set the IP address version to IPv4. The sin_addr.s_addr field is set to INADDR_ANY to let the socket bind to any interface on the device. We set sin_port to the port number passed to the constructor using the htons() function.

The htonl() and htons() functions convert the byte order of the values from host byte order to network byte order so the values can be properly interpreted when making the network calls. If you are unsure what byte order is, you can refer to the *Finding the byte order of your device* recipe from *Chapter 1*, *BSD Socket Library*.

After we have our sockaddr structure set, we use it to bind the socket to the address(es) specified in the servaddr structure. If the bind() function call was successful, we attempt to listen to the socket for new connections. We set the maximum number of backlog connection attempts to the LISTENQ constant, which is defined as 1024.

If the server type is set to SERVERTYPEECHO (for an echo server), the run loop will call the acceptConnectionEcho() function when an incoming connection is detected.

If the server type is set to SERVERTYPEIMAGE (for an image server), the run loop will call the acceptConnectionImage() function when an incoming connection is detected.

If the server type is neither SERVERTYPEECHO nor SERVERTYPEIMAGE, we set sRef to NULL. If sRef is NULL, we set the errorCode property and skip the rest of the connection code.

We now need to add our CFRunLoopSourceRef to a run loop. This is done using the CFRunLoopAddSource() function. The CFRunLoopAddSource() function has three parameters in the following order:

- ▶ CFRunLoopRef: This is the run loop to add to our CFRunLoopSourceRef.
- ▶ CFRunLoopSourceRef: This is the run loop source reference that we created.
- ▶ CFStringRef: This is the run loop mode to add to the source. The only option at this time is kCFRunLoopDefaultMode.

Once we add our `CFRunLoopSourceRef` reference to a run loop, we can clean up the references that are no longer needed. This is done using the `CFRelease()` function and is very important to avoid memory leaks in our application.

The last thing we call is the `CFRunLoopRun()` function to run the current thread's `CFRunLoop`. At this point, our server is listening on the port defined by our `port` variable, and will call the appropriate `acceptConnection` function (either `acceptConnectionEcho()` or `acceptConnectionData()`) defined in the `CFSocketCreateWithNative()` function every time a new connection comes in.

The next two functions can be seen in the *Creating an echo server* recipe of this chapter. They are for our echo server:

```
//For Echo server
void receiveDataEcho(CFSocketRef sRef, CFSocketCallBackType
  cType,CFDataRef address, const void *data, void *info)
{...}

void acceptConnectionEcho(CFSocketRef sRef, CFSocketCallBackType
  cType, CFDataRef address, const void *data, void *info)
{...}
```

Now let's write our function to accept the incoming connections for our data server:

```
void acceptConnectionData(CFSocketRef sRef, CFSocketCallBackType
  cType, CFDataRef address, const void *data, void *info)
{
  CFSocketNativeHandle csock = *(CFSocketNativeHandle *)data;
  CFSocketRef sn;
  CFRunLoopSourceRef source;

  const CFSocketContext context = {0, NULL, NULL, NULL, NULL};

  sn = CFSocketCreateWithNative(NULL, csock,
    kCFSocketDataCallBack, receiveDataData, &context);

  source = CFSocketCreateRunLoopSource(NULL, sn, 0);
  CFRunLoopAddSource(CFRunLoopGetCurrent(), source,
    kCFRunLoopDefaultMode);
  CFRelease(source);
  CFRelease(sn);
}
```

The `acceptConnectionImage()` function begins by retrieving the native socket handle from the incoming data and putting it in `csock`, which is `CFSocketNativeHandle`. `CDSocketNativeHandle` is `typedef` from an `int` type.

We use the `CFSocketCreateWithNative()` function to create a new `CFSocketRef` from csock. In the `CFSocketCreateWithNative()` function, we define a callback of type `kCFSocketDataCallBack`. This callback will call the `receiveDataData()` function every time new data is received.

We then create a `CFRunLoopSourceRef` using the `CFSocketCreateRunLoopSource()` function, and add the `CFRunLoopSourceRef` to the current run loop.

Let's create the `receiveDataData()` function. This function gets called whenever data is received on an established connection. This function accepts the standard parameters for a CFSocket callback.

```
//For Data server
void receiveDataData(CFSocketRef sRef, CFSocketCallBackType
cType,CFDataRef address, const void *data, void *info)
{
  CFDataRef df = (CFDataRef) data;
  NSData *imgData = (NSData *)df;
  struct sockaddr_in addr = *(struct
    sockaddr_in*)CFDataGetBytePtr(address);
  char buf[INET6_ADDRSTRLEN];
  NSString *connStr = [NSString stringWithFormat:@"Connection from
    %s, port %d", inet_ntop(AF_INET, &addr.sin_addr,buf,
    sizeof(buf)),ntohs(addr.sin_port)];
  NSLog(@"%@", connStr);
  [[NSNotificationCenter defaultCenter]
    postNotificationName:NOTIFICATIONIMAGE object:imgData];
}
```

In the `receiveDataData()` function, the data parameter contains the incoming data. This is standard for a `kCFSocketDataCallBack` callback. So the first thing we do in the `receiveDataData()` function is convert the data to a `CFDataRef` reference, and then convert the `CFDataRef` to an `NSData` object.

Once we have the `NSData` object, we post the data with a notification, so anything listening for the `"postimage"` notification will receive the data.

> You will notice that the `acceptConnectionEcho()` function uses almost the exact same code as the `acceptConnectionData()` function. The only difference is we have different callback functions defined in the `CFSocketCreateWithNative()` function. We could combine the two functions and make separate `CFSocketCreateWithNative()` function calls depending on the server type, but I prefer to separate them so each server type has its own workflow and the only common function is when we initiate the sockets. It really is a matter of preference.

Using the CFSocketServer class

The code bundle provided with this book and the code snippet in this chapter is not designed to handle multiple connections at the same time. For example, if you have two clients sending data at the same time, the data from the two clients will get combined and that would not be good.

When you write an application that is designed for multiple clients, you will want to use the information in the CFDataRef address parameter to distinguish between the different clients. From the logging information, you will see that each connection has a unique IP address and port number combination.

One of the simplest ways to create a server that can handle multiple connections is to create an NSDictionary object that contains the IP address, port number, and NSdata object. Then post the NSDictionary object to the notification rather than just the NSData object. The method that receives the notification will then be able to distinguish the data from different clients.

The downloadable code contains examples for both iOS and OS X. These samples will accept the incoming images, and either save the image to the disk (OS X project) or display it in a UIImageView object (iOS project).

How it works...

In order to create our CFSocket, we start off by creating a native (BSD) socket, and then use the CFSocketCreateWithNative() method to create the CFSocket.

To create a server using BSD sockets, you must first create a socket using the socket() function. The function returns an integer descriptor that can be used to identify the socket in all future function calls.

Once we have the socket descriptor, we need to bind the network interface and port to the socket. We will need to create a sockaddr structure with the IP address version, address, and the port number to bind the socket to. We will then call the bind() function to bind the sockaddr structure and the socket together.

Finally, we will need to listen on the socket for new connections. This is done with the listen() function.

The socket's bind and listen steps are the normal steps needed to prepare a TCP server and to create a listening descriptor. The listening descriptor will be used to accept incoming connections. Once we have created the native socket, we can create the CFSocket using the CFSocketCreateWithNative() function. The CFSocket is used to create a run-loop source with the CFSocketCreateRunLoopSource() function, which is then added to the run loop.

When we created the CFSocket using the `CFSocketCreateWithNative()` function, we then created a callback that would call the appropriate `acceptConnection` method (`acceptConnectionEcho()` for the echo server or `acceptConnectionData()` for the data server) each time a new connection came in.

The `acceptConnection()` method creates a new socket for each incoming connection, and then removes the connection from the listen queue. When we create the CFSocket for the incoming connections, we use the `CFSocketCreateWithNative()` function again; however, this time we create a callback that will call the appropriate `receiveData()` method whenever data is received on the socket.

Creating a client to send data

In the *Creating a data server* recipe from *Chapter 1*, *BSD Socket Library*, we created a server that can receive incoming data. In this recipe, we will create a client application that will send images to that server.

Also note that the data client and server applications created in *Chapter 1*, *BSD Socket Library*, can be used interchangeably with the data client and server applications created in this chapter.

We will be expanding the `CFSocketClient` class that we wrote in the *Creating a data client* recipe from *Chapter 1*, *BSD Socket Library*, to handle both the echo client and the data client.

Getting ready

This recipe is compatible with both iOS and OS X. No extra frameworks or libraries are required.

How to do it...

Let's get started!

Updating the CFSocketClient header file

In the header file, we add the `sendDataToSocket:withData:` method:

```
#import <Foundation/Foundation.h>

typedef NS_ENUM(NSUInteger, CFNetworkClientErrorCode) {
    NOERRROR,
    SOCKETERROR,
    CONNECTERROR,
    READERROR,
    WRITEERROR
};
```

```
#define MAXLINE 4096
@interface CFSocketClient : NSObject

@property (nonatomic) int self.errorCode;
@property (nonatomic) CFSocketRef sockfd;

-(id)initWithAddr:(NSString *) addr andPort:(int)port;

-(ssize_t) writtenToSocket:(CFSocketRef)sockfdNum withChar:(NSString
*)vptr;
-(ssize_t)sendDataToSocket:(CFSocketRef)lsockfd withDAta:NSData *)
data;

@end
```

Updating the CFSocketClient implementation file

This is the same CFSocketClient file as in the *Creating an echo client* recipe, except
that we are adding the sendDataToSocket:withData: method as shown in the following
code snippet:

```
-(ssize_t)sendDataToSocket:(CFSocketRef)lsockfd withData: (NSData
 *)data
{
  NSLog(@"sending");
  ssize_t n;
  const UInt8 *buf = (const UInt8 *)[data bytes];
  CFSocketNativeHandle sock = CFSocketGetNative(self.sockfd);

  if ((n = send(sock, buf,[data length],0)) <=0) {
    self.errorCode = WRITEERROR;
    n=-1;
  } else {
    self.errorCode = NOERRROR;
  }
  NSLog(@"Done");
  CFSocketInvalidate(lsockfd);
  CFRelease(lsockfd);
  lsockfd = NULL;
  return n;

}
```

The sendDataToSocket:withData: method will write the data to the already established
socket. This method begins by converting the NSData object to a UInt8 buffer. We then
convert the CFSocketRef to a BSD socket handle using the CFSocketGetNative()
function call.

The send() function is used to send the data to the server. If the send() function returns 0 or less sent bytes, it means there was a problem with sending the data, and we set the errorCode property to WRITERROR.

After the data is sent, we close the socket connection. If your client application requires you to send multiple files over the same socket, you will want to comment these out and close the connection when you are done.

The downloadable code contains examples for both iOS and OS X.

How it works...

The following are the steps to create a CFSocket connection to a server:

1. Create a CFSocket reference using the CFSocketCreate() function.
2. Create a sockaddr structure with the IP address version, IP address, and port number.
3. Use the CFDataCreate() function to create a reference to a CFData object that represents the sockaddr structure from step 2.
4. Use the CFSocketConnectToAddress() function to create a connection to the server. At this point, if nothing fails, we will have an open socket connection to the server, and we can send our data across.

Checking the network status

Any time you create an iOS application that communicates to other devices over the Internet, you will eventually need to verify that you have a connection prior to making your network calls. This can be done pretty easily by verifying that the address we are trying to connect is reachable, but only lets you know if you have a network connection or not.

When you write applications that communicate with mobile devices over the Internet, one of the things you need to keep in mind is that your users probably have a data plan that limits the amount of data they can send in a month. If they exceed that limit, they may have to pay an extra fee. If your application sends large amounts of data, it would be good to know what type of network connection the user currently has; if it is a mobile connection (as opposed to a Wi-Fi connection), warn the user prior to sending the data.

This recipe will check the type of network connection our device has. For this project, we will be using Apple's System Configuration framework, so you will need to import it into your project when you use this recipe.

This recipe is compatible with iOS and you will need to import Apple's System Configuration framework into your project.

How to do it...

Let's get started!

Creating the NetworkDetect header file

Let's create the `NetworkDetect` header file as follows:

```
#import <Foundation/Foundation.h>

typedef NS_ENUM(NSUInteger, NetworkTypes) {
  NONETWORK,
  MOBILE3GNETWORK,
  WIFINETWORK
};

@interface NetworkDetect : NSObject

+(int)networkConnectionType;

@end
```

The `NetworkDetect` header file starts out by defining the three network types that we will be looking for in an `enum` datatype. We also define the one method that we will use to check the network connection type; it is the `networkConnectionType:` method.

Creating the NetworkDetect implementation file

The following is the code snippet for creating the `NetworkDetect` implementation file:

```
#import "NetworkDetect.h"
#import <SystemConfiguration/SystemConfiguration.h>
#import <net/if.h>

@implementation NetworkDetect

+(int)networkConnectionType
{
  const char *hostname = "www.packtpub.com";
  SCNetworkReachabilityRef reachabilityRef =
    etworkReachabilityCreateWithName(NULL, hostname);
```

```
SCNetworkReachabilityFlags flags;
SCNetworkReachabilityGetFlags(reachabilityRef, &flags);
BOOL isReachable = ((flags & kSCNetworkFlagsReachable) != 0);
BOOL needsConnection = ((flags &
  kSCNetworkFlagsConnectionRequired) != 0);
NSLog(@"%d  %d", isReachable, needsConnection);
if(isReachable && !needsConnection) // connection is available
{
  // determine what type of connection is available
  BOOL isCellularConnection = ((flags &
    kSCNetworkReachabilityFlagsIsWWAN) != 0);

  if(isCellularConnection)
    return MOBILE3GNETWORK; // cellular connection available
  else
    return WIFINETWORK; // Wi-Fi connection available
}
return NONETWORK; // no connection at all
}


@end
```

The networkConnectionType: method begins by setting hostname to the URL of the server we are connecting to. To determine if we have a network connection and the type of connection, we need to create a SCNetworkReachability reference. To get the SCNetworkRechabilityRef, we use the SCNetworkReachabilityCreateWithName() function, which requires a hostname to connect to.

After we get our SCNetworkReachabilityRef, we need to retrieve the SCNetworkReachabilityFlags enum from the reference. This is done with the SCNetworkReachabilityGetFlags() function.

Once we have the network reachability flags, we can begin testing our connection. We use the bitwise AND operator to see if the host is reachable (isReachable) and if it needs to establish a connection before we can communicate with the host (needsConnection). If the isReachable flag is false or needsConnection is true, we return NONETWORK, meaning the host is not reachable.

If we are able to connect to the host, we then check to see if we have a cellular connection by checking the network reachability flags again. If we have a cellular connection, we return MOBILE3GNETWORK; otherwise, we assume we have a Wi-Fi connection and return WIFINETWORK.

The downloadable code contains a sample iOS application for this recipe.

How it works...

In this recipe, we use the SCNetworkReachibility API to determine the reachability of a remote host and the current network configuration. One thing to keep in mind is that the SCNetworkReachability API does not actually determine if the host received the data packet. It only has the ability to determine if we can send packets to the remote host.

Once we create the SCNetworkReachability reference with the SCNetworkReachibilityCreateWithName() function, we pull the reachability flags using the SCNetworkReachibilityGetFlags() function. We can then determine if the network is reachable, if it needs a connection, and what type of connection it has, by examining the flags.

3
Using Libnet

In this chapter, we will cover:

- ▶ Installing libnet
- ▶ Adding libnet to your project
- ▶ Resolving names to addresses with libnet
- ▶ Retrieving local addresses with libnet
- ▶ Constructing a Ping packet with libnet
- ▶ Constructing a UDP packet with libnet
- ▶ Constructing a TCP packet with libnet

Introduction

Libnet is a library that allows developers to construct and inject individual network packets. The libnet API hides most of the packet creation low-level details from the developer and allows the developer to quickly create and inject simple packets. Not only can libnet be used to create very powerful network security and monitoring tools, but it can also be used for malicious activities.

 While it is possible to compile libnet for the iPhone, if your app constructs custom packets and injects them into the network, Apple will probably reject your app. The code in this chapter is written and tested for OS X; it may or may not work on iOS.

When computers on an IP network wish to communicate, they exchange packets. These packets contain two types of information that are as follows:

- **Control information (header)**: The header provides information that the network needs to route the packet to the correct destination. This includes source and destination addresses, checksums, control flags, sequence numbers, and Time to Live.

- **User data (payload)**: The user data, more commonly known as the payload, is the information that the computers wish to exchange. This can be anything from web pages to encrypted files to streaming video.

Large chunks of data are broken apart into multiple packets. For protocols such as TCP that require reliable communication, a sequence number in the header is used to reassemble the data in the correct order, regardless of the order in which the packets were received.

A packet is built in layers as shown in the following diagram:

		Data		Application Layer		FTP	HTTP	SMTP	DNS
	Protocol Header			Protocol Layer		TCP		UDP	
IP Header				Internet Layer		ICMP	IP	ARP	
Frame Header				Link Layer		ethernet	802.11 WIFI	Point to Point	

The four layers of the packet are as follows:

- **Application layer**: In this layer, an application creates the payload. This is where higher level protocols, such as FTP, HTTP, or SMTP do their work. The application headers and the payload are added to this layer.

- **Protocol layer**: This layer provides a uniform networking interface that hides the underlying network connections. This is where the payload is broken into multiple packets (if needed) and reassembled. This layer is where a protocol-specific header, such as TCP, UDP, or ICMP, is added.

- **Internet layer**: Every device on an IP network is identified by a unique address known as an IP address. There are two versions of IP addresses: IPv4 and IPv6. This is the layer where the IP header is added.

- **Link layer**: There are many different types of network connections, such as Ethernet, 802.11 Wi-Fi, and **Point-to-Point Protocol** (**PPP**). The Link layer defines the method in which the host communicates to the network.

Each of these layers wraps (or a better term would be encapsulates) the layers below it. We can think of it as an onion where each layer of the onion completely encompasses all layers below.

The biggest strength of this model is that each layer is independent of all the other layers. For example, the Internet layer does not need to know, nor does it rely on, anything from the Protocol layer.

With this in mind, a packet is constructed in the following order:

1. Get the data (the payload) we wish to send across.
2. Construct the Application header that contains the payload.
3. Construct the Protocol header that encapsulates the Application header and the payload.
4. Construct the IP header that encapsulates the Protocol header (the Protocol header encapsulates the Application header and the payload).
5. Construct the Frame header that encapsulates the IP header (the IP header encapsulates the Protocol header that encapsulates the Application header and the payload).

When we are constructing our packets, it is very important to understand how the different layers wrap or encapsulate the layer above them. We also need to understand that when a device receives a packet, it peels the layers away. Using the preceding onion analogy, each layer of the onion needs to be completely peeled away to get to the next layer. Refer to the following diagram:

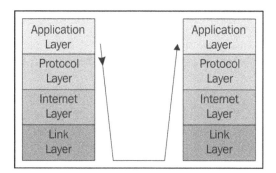

The examples in this chapter use the libnet raw socket interface (rather than the link-layer interface), which means we do not need to worry about coding the Link layer. The link-layer interface is slightly more complex but gives you control over how the Frame layer headers are created. The following steps show how we will build packets in this chapter:

1. Get the data (the payload) we wish to send across. Typically, this will be a text string or data.
2. Build the Protocol header that encapsulates the payload. Depending on the protocol we are using, we would use one of the `libnet_build` functions, such as `libnet_build_tcp`, `libnet_build_udp`, or `libnet_build_icmpv4_echo`.

3. Build the IP header that encapsulates the Protocol header. We can use `libnet_build_ipv4` or `libnet_autobuild_ipv4` to do this.

4. Use the `libnet_write()` function to set the packet out.

The various Protocol headers will be covered in their respective recipes. The IP header is constant for each of the protocols so we will cover this header here:

The following list gives a brief explanation about each of the fields in the IP header:

▸ `Version`: This refers to the version of the IP packet. Its value can be either 4 (IPv4) or 6 (IPv6). For our examples, we will only be using IPv4, but libnet does have IPv6 versions for all of the functions discussed in this chapter.

▸ `Header Length`: This is the number of 32-bit words in the TCP header. The minimum value is 5. Since the IP header may contain a variable number of options, this field specifies the size of the header.

▸ `Type of Service`: This field, now known as **Differentiated Services Code Point** (**DSCP**), may indicate a particular quality of service needs. Libnet still refers to TOS and is usually set to 0.

▸ `Total Length`: This gives the total length of the entire packet, including that of the header and the data, in bytes. The minimum size is 20 and the maximum size is 65535. Some networks set restrictions on the packet size, which may fragment the packet.

▸ `Identification`: This field is primarily used to uniquely identify fragments of an original packet.

▸ `Flags`: This refers to three flags that are defined in the IP packet. They are as follows:
  ❑ **Bit 0**: This is reserved and must be 0.
  ❑ **Bit 1**: If the **Don't Fragment** (**DF**) flag is set and fragmentation is needed to route the packet, the packet will be dropped.
  ❑ **Bit 2**: If a packet is fragmented, all the fragments will have the **More Fragment** (**MF**) flag set except for the last one. The flag is cleared for the packets that are not fragmented.

▸ `Fragment Offset`: This specifies the offset of a particular fragment and is relative to the beginning of the original unfragmented packet.

- ▶ Time to Live: This indicates the number of hops the packet can be routed. This number is decremented at each hop until it reaches its destination or it reaches 0. If the Time to Live reaches 0 before the packet reaches its destination, the packet is discarded.

- ▶ Protocol: This is the IP Protocol ID.

- ▶ Header Checksum: This is the checksum of the IP header.

- ▶ Source Address: This is the IPv4 address of the sender.

- ▶ Destination Address: This is the IPv4 address of the destination.

- ▶ IP Option: This field is normally not used.

The libnet_build_ipv4() functions take the parameters mentioned in the following list; the list also shows how they are mapped to the fields in the IP header:

- ▶ ip_len: This maps to the Total Length field.

- ▶ tos: This maps to the Type of Service field.

- ▶ id: This maps to the Identification field.

- ▶ frag: This maps to the Fragmentation Offset field.

- ▶ ttl: This maps to the Time to Live field.

- ▶ prot: This maps to the Protocol field.

- ▶ sum: This maps to the Checksum field and is set to 0 (zero) to have libnet autofill the checksum.

- ▶ src: This maps to the Source Address field.

- ▶ dst: This maps to the Destination Address field.

- ▶ payload: This is the Option payload that is null if there is no payload. It does not directly map to anything in the header.

- ▶ payload_s: This denotes the size of the payload or 0. It does not directly map to anything in the header.

- ▶ libnet_t: This is the libnet context that is to be used.

- ▶ ptag: This refers to the Protocol tag if we are modifying an existing header or 0 if we build a new one.

Whenever we use the libnet library in a project, we will need to run the project as the root (the super user). This has to do with creating and injecting packets into the network. Generally, this operation is not permitted for normal users. Luckily for us, **Xcode** allows us to run our project as a root.

To run your project as a root, navigate to **Project | Scheme | Edit Scheme** from the top menu as shown in the following screenshot:

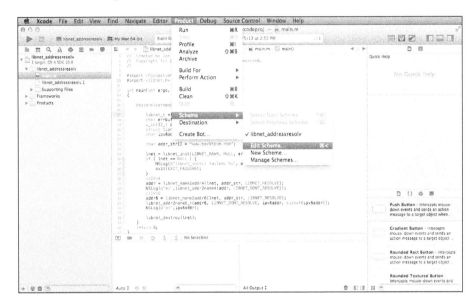

In the window that opens up, change the **Debug Process As** selection from **Me** to **root** as shown in the following screenshot:

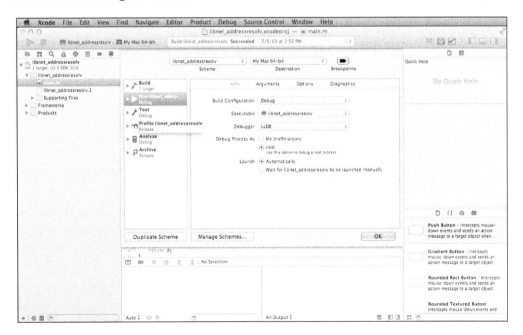

Note that when you debug your process as root, you will periodically be asked for your password. Your user needs to be an administrator on the computer for this to work. If you are not an administrator, you will not be able to debug your application as a root.

Before we get into actually constructing packets, we will need to download and install the libnet library.

Installing libnet

In this recipe, we will show you how to download and install libnet on your computer. Libnet was originally maintained on the `http://packetfactory.openwall.net/` site; however, this site has not been updated since 2007. Since then, a number of individuals have forked the library in an attempt to maintain it. The version that we will be using is the `libnet-dev` project located at `http://sourceforge.net/`.

Getting ready

To get ready for the installation, we will need to download libnet. The projects in this chapter have been tested with the 1.2-RC2 Version, and you can find this version at `http://sourceforge.net/projects/libnet-dev/files/libnet-1.2-rc2.tar.gz/download`.

> Some of the code in this chapter have issues with Version 1.16. If you currently have 1.16 installed, you will need to update it to 1.2.

How to do it...

Once libnet is downloaded, we can install it by performing the following steps:

1. Open a terminal window by going to **Applications | Utilities | Terminal**.

   Assuming that libnet was downloaded to the `Downloads` directory, we will want to go to the `Downloads` directory, untar the libnet tar file, and then move to the libnet directory that was created when we untared the libnet tar file:

   ```
   cd ~/Downloads
   tar xopf libnet-1.2-rc2.tar
   cd libnet-1.2-rc2
   ```

The actual libnet download is in gzip format with the file name `libnet-1.2-rc.tar.gz`. However, if you download the file with Safari, it will automatically unzip the file for you, leaving you with the file `libnet-1.2-rc2.tar`. If you use another browser, you may need to unzip the file manually before you run the `tar` command. To unzip the file manually, run the following command:

`gunzip libnet-1.2-rc.tar.gz`

2. Now we need to compile and install libnet. If you are familiar with compiling libraries or applications on other Unix platforms, this should seem pretty familiar to you. From the libnet directory, run the following commands:

`./configure`

`make`

`sudo make install`

When you run the `sudo make install` command, you will need to enter your password to let you run the command as a super user.

3. Let's verify whether we have successfully installed libnet by running the following two commands:

❑ The output should show the libnet directory and the `libnet.h` file on using the following command:

`ls /usr/local/include | grep libnet`

❑ The output should show multiple libnet library files: `libnet.1.dylib`, `libnet.9.dylib`, `libnet.a`, `libnet.dylib`, and `libnet.la` on using the following command:

`ls /usr/local/lib | grep libnet`

How it works...

The `./configure`, `make`, and `sudo make install` commands are pretty much the standard commands used for installing applications and libraries from source on a Unix-based system. The `./configure` command configures the source for your system. The `make` command reads the `Makefile` created by the `./configure` command and builds the application/library. The `sudo make install` command installs the application/library. The `make install` command usually requires super user privileges so it can install files to a system directory, which is why we have `sudo` before it.

Adding libnet to your project

Once libnet is installed, we need to add it to our project to be able to use it. There are a number of ways to do this; we will be covering the recommended way in this recipe.

Getting ready

Before we can add libnet to our project, we need to install it on our system. The *Installing libnet* recipe in this chapter covers how to do this.

How to do it...

Once the project is created, we will need to follow the ensuing steps to add libnet to it:

1. Begin by selecting the project in Xcode. Select **Target** and then select **Build Settings**; you should be able to see something similar to the following screenshot:

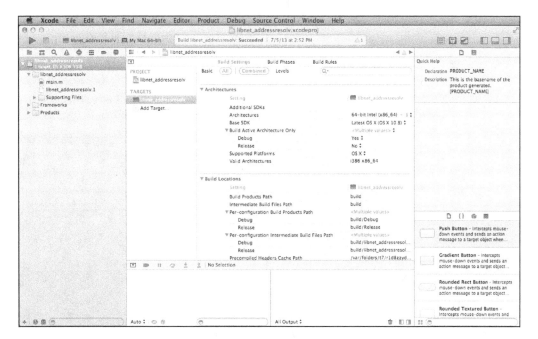

2. Scroll down in the **Build Settings** until you get to the **Linking** section. Under the **Other Linker Flags** option, add **-lnet**.

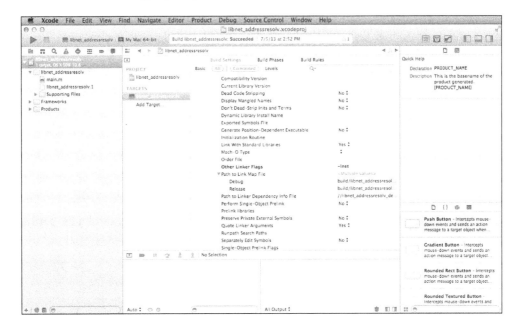

3. Now scroll down until you reach the **Search Paths** section and add /usr/local/lib to **Library Search Paths** as shown in the following screenshot:

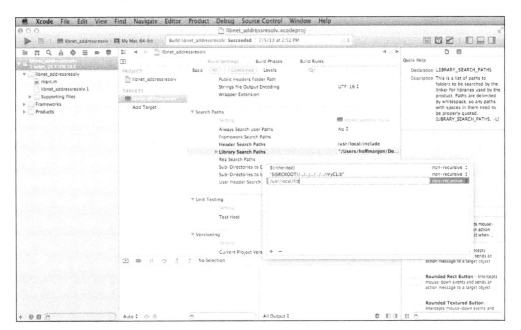

4. Finally, we will want to add `/usr/local/include` to the header's search path. This will allow us to import the `libnet.h` header file without having to give the full path to it.

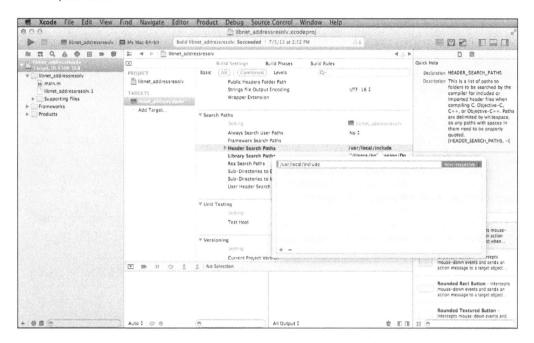

How it works...

When we add **-lnet** to **Other Linker Flags**, we are telling Xcode to link the libnet library to our project. The only problem with linking libnet to our project is that the library is located in the `/usr/local/lib` directory, which Xcode does not know about. This is why we add `/usr/local/lib` to the **Library Search Path** setting. This tells Xcode to also look in `/usr/local/lib` for libraries that it needs.

Resolving names to addresses with libnet

In this recipe, we learn how to resolve DNS names (such as `www.packtpub.com`) to IP addresses using libnet. This recipe will introduce libnet functions that will resolve the address from the DNS name and display the address. It will also introduce the `libnet_init()` and `libnet_destroy()` functions.

The `libnet_init()` function initializes and returns a libnet context. This context is the center of everything that libnet does. A libnet context should be initialized prior to using any of the libnet functions. The context should also be destroyed, using the `libnet_destroy()` function, once it is no longer needed.

Getting ready

Prior to running the examples in the chapter, we will need to download and install libnet (see the *Installing libnet* recipe of this chapter). You will also need to add libnet to your project (see the *Adding libnet to your project* recipe of this chapter).

Don't forget that if we wish to run our project within Xcode, we will need to change the scheme **Debug Process As** setting to run the project as **root** (see the *Introduction* of this chapter for directions on how to do this).

How to do it...

We will be resolving www.packtpub.com to its IPv4 and IPv6 addresses.

Importing the libnet header

At the top of your class, you will need to have the following line to import the libnet header:

```
#import "libnet.h"
```

For resolving www.packtpub.com to its IPv4 and IPv6 addresses, use the following code:

```
libnet_t *lnet;
char errbuf[LIBNET_ERRBUF_SIZE];
u_int32_t addr;
struct libnet_in6_addr addr6;
char ipv6addr[64];

char addr_str[] = "www.packtpub.com";

lnet = libnet_init(LIBNET_RAW4, NULL, errbuf);
if ( lnet == NULL ) {
    NSLog(@"libnet_init() failed: %s", errbuf);
    exit(EXIT_FAILURE);
}
//IPv4
addr = libnet_name2addr4(lnet, addr_str, LIBNET_RESOLVE);
NSLog(@"%s",libnet_addr2name4(addr, LIBNET_DONT_RESOLVE));
//IPv6
addr6 = libnet_name2addr6(lnet, addr_str, LIBNET_RESOLVE);
libnet_addr2name6_r(addr6, LIBNET_DONT_RESOLVE, ipv6addr,
sizeof(ipv6addr));
NSLog(@"%s",ipv6addr);

libnet_destroy(lnet);
```

We start off by declaring the variables we will be using within our code.

 Most lnet examples you see in books or on the Internet use the name 1 for the libnet context, so usually, the declaration looks like this: libnet_t *1. Personally, I like using variable names that are longer than one character so they have meaning when I read code. So I usually use the variable name of lnet for the libnet context.

This is just my personal preference and either 1 or lnet will work equally well.

The libnet_init() function is used to initiate the libnet context. We should initiate the context before calling any other libnet functions. The libnet_init() function takes the following three arguments:

- **Injection type**: For everything in this chapter we will be using LIBNET_RAW4. The other types are LIBNET_LINK, LIBNET_LINK_ADV, LIBNET_RAW4, LIBNET_RAW4_ADV, LIBNET_RAW6, and LIBNET_RAW6_ADV.

- **Device**: This is the name of the interface to be used, or we set it to NULL to let libnet choose the interface.

- **Error Buffer**: This is a buffer that will contain any errors if something goes wrong with the request.

After we initiate the libnet context, we verify that the libnet context was properly initialized. If it wasn't initialized properly, we display the error and exit, otherwise we call the libnet_name2addr4() function. This function will take a char array and return a network-byte-ordered IPv4 address. In our example, the char array contains a hostname (such as www.packtpub.com), but it can also contain an IP address.

The libnet_name2addr4() function accepts the following three arguments:

- libnet_t *lnet: This is a pointer to the libnet context to use.

- host_name: This is a pointer to the char array containing the name.

- uint8_t use_name: This can be either LIBNET_RESOLVE or LIBNET_DONT_RESOLVE. If the char array contains a hostname such as www.packtpub.com, we would want the libnet_name2addr() function to perform a DNS lookup prior to creating the network-byte-ordered IPv4 address; therefore, we would set this to LIBNET_RESOLVE. If the hostname contained an IP address, we would not want libet_name2addr4() to perform a DNS lookup, so we would use LIBNET_DONT_RESOLVE.

Once we have the address in a network-byte-ordered format, we need to convert it to a presentable form. In the preceding example, we used the `libnet_addr2name4()` function but we set the `use_name` parameter to `LIBNET_DONT_RESOLVE`. This function takes a network-byte-ordered IPv4 address and returns a pointer to a `char` array containing the IP address in a format that we can present. This function takes two arguments:

- ► `uint32_t in`: The network-byte-ordered IPv4 address.
- ► `uint8_t use_name`: This can be either `LIBNET_RESOLVE` or `LIBNET_DONT_RESOLVE`. If we wish to get the hostname of the device we would set this to `LIBNET_RESOLVE`. If we wish to get the IP address to a presentable format, we would set this to `LIBNET_DONT_RESOLVE`.

The `libnet_name2addr4()` and `libnet_addr2name4()` functions work only with IPv4 addresses. Libnet also provides functions for IPv6 functions. We use the `libnet_name2addr6()` function to return the `libnet_in6_addr` structure containing a network-byte-ordered IPv6 address. This function takes the same arguments as the `libnet_name2addr4()` function described previously.

Once we have the IPv6 address in the `libnet_in6_addr` structure, we need to convert it to a presentable form. We can do this with the `libnet_addr2name6_r()` function. This function accepts the following four arguments:

- ► `libnet_in6_addr *addr`: This is the `libnet_in6_addr` structure we previously created using the `libnet_name2addr6()` function.
- ► `uint8_t use_name`: This can be either `LIBNET_RESOLVE` or `LIBNET_DONT_RESOLVE`. If we wish to get the hostname of the device we would set this to `LIBNET_RESOLVE`. If we wish to get the IP address to a presentable form, we would set this to `LIBNET_DONT_RESOLVE`.
- ► `char* ipv6addr`: This is the `char` array that will contain the hostname or IPv6 address if the `libnet_addr2name6_r()` function was successful.
- ► `int ipv6addr_len`: This gives the maximum size of the `ipv6addr` char array.

Finally, we call the `libnet_destroy()` function to properly release our libnet context.

How it works...

When you use libnet, the first thing you need to do is to create a libnet context. This is done using the `libnet_init()` function. Once you create a libnet context, always remember to release it properly by using the `libnet_destroy()` function. If you do not release the context properly, your application will have leaks.

Once we had the libnet context, we use the `libnet_name2addr4()` function to perform a DNS lookup for the hostname and return a network-byte-ordered IPv4 address. We then used the `libnet_addr2name4()` function to convert the network-byte-ordered IPv4 address into a form that we could display.

For the IPv6 address, we used the `libnet_name2addr6()` function to perform a DNS lookup for the hostname and return a `libnet_in6_addr` structure containing the network-byte-ordered IPv6 address. We then used the `libnet_addr2name6()` function to convert the `libnet_in6_addr` structure to a form that we could display.

Retrieving local addresses with libnet

Within the libnet library, there are a number of instances where you will need the local addresses (hardware and/or IP addresses). If we were sending a packet, we will need to know the hardware address of the device at the Link layer. For the IP headers, we need to know the IP addresses (either IPv4 or IPv6) so that we can put it in the `Source Address` field.

In this recipe, we will show how to retrieve and display the hardware, IPv4, and IPv6 addresses using libnet.

Getting ready

Prior to running the examples in the chapter, we will need to download and install libnet (see the *Installing libnet* recipe of this chapter). You will also need to add libnet to your project (see the *Adding libnet to your project* recipe of this chapter.

If we wish to run our project within Xcode, we will need to change the scheme **Debug Process As** setting to run as **root,** as described in the *Introduction* section of this chapter.

How to do it...

Let's get the local addresses of our device.

Importing the libnet header

At the top of your class, you will need to import the libnet header:

```
#import <libnet.h>
```

Retrieving the local IP and hardware addresses of our device

Use the following code for retrieving the local IP and hardware addresses of our device:

```
libnet_t *lnet;
char errbuf[LIBNET_ERRBUF_SIZE];
u_int32_t addr;
struct libnet_in6_addr addr6;
char ipv6addr[64];
struct libnet_ether_addr *mac_addr;
lnet = libnet_init(LIBNET_RAW4, NULL, errbuf);
```

```
if ( lnet == NULL ) {
    NSLog(@"Error with libnet_init():  %s", errbuf);
    exit(EXIT_FAILURE);
}
//IPv4
addr = libnet_get_ipaddr4(lnet);
if ( addr != -1 )
    NSLog(@"IPv4 address: %s\n", libnet_addr2name4(addr,LIBNET_DONT_
RESOLVE));
else {
    NSLog(@"Error retrieving IP address: %s",libnet_geterror(lnet));
    exit(EXIT_FAILURE);
}
//IPv6
addr6 = libnet_get_ipaddr6(lnet);
libnet_addr2name6_r(addr6, LIBNET_DONT_RESOLVE, ipv6addr,
sizeof(ipv6addr));
NSLog(@"%s",ipv6addr);
  //MAC
mac_addr = libnet_get_hwaddr(lnet);
if ( mac_addr != NULL )
    NSLog(@"MAC address: %02X:%02X:%02X:%02X:%02X:%02X\n",mac_addr-
>ether_addr_octet[0],mac_addr->ether_addr_octet[1],mac_addr->ether_
addr_octet[2],mac_addr->ether_addr_octet[3],mac_addr->ether_addr_
octet[4],mac_addr->ether_addr_octet[5]);
else
    NSLog(@"Couldn't get my MAC address: %s\n",libnet_
geterror(lnet));
libnet_destroy(lnet);
```

We begin by declaring the variables that we will be using to retrieve the local IP and hardware addresses. We use the `libnet_init()` function to initiate the libnet context. We need to initiate the context before calling any other libnet functions. The `libnet_init()` function takes the following three arguments:

- `Injection Type`: For everything in this chapter, we will be using `LIBNET_RAW4`. The other types are: `LIBNET_LINK`, `LIBNET_LINK_ADV`, `LIBNET_RAW4`, `LIBNET_RAW4_ADV`, `LIBNET_RAW6`, and `LIBNET_RAW6_ADV`.

- `Device`: This is the name of the interface to use, or we set it to `NULL` to let libnet choose the interface.

- `Error Buffer`: This buffer contains any errors that occur if something goes wrong with the request.

We should always verify that the libnet context is properly initialized. If it isn't properly initialized, we display the error and exit.

We then retrieve and display the IPv4 address for the local device. We do this by using the `libnet_get_ipaddr4()` function. This function takes a libnet context as the only argument. If the context was initialized without a device, this function will attempt to find one. If the function fails, it will return `-1`.

If the `libnet_get_ipaddr4()` function was successful, we use the `libnet_addr2name4()` function to convert the network-byte-ordered IPv4 address to a `char` array that we can display. The `libnet_addr2name4()` function takes the following two arguments:

- `uint32_t in`: This is the network-byte-ordered IPv4 address.
- `uint8_t use_name`: This can be either `LIBNET_RESOLVE` or `LIBNET_DONT_RESOLVE`. If we wish to get the hostname of the device, we would set this to `LIBNET_RESOLVE`. If we wish to get the IP address to a presentable form, we would set it to `LIBNET_DONT_RESOLVE`.

Now, we retrieve and display the IPv6 address of the local device. To do this, we use the `libnet_get_addr6()` function. This function takes a libnet context as its only argument. If the context was initialized without a device, the function will attempt to find one, just like the `libnet_get_addr4()` function does. If the function fails and returns an `in6addr_error`, we can use `libnet_geterror()` to tell us what happened.

We use the `libnet_addr2name6_r()` function to convert the `libnet_in6_addr` structure to a form that we can display. This function accepts the following four arguments:

- `libnet_in6_addr *addr`: This is the `libnet_in6_addr` structure we previously created using the `libnet_name2addr6()` function.
- `uint8_t use_name`: This can be either `LIBNET_RESOLVE` or `LIBNET_DONT_RESOLVE`. If we wish to get the hostname of the device, we would set this to `LIBNET_RESOLVE`. If we wish to get the IP address to a presentable form, we would set this to `LIBNET_DONT_RESOLVE`.
- `char* ipv6addr`: This is the `char` array that will contain the hostname or IPv6 address if the `libnet_addr2name6_r()` function was successful.
- `int ipv6addr_len`: This is the maximum size of the `ipv6addr` char array.

If there was an error retrieving the IPv6 address, the `char` array will contain `ffff:ffff:ffff:ffff:ffff:ffff:ffff:ffff`.

Finally, we retrieve and display the hardware address for the local device. To do this, we use the `libnet_get_hwaddr()` function. This function takes a libnet context as the only argument. If the context was initialized without a device, the function will attempt to find one. If the function fails, it will return `NULL`, otherwise it will return a `libnet_ether_addr` structure that contains the hardware address.

We need to call the `libnet_destroy()` function to release our libnet context properly. It is important that we remember to call this function, otherwise our application will have memory leaks.

How it works...

To retrieve the local addresses, we used the following libnet functions:

- `libnet_get_ipaddr4()`: This retrieves the local IPv4 address
- `libnet_get_ipaddr6()`: This retrieves the local IPv6 address
- `libnet_get_hwaddr()`: This retrieves the local hardware address

If we were to use the addresses in conjunction with other libnet functions (such as populating fields of a header), we would use the results as they are returned by these functions. However, in this recipe, we convert the results to a form that we could display.

Constructing a Ping packet with libnet

In this recipe, we will construct an ICMP (Ping) packet and inject it into the network. The device that receives the packet should respond back with an ICMP response packet. However, libnet is a packet construction and an injection library, not a packet capture library, so we will use **Wireshark** (`http://www.wireshark.org`) to see the packets that we send out and the packet that is returned. In *Chapter 4, Using Libpcap*, we will see how to capture packets.

In order to create an ICMP packet and inject it into the network, we will need to create an ICMP header and an IP header. The IP header and the corresponding `libnet_build_ipv4()` function were covered in the *Introduction* section of this chapter, so we will not cover that in detail here. We will cover the ICMP header and the `libnet_build_icmpv4_echo()` function in depth. There are a number of different ICMP types; in this recipe, we will be covering the Echo (request). The following diagram shows what the ICMP header looks like:

The following list gives a brief explanation of each of the fields in the ICMP header:

- `ICMP Type`: This identifies the ICMP message type. The Echo request message is type `8`, while the Echo reply is type `0`.
- `code`: This is not used in the Echo reply so this is set to `0`.
- `Checksum`: This is the checksum for the ICMP header.
- `Identifier`: This is the identification field that can be used to match up the Echo request with the Echo reply.

▸ Sequence Number: This is a sequence number that can also be used to match up an Echo request with the Echo reply.

▸ Optional Data (payload): This is the additional data that is sent with the header.

The libnet_build_icmpv4_echo() function takes the following arguments. The list also shows how they match up with the ICMP header fields:

▸ type: This maps to the ICMP Type field. In our example, we will use the ICMP_ECHO type defined in the libnet-headers.h file. This header is included when you import the libnet.h header.

▸ code: This maps to the Code field. It will be 0 in our example.

▸ sum: This maps to the Checksum field. If we set it to 0, libnet will autofill it.

▸ id: This maps to the Identifier field.

▸ seq: This maps to the Sequence Number field.

▸ payload: This maps to the Optional Data (payload) field.

▸ payload_s: This is the size of the payload.

▸ lnet: This is the libnet context that is to be used.

▸ ptag: This is the protocol tag we use if we are modifying an existing header or 0 to build a new one.

Getting ready

Prior to running the examples in the chapter, we will need to download and install libnet (see the *Installing libnet* recipe of this chapter). You will also need to add libnet to your project (see the *Adding libnet to your project* recipe of this chapter).

If we wish to run our project within Xcode, we will need to change the scheme **Debug Process As** setting to run as **root**, as described in the *Introduction* section of this chapter.

How to do it...

Let's create and inject our first packet.

Importing the libnet header

At the top of your class, you will need to import the libnet header:

```
#import <libnet.h>
```

Defining variables

Use the following code for defining variables:

```
libnet_t *lnet;
u_int32_t target, source;
u_int16_t id,seq;
char payload[] = "Hello from libnet";
char errbuf[LIBNET_ERRBUF_SIZE];
```

We start by setting up the variables that we will be using. We will be including an optional payload, which is the text in the payload `char` array.

Initiating the libnet context

Use the following code for initiating the libnet context:

```
lnet = libnet_init(LIBNET_RAW4, NULL, errbuf);
if ( lnet == NULL ) {
    NSLog(@"Error with libnet_init():  %s", errbuf);
    exit(EXIT_FAILURE);
}
```

We use the `libnet_init()` function to initiate the libnet context. We need to initiate the context before calling any other libnet functions. The `libnet_init()` function takes the following three arguments:

▶ `Injection Type`: For everything in this chapter we will be using `LIBNET_RAW4`. The other types are: `LIBNET_LINK`, `LIBNET_LINK_ADV`, `LIBNET_RAW4`, `LIBNET_RAW4_ADV`, `LIBNET_RAW6`, and `LIBNET_RAW6_ADV`.

▶ `Device`: This is the name of the interface that is to be used, or else we set it to `NULL` to let libnet choose the interface.

▶ `Error Buffer`: This is a buffer that contains the errors if something goes wrong with the request.

Setting the target and source IP addresses

Use the following code for setting the target and source IP addresses:

```
target = libnet_name2addr4(lnet, 10.0.0.1, LIBNET_DONT_RESOLVE);
source = libnet_get_ipaddr4(lnet);
if ( source == -1 ) {
    NSLog(@"Error retrieving IP address: %s",libnet_geterror(lnet));
    libnet_destroy(lnet);
    exit(EXIT_FAILURE);
}
```

We use the `libnet_name2addr4()` function to get the network-byte-ordered IPv4 address of the target device (the device we are sending the ICMP packet to). The `libnet_name2addr4()` function accepts the following three arguments:

- `libnet_t *lnet`: This is a pointer for the libnet context to be used.
- `host_name`: This is a pointer to the `char` array containing the name.
- `uint8_t use_name`: This can be either `LIBNET_RESOLVE` or `LIBNET_DONT_RESOLVE`. If the `char` array contained a hostname such as `www.packtpub.com`, we would want `libnet_name2addr4()` to perform a DNS lookup to resolve the name prior to creating the network-byte-ordered IPv4 address; therefore, we would use `LIBNET_RESOLVE`. If the `char` array contains an IP address we would not want `libet_name2addr4()` to perform a DNS lookup, so we would use `LIBNET_DONT_RESOLVE`.

We then use the `libnet_get_ipaddr4()` function to retrieve the IPv4 address of our local device. This function takes a libnet context as the only argument. If the context was initialized without a device, the function will attempt to find one. If the function fails, it will return -1.

Creating a random number to be used as an identifier

To create a random number to be used as an identifier, use the following code:

```
/* Generating a random id */
libnet_seed_prand (lnet);
id = (u_int16_t)libnet_get_prand(LIBNET_PR16);
```

The `libnet_seed_prand()` seeds the pseudo-random number generator. The `LIBNET_PR16 constant` specifies a number between 0 and 32767.

Building the ICMP header

Use the following code for building the ICMP header:

```
/* Building ICMP header */
seq = 1;

if (libnet_build_icmpv4_echo(ICMP_ECHO,
                    0,
                    0,
                    id,
                    seq,
                    (u_int8_t*)payload,
                    sizeof(payload),
                    lnet,
                    0) == -1)
    {
```

```
        NSLog(@"Error building UDP header: %s\n",libnet_geterror(lnet));
        libnet_destroy(lnet);
        exit(EXIT_FAILURE);
    }
```

To build the ICMP header, we use the `libnet_build_icmpv4_echo()` function. We covered how the parameters map to the ICMP Echo header in the introduction section of this recipe. The values of each parameter are as follows:

- `type`: This is `ICMP_ECHO (8)`, which specifies that this is an Echo request
- `code`: This is `0` and it is not used for the ICMP Echo request
- `sum`: This is set to `0` to let libnet generate the checksum
- `id`: This is the pseudo-random number that we generated
- `seq`: This is the `seq` variable that is set to `1`
- `payload`: This is our payload
- `payload_s`: This is our payload sized
- `lnet`: This is the libnet context to be used with this header
- `ptag`: This is set to `0` to generate a new header

Building the IPv4 header

Use the following code for building the IPv4 header:

```
/* Building IP header */
if( libnet_build_ipv4(LIBNET_IPV4_H + LIBNET_ICMPV4_ECHO_H +
sizeof(payload),
                        0,
                        id,
                        0,
                        64,
                        IPPROTO_ICMP,
                        0,
                        source,
                        target,
                        NULL,
                        0,
                        lnet,
                        0) == -1)
{
    NSLog(@"Error building IP header: %s\n",libnet_geterror(lnet));
     libnet_destroy(lnet);
     exit(EXIT_FAILURE);
}
```

To generate the IPv4 header, we use the `libnet_build_ipv4()` function. We covered this function and how the parameters map to the header fields in the *Introduction* section of this chapter. The values for each parameter are as follows:

- `ip_len`: This is the size of the IPv4 header, the ICMPv4 header, and the payload added together
- `tos`: We are not using this, so we set it to `0`
- `id`: This is the pseudo-random number that is generated
- `frag`: This is not fragmented, so the offset is `0`
- `ttl`: This is set to a maximum of 64 hops
- `prot`: Protocol type is set to `IPPROTO_ICMP`
- `sum`: This is set to `0` to let libnet autofill
- `src`: This is the source IPv4 address
- `dst`: This is the destination IPv4 address
- `payload`: This sets the payload to `Null`
- `payload_s`: This sets the payload size to `0`
- `libnet_t`: This is the libnet context
- `ptag`: This is set to `0` and, therefore, a new header is built

Injecting the ICMP packet

We use the `libnet_write()` function to inject the ICMP packet in the following manner:

```
/* Writing packet */
int bytes_written = libnet_write(lnet);
if ( bytes_written != -1 )
    printf("%d bytes written to device %s.\n", bytes_written,
        libnet_getdevice(lnet));
else
    NSLog(@"Error writing packet: %s\n",libnet_geterror(lnet));

libnet_destroy(lnet);
```

The `libnet_write()` function returns the number of bytes written, or `-1` if the operation fails. If the operation is successful, we log the number of bytes written; otherwise, we log the error message .

Don't forget to release the libnet context using the `libnet_destory()` function.

How it works...

The steps to create and send an ICMP packet are as follows:

1. Create the libnet context using the `libnet_init()` function.

2. Get the target IPv4 address using the `libnet_namte2addr4()` function.

3. Get the source IPv4 address using the `libnet_getaddr4()` function.

4. Create the ICMPv4 Echo header using the `libnet_build_icmpv4_echo()` function.

5. Create the IPv4 header using the `libnet_build_ipv4()` function.

6. Send the packet out with the `libnet_write()` function.

7. Release the libnet context with the `libnet_destroy()` function.

If you use Wireshark to watch the packet go out and to see the response, it would look something like this:

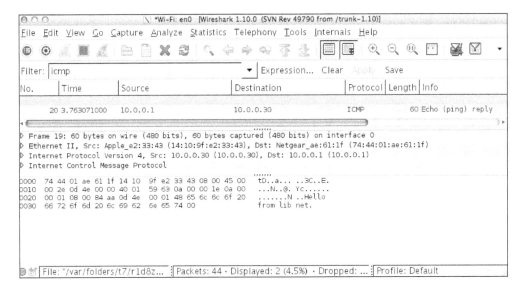

Constructing a UDP packet with libnet

The **User Datagram Protocol** (**UDP**) sends datagrams to other hosts on an IP network without any prior handshaking to set up the communication channel between the devices. A datagram is just a packet (like an ICMP or TCP packet), except that the delivery, arrival time, and sequence are not guaranteed. The UDP protocol is considered to be an unreliable protocol because there is no guarantee of delivery.

The minimalist approach of UDP makes it ideal for real-time applications, such as Voice over IP, online games and streaming media, where dropping of packets is preferred over waiting for delayed packets. If guarantee of delivery is needed so that packets are not dropped, applications should use TCP or SCTP instead of UDP.

In this recipe, we will be creating a UDP packet and sending it to a remote device. We will use Wireshark (`http://www.wireshark.org`) to see the packets that we send out, however, we will not see any return packet because UDP on its own does not send a response.

In order to create a UDP packet and write it to the network, we will need to create a UDP header and an IP header. The IP header and the corresponding `libnet_build_ipv4()` function were covered in the *Introduction* section of this chapter, so it will not be covered here in detail. We will be looking at the `libnet_build_udp()` function and the UDP header as shown in the following diagram:

The following list gives a brief explanation of each of the fields in the UDP header:

 ▶ `Source Port`: This identifies the port used by the sender, and we can assume that any reply can be sent to this port. If no reply is needed or wanted, then we should set this port to `0`, indicating that we are not expecting a reply.

 ▶ `Destination Port`: This identifies the port on the client that the datagram packet is going to. This port should be a valid port number between `0` and `65535`.

 ▶ `Length`: This is the size of the UDP header and the payload.

 ▶ `Checksum`: This is the checksum for the UDP header.

The arguments taken by the `libnet_build_udp()` function and how they match up with the UDP header fields are mentioned in the following list:

 ▶ `sp`: This maps to the `Source Port` field

 ▶ `dp`: This maps to the `Destination Port` field

 ▶ `len`: This maps to the `Length` field

 ▶ `sum`: This maps to the `Checksum` field

 ▶ `payload`: This maps to the `Optional Data (payload)` field

 ▶ `payload_s`: This is the payload size

 ▶ `lnet`: This is the libnet context that is used with this header

 ▶ `ptag`: This is a protocol tag that is used if we are modifying an existing header or `0` to build a new one

Getting ready

Prior to running the examples in the chapter, we will need to download and install libnet (see the *Installing libnet* recipe of this chapter). We will also need to add libnet to our project (see the *Adding libnet to your project* recipe of this chapter).

If we wish to run the project within Xcode, we will need to change the scheme **Debug Process As** setting to run as **root**, as described in the *Introduction* section of this chapter.

How to do it...

Let's create and inject a UDP packet.

Importing the libnet header

At the top of your class, you will need to import the libnet header using the following code:

```
#import <libnet.h>

Defining Variables
 libnet_t *lnet;
 u_int32_t target, source;
 u_int16_t id,seq;
 char payload[] = "Hello from libnet";
 char errbuf[LIBNET_ERRBUF_SIZE];
```

We start off by setting up the variables that we will be using to create and inject our UDP packet. We will be including an optional payload, which is the text of the payload `char` array.

Initiating the libnet context

Use the following code for initiating the libnet context:

```
lnet = libnet_init(LIBNET_RAW4, NULL, errbuf);
if ( lnet == NULL ) {
    NSLog(@"Error with libnet_init():  %s", errbuf);
    exit(EXIT_FAILURE);
}
```

We use the `libnet_init()` function to initiate the libnet context. The libnet context needs to be initiated before calling any other libnet functions. The `libnet_init()` function takes three arguments:

- ▶   `Injection Type`: For everything in this chapter, we will be using `LIBNET_RAW4`. The other types are: `LIBNET_LINK`, `LIBNET_LINK_ADV`, `LIBNET_RAW4`, `LIBNET_RAW4_ADV`, `LIBNET_RAW6`, and `LIBNET_RAW6_ADV`.

- ▶ `Device`: The interface to use or `NULL` to let libnet choose the interface.

- ▶ `Error Buffer`: This is a buffer that will contain any errors if something goes wrong with the request.

We then verify that the libnet context was properly initialized. If it wasn't properly initialized, we display the error and exit.

Setting the target and source IP addresses

Use the following code for setting the target and source IP addresses:

```
target = libnet_name2addr4(lnet, "10.0.0.1", LIBNET_DONT_RESOLVE);
source  = libnet_get_ipaddr4(lnet);
 if ( source == -1 ) {
     NSLog(@"Error retrieving IP address:
 %s",libnet_geterror(lnet));
     libnet_destroy(lnet);
     exit(EXIT_FAILURE);
 }
```

The `libnet_name2addr4()` function gets the network-byte-ordered IPv4 address. This function accepts the following three arguments:

- ▶ `libnet_t *lnet`: This is a pointer to the libnet context to be used.

- ▶ `host_name`: This is a pointer to the `char` array containing the name.

- ▶ `uint8_t use_name`: This can be either `LIBNET_RESOLVE` or `LIBNET_DONT_RESOLVE`. If the `char` array contained a hostname such as `www.packtpub.com`, we would want `libnet_name2addr4()` to perform a DNS lookup to resolve the name prior to creating the network-byte-ordered IPv4 address, therefore, we would use `LIBNET_RESOLVE`. If the hostname contained an IP address, we would not want `libnet_name2addr4()` to perform a DNS lookup so we would use `LIBNET_DONT_RESOLVE`.

We use the `libnet_get_ipaddr4()` function to retrieve the IPv4 address. This function takes the libnet context as the only argument. If the context was initialized without a device, the function will attempt to find one; if it fails it will return `-1`.

Creating a random number to be used as an identifier

Use the following code to create a random number to be used as an identifier:

```
/* Generating a random id */
libnet_seed_prand (lnet);
id = (u_int16_t)libnet_get_prand(LIBNET_PR16);
```

The `libnet_seed_prand` seeds the pseudo-random number generator. The `libnet_get_prand()` function generates a pseudo-random value within the `rand` value specified. The `LIBNET_PR16` constant specifies a number between `0` and `32767`.

Building the UDP header

Use the following code to build the UDP header:

```
/* Building UDP header */
seq = 1;

if (libnet_build_udp(
                    libnet_get_prand (LIBNET_PRu16),
                    101,
                    LIBNET_UDP_H+ sizeof(payload),
                    0,
                    (u_int8_t*)payload,
                    sizeof(payload),
                    lnet,
                    0) == -1)
{
    NSLog(@"Error building ICMP header: %s\n",libnet_
geterror(lnet));
    libnet_destroy(lnet);
    exit(EXIT_FAILURE);
}
```

The UDP header is generated using the `libnet_build_udp()` function. We covered how the parameters map to the UDP header in the introduction section of this recipe. The values of each parameter are as follows:

- ▶ `sp`: We use the `libnet_get_prand()` function to generate a random port to be used for the source port.
- ▶ `dp`: This is the destination port. We are sending packets to port `101` on the destination device.
- ▶ `len`: This is the size of the UDP header and the payload size added together to give us the total size.
- ▶ `sum`: This is set to `0`, so libnet will autofill.
- ▶ `payload`: This is our payload.
- ▶ `payload_s`: This is our payload size.
- ▶ `lnet`: This is the libnet context to be used with this header.
- ▶ `ptag`: This is set to `0` for generating a new header.

Building the IPv4 header

Use the following code to build the IPv4 header:

```
/* Building IP header */

if ( libnet_build_ipv4(LIBNET_IPV4_H + LIBNET_UDP_H + sizeof(payload),
                       0,
                       id,
                       0,
                       64,
                       IPPROTO_UDP,
                       0,
                       source,
                       target,
                       NULL,
                       0,
                       lnet,
                       0) == -1)
{
    NSLog(@"Error building IP header: %s\n",libnet_geterror(lnet));
    libnet_destroy(lnet);
    exit(EXIT_FAILURE);
}
```

We generate the IPv4 header using the `libnet_build_ipv4()` function. We covered the `libnet_build_ipv4()` function and how the parameters map to the header fields in the *Introduction* section of this chapter. The values for each parameter are as follows:

- ▸ `ip_len`: This is the size of the IPv4 header, the UDP header, and the payload added together
- ▸ `tos`: We are not using this so we set it to 0
- ▸ `id`: This is the pseudo-random number
- ▸ `frag`: This is not fragmented so the offset is 0
- ▸ `ttl`: This is set to a maximum of sixty-four hops
- ▸ `prot`: The protocol type is set to `IPPROTO_UDP`
- ▸ `sum`: This is set to 0 to have libnet autofill
- ▸ `src`: This is the source IPv4 address
- ▸ `dst`: This is the destination IPv4 address
- ▸ `payload`: This is set to `Null`
- ▸ `payload_s`: The payload size is 0

> ▸ `libnet_t`: This is the libnet context
>
> ▸ `ptag`: This is set to `0` to build a new header

Injecting the packet

Use the following code for injecting the packet:

```
/* Writing packet */
int bytes_written = libnet_write(lnet);
if ( bytes_written != -1 )
    NSLog(@"%d bytes written to device %s.\n", bytes_written, libnet_
getdevice(lnet));
else
    NSLog(@"Error writing packet: %s\n",libnet_geterror(lnet));

libnet_destroy(lnet);
```

We use the `libnet_write()` function to inject the UDP packet. The `libnet_write()` function returns the number of bytes written, or `-1` if the operation fails. If the operation is successful, we log the number of bytes written, otherwise we log the error message.

Finally, we use the `libnet_destory()` function to release the libnet context.

How it works...

The steps to create and send a UDP packet are as follows:

1. Create the libnet context using the `libnet_init()` function.
2. Get the target IPv4 address using the `libnet_namte2addr4()` function.
3. Get the source IPv4 address using the `libnet_getaddr4()` function.
4. Create the UDP header using the `libnet_build_udp()` function.
5. Create the IPv4 header using the `libnet_build_ipv4()` function.
6. Send out the packet with the `libnet_write()` function.
7. Release the libnet context with the `libnet_destroy()` function.

If you use Wireshark to watch the packet get injected it would look like the following screenshot:

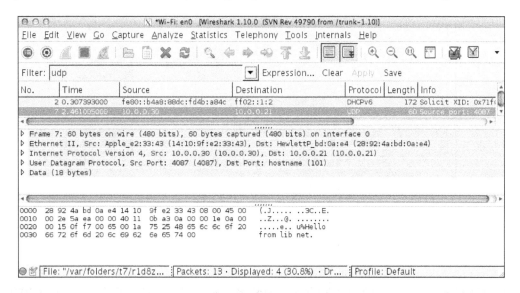

Constructing a TCP packet with libnet

Using **Transmission Control Protocol** (**TCP**), a device sends packets to other devices on an IP network. TCP is designed to provide a reliable, ordered, and error-checked delivery of packets between applications. This does add additional overheads as compared to UDP, so applications that do not require reliability should use UDP instead.

When a device wants to communicate with another device using TCP, a three-way handshake must occur. The first device begins by sending a TCP packet with the SYN flag set. This is like saying, "Hi Joe. Can we talk?" The remote device is supposed to respond with a packet that has the SYN/ACK (synchronize/acknowledge) flags set, which is like Joe saying, "Sure, we can talk. What's up?" The three-way handshake is completed when the first device responds again with a packet that has the ACK flag set. This is like responding to Joe by saying, "Good, because I have something important to tell you."

The following diagram shows the three-way handshake:

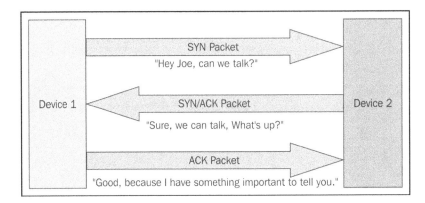

Once the three-way handshake is completed, the connection is considered to be established, which means the communication between the two devices can begin.

In order to create a TCP packet and inject it to the network, we will need to create a TCP header and an IP header. The IP header and the corresponding `libnet_build_ipv4()` function were covered in the *Introduction* section of this chapter, so we will not cover it in detail here. We will be looking at the TCP header and the `libnet_build_TCP()` function here.

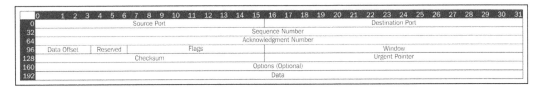

The following list explains the fields in the preceding diagram:

▸ `Source Port`: This identifies the port from where the packet is being sent.

▸ `Destination Port`: This identifies the port on the client that the TCP packet is going to.

▸ `Sequence Number`: This is the initial sequence number for this session if the SYN flag is set. If the SYN flag is not set then this is the sequence number of the first data byte of this segment for this session.

▸ `Acknowledgement Number`: If the ACK flag is set, this value is the next sequence number that the receiver is expecting. The first ACK that is sent by both ends of the communication acknowledges the other end's initial sequence number.

▸ `Data Offset`: This gives the size of the TCP header.

▸ `Reserved`: This is reserved for future use and should be set to `0`.

- ▶ Flags: This refers to the TCP flags, which are as follows:
  - ❏ NS: **Explicit Congestion Notification** (**ECN**)-nonce that protects against concealment.
  - ❏ CWR: This stand for Congestion Window Reduced.
  - ❏ ECE: This indicates that the TCP peer is ECN capable if the SYN flag is also set.
  - ❏ URG: This indicates that the Urgent Pointer field of the header is significant.
  - ❏ ACK: This indicates that the acknowledgment field is significant. All packets after the initial SYN packet should have this flag set.
  - ❏ PSH: This indicates the need to push the data up to the receiving application immediately and not wait for additional packets to fill the buffer.
  - ❏ RST: This resets the connection.
  - ❏ SYN: This synchronizes the sequence numbers; this flag is set in the first packet sent from one device to another.
  - ❏ FIN: This indicates that the device has finished talking.
- ▶ Window: This is the maximum size of data the sender of this segment is willing to accept from the receiver at one time.
- ▶ Checksum: This is the checksum for the TCP header.
- ▶ Urgent Pointer: This is used in conjunction with the URG flag. This field contains the sequence number for the last byte of urgent data.

The following list shows the arguments the libnet_build_tcp() function takes and how they match up with the TCP header fields:

- ▶ sp: This maps to the Source Port field
- ▶ dp: This maps to the Destination Port field
- ▶ seq: This maps to the Sequence Number field
- ▶ ack: This maps to the Acknowledgment Number field
- ▶ control: This maps to the Flags field
- ▶ win: This maps to the Window field
- ▶ sum: This maps to the Checksum field
- ▶ urg: This maps to the Urgent Pointer field
- ▶ len: This shows the size of the TCP packet field
- ▶ payload: This maps to the optional data (payload) field
- ▶ payload_s: This gives the payload size

- ▶ `lnet`: This is the libnet context to be used with this header
- ▶ `ptag`: This is the protocol tag if we are modifying an existing header or `0` to build a new one

Getting ready

Prior to running the examples in the chapter, we will need to download and install libnet (see the *Installing libnet* recipe of this chapter). We will also need to add libnet to our project (see the *Adding libnet to your project* recipe of this chapter).

If we wish to run our project within Xcode, we will need to change the scheme **Debug Process As** setting to run as **root**, as described in the *Introduction* section of this chapter.

How to do it...

Let's create and inject a TCP packet.

Importing the libnet header

At the top of your class, you will need to import the libnet header:

```
#import <libnet.h>
```

Defining variables

Use the following code for defining variables:

```
libnet_t *lnet;
u_int32_t target, source;
u_int16_t id,seq;
char payload[] = "Hello from libnet";
char errbuf[LIBNET_ERRBUF_SIZE];
```

We start off by declaring the variables we will be using to create and inject our TCP packet. We will be including an optional payload, which is the text in the payload `char` array.

Initiating the libnet context

To initiate the libnet context, use the following code:

```
lnet = libnet_init(LIBNET_RAW4, NULL, errbuf);
if ( lnet == NULL ) {
    NSLog(@"Error with libnet_init():  %s", errbuf);
    exit(EXIT_FAILURE);
}
```

We use the `libnet_init()` function to initiate the libnet context. We should initiate the context before calling other libnet functions. The `libnet_init()` function takes three arguments:

- ▶ `Injection Type`: For everything in this chapter, we will be using `LIBNET_RAW4`. The other types are: `LIBNET_LINK`, `LIBNET_LINK_ADV`, `LIBNET_RAW4`, `LIBNET_RAW4_ADV`, `LIBNET_RAW6`, and `LIBNET_RAW6_ADV`.

- ▶ `Device`: The interface to use or `NULL` to let libnet choose the interface.

- ▶ `Error Buffer`: This is a buffer that will contain any errors if something goes wrong with the request.

We then verify whether the libnet context was properly initialized. If it wasn't, we display the error and exit.

Setting the target and source IP addresses

We use the `libnet_name2addr4()` function to get the network-byte-ordered IPv4 address.

The `libnet_name2addr4()` function accepts the following three arguments:

- ▶ `libnet_t *lnet`: This is a pointer to the libnet context to use.

- ▶ `host_name`: This is a pointer to the `char` array containing the name.

- ▶ `uint8_t use_name`: This can be either `LIBNET_RESOLVE` or `LIBNET_DONT_RESOLVE`. If the `char` array contained a hostname such as `www.packtpub.com`, we would want `libnet_name2addr4()` to perform a DNS lookup to resolve the name prior to creating the network-byte-ordered IPv4 address; therefore, we would use `LIBNET_RESOLVE`. If the hostname contained an IP address, we would not want `libet_name2addr4()` to perform a DNS lookup, so we would use `LIBNET DONT_RESOLVE`.

```
target = libnet_name2addr4(lnet, "10.0.0.1", LIBNET_DONT_RESOLVE);
source  = libnet_get_ipaddr4(lnet);
if ( source == -1 ) {
    NSLog(@"Error retrieving IP address: %s",libnet_
geterror(lnet));
    libnet_destroy(lnet);
    exit(EXIT_FAILURE);
 }
```

We use the `libnet_name2addr4()` function to get the network-byte-ordered IPv4 address. It accepts the following three arguments:

- ▶ `libnet_t *lnet`: This is a pointer to the libnet context to be used.

- ▶ `host_name`: A pointer to the `char` array containing the name.

> ▸ `uint8_t use_name`: This can be either `LIBNET_RESOLVE` or `LIBNET_DONT_RESOLVE`. If the `char` array contained a hostname such as www.packtpub.com, we would want `libnet_name2addr4()` to perform a DNS lookup to resolve the name prior to creating the network-byte-ordered IPv4 address, therefore, we would use `LIBNET_RESOLVE`. If the hostname contained an IP address, we would not want `libet_name2addr4()` to perform a DNS lookup, so we would use `LIBNET DONT_RESOLVE`.

We use the `libnet_get_ipaddr4()` function to retrieve the IPv4 address. This function takes a libnet context as the only argument. If the context was initialized without a device, the function will attempt to find one; if it fails, it will return -1.

Creating a random number to be used as an identifier

To create a random number to be used as an identifier, use the following code:

```
/* Generating a random id */
libnet_seed_prand (lnet);
id = (u_int16_t)libnet_get_prand(LIBNET_PR16);
```

The `libnet_seed_prand` seeds the pseudo-random number generator. The `libnet_get_prand()` generates a pseudo-random value within the `rand`-specified value. The `LIBNET_PR16` specifies a number between 0 and 32767.

Building the TCP header

Use the following code for building the TCP header:

```
/* Building TCP header */
seq = 1;
if (libnet_build_tcp (libnet_get_prand (LIBNET_PRu16),
                      80,
                      0,
                      0,
                      TH_SYN,
                      1024,
                      0,
                      0,
                      LIBNET_TCP_H,
                      (u_int8_t*)payload,
                      sizeof(payload),
                      lnet,
                      0) == -1)
{
    NSLog(@"Error building TCP header: %s\n",libnet_geterror(lnet));
    libnet_destroy(lnet);
    exit(EXIT_FAILURE);
}
```

We build the TCP header using the `libnet_build_tcp()` function. In the introduction section of this recipe, we covered how the parameters map to the TCP header. The values of each of the parameter are as follows:

- ▸ sp: We use the `libnet_get_prand()` function to generate a random port to use for the source port.

- ▸ dp: We use this for sending to port 80 on the destination computer.

- ▸ seq: This denotes the sequence number 0.

- ▸ ack: This is the acknowledgement number of 0.

- ▸ control: This sets the SYN (synchronize flag). For multiple flags, we would OR them together. For example, if we wanted to set both the SYN and ACK flag, we would set this field to `TH_SYN|TH_ACK`.

- ▸ win: This denotes the maximum window size in 1024 octets (bytes).

- ▸ sum: This sets the `Checksum` to 0 so that libnet autofills.

- ▸ urg: This sets the `Urgent Pointer` field to 0 because we are not using it.

- ▸ len: This is the size of the TCP header.

- ▸ payload: This is our payload.

- ▸ payload_s: This is the payload size.

- ▸ lnet: This is the libnet context to be used with this header.

- ▸ ptag: This is 0 and is used to generate a new header.

Building the IPv4 header

Use the following code for building the IPv4 header:

```
/* Building IP header */

if ( libnet_build_ipv4(LIBNET_TCP_H + LIBNET_IPV4_H + sizeof(payload),
                 0,
                 id,
                 0,
                 64,
                 IPPROTO_TCP,
                 0,
                 source,
                 target,
                 NULL,
                 0,
                 lnet,
                 0) == -1)
```

```
{
    NSLog(@"Error building IP header: %s\n",libnet_geterror(lnet));
    libnet_destroy(lnet);
    exit(EXIT_FAILURE);
}
```

We generate the IPv4 header using the `libnet_build_ipv4()` function. We covered the `libnet_build_ipv4()` function and how the parameters map to the header fields in the *Introduction* section of this chapter. The values for each parameter are as follows:

- `ip_len`: This is the size of the IPv4 header, the TCP header, and the payload added together
- `tos`: We are not using this so we set it to 0
- `id`: This is the pseudo-random number generated on line 24
- `frag`: This is not fragmented, so the offset is 0
- `ttl`: This is set to a maximum of sixty-four hops
- `prot`: This sets the protocol type to `IPPROTO_TCP`
- `sum`: This is set to 0 to have libnet autofill
- `src`: This is the source IPv4 address
- `dst`: This is the destination IPv4 address
- `payload`: The payload is set to `Null`
- `payload_s`: This denotes the payload size as 0
- `libnet_t`: This is the libnet context
- `ptag`: This is set to 0 to build a new header

Injecting the packet

Use the following code for injecting the packet:

```
/* Writing packet */
int bytes_written = libnet_write(lnet);
if ( bytes_written != -1 )
    printf("%d bytes written.\n", bytes_written);
else
    NSLog(@"Error writing packet: %s\n",libnet_geterror(lnet));

libnet_destroy(lnet);
```

We use the `libnet_write()` function to send out the TCP packet. The `libnet_write()` function returns the number of bytes written, or `-1` if the operation fails. If the operation is successful, we log the number of bytes written, otherwise we log the error message.

Finally, we use the `libnet_destory()` function to release the libnet context.

How it works...

The steps to create and send a TCP packet are as follows:

1. Create the libnet context using the `libnet_init()` function.
2. Get the target IPv4 address using the `libnet_namte2addr4()` function.
3. Get the source IPv4 address using the `libnet_getaddr4()` function.
4. Create the TCP header using the `libnet_build_tcp()` function.
5. Create the IPv4 header using the `libnet_build_ipv4()` function.
6. Send out the packet with the `libnet_write()` function.
7. Release the libnet context with the `libnet_destroy()` function.

If you use Wireshark to watch the packet getting injected and to see the response, it should look like the following screenshot:

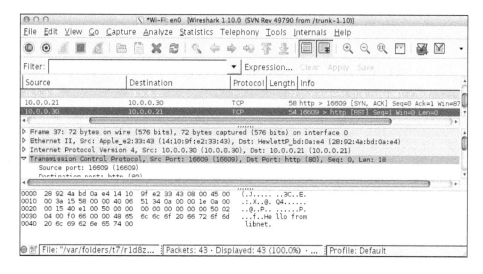

A lot of experimenting can be done with libnet, especially with the TCP packets. Try setting different flags and seeing what type of response comes back. In the next chapter, we'll discuss the libpcap library, which is a packet capture library. In that chapter, we will also discuss how to use libnet and libpcap together.

4

Using Libpcap

In this chapter, we will cover:

- ▶ Adding libpcap to your project
- ▶ Retrieving network device information
- ▶ Capturing packets
- ▶ Decoding Ethernet headers
- ▶ Decoding IP headers
- ▶ Decoding ARP headers
- ▶ Decoding TCP headers
- ▶ Decoding UDP headers
- ▶ Decoding ICMP headers
- ▶ Filtering packets
- ▶ Saving a capture file
- ▶ Creating a simple port scanner using libnet and libpcap together

Introduction

In the previous chapter, we discussed libnet, which is a library for constructing and injecting individual network packets. Being able to create and inject packets into the network is a very powerful feature, but to really make it useful, we need to be able to read the packets that come back. This is where libpcap comes in.

While it is possible to compile libpcap for iOS and jailbreak the phone to run the application as root, Apple would almost certainly reject your application. The code in this chapter is written and tested for OS X. It may or may not work for iOS.

The libpcap library is a packet-capturing library that is used by many popular network packet analyzers, including tcpdump (which maintains the libpcap library) and Wireshark (used in *Chapter 3, Using Libnet*). It can also be used for network monitors, intrusion detection systems, and network testers.

This library provides a cross-platform API to capture, filter, and save packets. It was originally developed as part of the tcpdump project. The low-level packet capture code was extracted from the main tcpdump project and made into a library that tcpdump now links to.

Typically, when a network interface receives a packet, it checks to see if the destination MAC address on the packet matches its own address. If it does match, the interface then sends the packet up through the protocol stack. When we run a packet analyzer and set the network interface to the promiscuous mode, copies of all of the packets that the interface receives (even if the packet is not destined for the device) are sent to the packet capture utility. Switched networks do offer some protection and require more than just putting a network interface into the promiscuous mode to see all of the traffic, but the packet capture utility still receives a copy of all of the packets destined for the device that it is running on.

When a packet is received by the packet capture utility, it is complete with all of the headers. If you recall from *Chapter 3, Using Libnet*, a packet is built in layers.

		Data		Application Layer		FTP	HTTP	SMTP	DNS
	Protocol Header			Protocol Layer		TCP		UDP	
IP Header				Internet Layer		ICMP	IP		ARP
Frame Header				Link Layer		Ethernet	Token Ring	Point-to-Point Protocol	

The four layers are as follows:

- **Application layer**: This layer is where the application creates the payload. This is where high-level protocols, such as FTP, HTTP, SMTP, and many more do their work. The application headers and payload are added in this layer.

- **Protocol layer**: This layer provides a uniform networking interface that hides the underlying network connections. This is where the payload is broken up into multiple packets (if needed) and reassembled. This layer is where the protocol-specific header, such as the TCP, UDP, or ICMP is added.

- ▸ **Internet layer**: Every device on an IP network is identified by a unique address called an IP address. There are two versions of IP addresses: IPv4 and IPv6. This layer is where the IP header is added.

- ▸ **Link layer**: There are many different types of network connections such as Ethernet, Wi-Fi, **Point-to-Point Protocol** (**PPP**), and so on. The Link layer defines the method by which the host communicates with the network.

Each of these layers wraps or encapsulates the layer above it. We can think of it as an onion where each layer of the onion completely encompasses all of the layers below it. When we built the packet with libnet, we built it using the top-down approach by adding the Application layer first followed by the Protocol, Internet, and Link layers. When we capture a packet with libpcap, we need to peel the layers away from the bottom-up, starting with the Link layer followed by the Internet, Protocol, and Application layers.

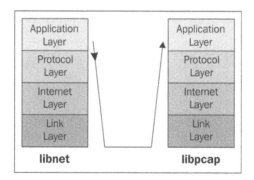

We will be discussing each header type and the information that it contains in the various decoding recipes of this chapter. We will also build a `PCAP_Headers.h` file as we go through the recipes of this chapter. The `PCAP_Headers.h` header will contain the structures and constants that are needed to decode the headers. You can see the entire `PCAP_Headers.h` file in the downloadable code for this chapter.

As we go through this chapter's recipes, we will be adding the functions for a packet capture library. You can see the complete code for the packet capture utility in the `PCAPcapture` project from the downloadable code.

Adding libpcap to your project

The first thing that we need to do is add libpcap to our project. Whenever there is a project that you need to add libpcap to, you need to follow the steps mentioned here.

Getting ready

We need to create an OS X project that we can add the libpcap library to.

How to do it...

Once the project is created, we need to add the library to our project using these steps:

1. Select the project name from the project navigator area within your Xcode project.
2. Select the project name from the **TARGET** section.
3. Select the **Build Phases** tab and open the **Link Binary With Libraries** section.
4. Click on the **+** sign.
5. Type `libpcap` in the search box and select the **libpcap.dylib** library.

Now that we have the library linked to the project, we need to set the application to run as root for debugging. To do so, follow these steps:

1. To run your project as root, navigate to **Product** | **Scheme** | **Edit Scheme** from the top menu as shown in the following screenshot:

2. In the window that opens up, change the **Debug Process As** selection from **Me** to **root**:

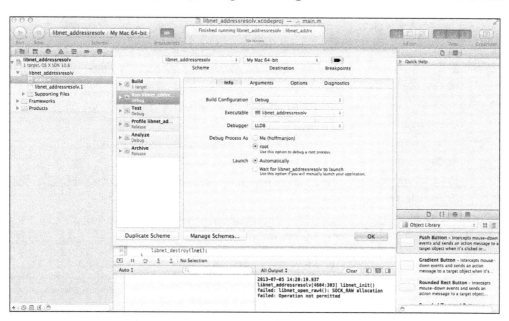

One thing to note is that when you debug the process as root, you will be periodically asked for your password. You also need to be an administrator for the computer you are working on.

How it works...

In this recipe, we added the libpcap library by linking the libpcap library to our target. We used the libpcap library that is compiled by Apple and comes with OS X. While you could compile our own version, if you want to distribute your app it is probably safer to use the version that comes along with your operating system.

The libpcap library requires root privileges to run since it accesses the network interfaces, so we set the application to run as root; this allows us to test it within Xcode.

Retrieving network device information

When we start using libpcap, we can specify a particular interface or let libpcap pick one up for us. In this recipe, we will retrieve a list of the network interfaces that are available and the address information for those interfaces.

To retrieve all of the devices, we use the `pcap_findalldevs()` function that returns a linked list of network interfaces. Each element in the list is of the `pcap_if_t` type. The `pcap_if_t` structure contains the following elements:

- `pcap_if *next`: This denotes the next element in the list. The value is NULL if it is the last element.

- `char *name`: This denotes the name of the device. This name can be passed to other functions to identify the device.

- `char *description`: This description provides a human-readable description of the device.

- `pcap_addr *addresses`: This is a pointer to the first element of a list of addresses for the interface.

- `u_int`: The `PCAP_IF_` interface flags. Currently the only possible flag is `PCAP_IF_LOOPBACK`, which is set if this interface is loopback.

You will see the `pcap_addr` structure within `pcap_if_t`. The `pcap_addr` structure is a linked list of addresses that belong to this interface. The `pcap_addr` structure contains the following elements:

- `pcap_addr *next`: This denotes the next element in the list. Its value is NULL if it is the last element.

- `sockaddr *addr`: This is a pointer to the `sockaddr` structure containing the IP address.

- `sockaddr *netmask`: This is a pointer to the `sockaddr` structure containing the netmask.

- `sockaddr *broadaddr`: This is a pointer to the `sockaddr` structure containing the broadcast address.

- ▶ sockaddr *dstaddr: This is a pointer to the sockaddr structure containing the destination address. Its value will be NULL if it is not a point-to-point interface.

Getting ready

Prior to running this recipe, we need to follow the *Adding libpcap to your project* recipe presented earlier in this chapter.

How to do it...

Let's retrieve the network interfaces by following the ensuing steps:

1. We start off by importing the following necessary header files:

```
#import <pcap.h>
#import <arpa/inet.h>
```

The first few lines are the header files that are to be imported. Notice that on the second line we are importing the pcap.h header; this is the header for the pcap library.

2. We need to define the following variables:

```
pcap_if_t *allDevs;
char errbuf[PCAP_ERRBUF_SIZE];
```

The allDevs pcap_if_t structure will contain the list of network interfaces when the pcap_findalldev() function is complete. The errbuf array will contain the error if the pcap_findalldevs function fails.

3. Let's get the list of network interfaces.

```
if (pcap_findalldevs(&allDevs, errbuf) == -1) {
    NSLog(@"Error: %s", errbuf);
    return -1;
}
```

We call the pcap_findalldevs() function to get the list of all of the network interfaces. If the pcap_findalldevs() function fails, it will return -1. The list of network interfaces will be returned in the allDevs structure.

4. Finally, we display the information about the network interfaces as follows:

```
for(pcap_if_t *dev=allDevs; dev; dev=dev->next)
{
    NSLog(@"\n");
    NSLog(@"%s", dev->name);
    NSLog(@"----------------------");
    char addr[INET6_ADDRSTRLEN];
```

```
            pcap_addr_t *adrs = dev->addresses;
            for(;adrs;adrs = adrs->next) {
                struct sockaddr *sa = adrs->addr;
                inet_ntop(sa->sa_family, &(((struct sockaddr_in *)
sa)->sin_addr),
                        addr, sizeof(addr));
                NSLog(@"    %s", addr);
            }
        }
    }
```

Here, we loop through the list of network interfaces returned from the `pcap_findalldevs()` call. The first thing we do is log the name of the network interface. This will be similar to **en0**, **lo0**, or **p2p0**.

Next, we set up a character array to hold the address when we convert the address within the `sockaddr` structure to a character array. We use the `INET6_ADDRSTRLEN` constant because it is large enough to hold both the IPv4 and IPv6 addresses.

The `pcap_if_t` structure contains a pointer to a `pcap_addr_t` structure that contains a list of addresses associated with this network interface. We retrieve a pointer to this structure and then loop through the addresses. Next, we pull out the `sockaddr` structure that represents the address itself.

We use the `inet_ntop()` function to convert the address into a human-readable format and log it.

How it works...

The pcap library provides a `pcap_findalldevs()` function that returns a linked list of all of the network interfaces on your device. Within the `pcap_if` structure, there is a pointer to a `pcap_addr` structure. This structure is a linked list that contains the addresses associated with the interface.

Capturing packets

In this recipe, we will show you how to use the libpcap library to capture packets. We will also introduce some basic libpcap concepts, such as the `pcap` handler and filters.

Getting ready

Prior to running this recipe, we need to follow the *Adding libpcap to your project* recipe presented earlier in this chapter.

How to do it...

Let's capture some packets by following the ensuing steps:

1. We start off by defining the following three symbols for use in our code:

    ```
    #define SNAPLEN 65535
    #define PROMISC 1
    #define TIMEOUT 500
    ```

    The SNAPLEN constant defines the maximum size of the packet to be captured. The PROMISC constant specifies whether we want to set the interface to the promiscuous mode or not; 1 is true and 0 is false. The TIMEOUT constant is the read timeout in milliseconds.

2. We need to define the following variables:

    ```
    pcap_t *handle;
    char errbuf[PCAP_ERRBUF_SIZE];
    bpf_u_int32 localNet, netMask;
    struct bpf_program filterCode;
    char filter[] = "arp or tcp or udp or icmp";
    ```

    The three variables to note are:

    - pcap_t *handle: This is the pcap handler. The pcap_t variable is a typedef from the pcap structure. This is the main monolithic structure that contains all of the details that make up the pcap descriptor and references a libpcap session.

    - Char filter[]: This is the filter code that will tell libpcap which types of packets should be captured. The arp or tcp or udp or icmp string specifies that we want to capture any ARP, TCP, UDP, or ICMP packet. We will discuss how to write filter code in the *Filtering packets* recipe.

    - Struct bpf_program filterCode: When we pass the filter code through the pcap_compile() function, filterCode will be populated with the compiled version of the filter string.

3. The first thing we are going to do is decide which network interface to capture the packets on:

    ```
    char *dev = pcap_lookupdev(errbuf);
    if (dev==NULL) {
        NSLog(@"Error finding default device %s", errbuf);
        exit(2);
    }
    ```

We can define the network interface by hardcoding the interface name like this: `char *dev = "en0"`, or we could allow libpcap to choose an interface by using the `pcap_lookupdev()` function. In our example, we will use the `pcap_lookupdev()` function that returns a pointer to a string; this string contains the name of the first network interface suitable for use with libpcap. If there is an error, the function will return `NULL` and populate the error buffer.

4. Once we have the network interface that will be used to capture the packets, we need to open it:

```
handle = pcap_open_live(dev, SNAPLEN, PROMISC, TIMEOUT, errbuf);
if (handle == NULL) {
    NSLog(@"Can not open device %s", errbuf);
    exit(2);
}
```

To open the network interface, we use the `pcap_open_live()` function. This function takes the following five arguments:

- ❏ `char *device`: This is a pointer to a string that contains the name of the network interface to use for the packet capture.

- ❏ `int snaplen`: This is the maximum size of the packet to be captured. The term `SNAPLEN` stands for "snapshot length". If the packet is larger than this value, the packet will be truncated to the length defined by `SNAPLEN`.

- ❏ `int promisc`: This specifies whether the interface should be put into the promiscuous mode or not. Defining it as `1` will put the interface into promiscuous mode; this will allow us to capture all of the packets rather than just the packets destined for our interface.

- ❏ `int to_ms`: This specifies the read timeout in milliseconds.

- ❏ `Char *errbuf`: This is the error buffer that will contain the error if libpcap cannot open the interface.

The function returns a `pcap_t` handler or `NULL` if the function fails. The `pcap_t` handler is needed for most of the libpcap functions.

5. Next, we do a network lookup to determine the network and netmask of the network interface:

```
if (pcap_lookupnet(dev, &localNet, &netMask, errbuf) == -1) {
    pcap_close(handle);
    NSLog(@"pcap_lookupnet failed");
    exit(2);
}
```

We look up the network and netmask of the network interface by using the `pcap_lookupnet()` function that takes the following four arguments:

- ❏ `char *device`: This is a pointer to a string containing the name of the network interface to be used for the packet capture.

- ❏ `bpf_u_int32 *netp`: This is the network that the network interface is on. For example, if the IP address of the network interface is 10.0.0.4 and that of the netmask is 255.255.255.0, then the network would be 10.0.0.0.

- ❏ `bpf_u_int32 *maskp`: This is the netmask of the network that the interface is on.

- ❏ `Char *errbuf`: This is the error buffer that will contain the error if libpcap cannot open the interface.

If the `pcap_lookupnet()` function is successful, it will return 0, otherwise it will return -1 and the `errbuf` array will be populated with the appropriate error message.

6. Now we need to set the filter:

```
if (pcap_compile(handle, &filterCode, filter, 1, netMask) == -1) {
    pcap_close(handle);
    NSLog(@"pcap_compile failed");
    exit(2);
}
if (pcap_setfilter(handle, &filterCode) == -1) {
    pcap_close(handle);
    NSLog(@"Can't install filter");
    exit(2);
}
```

The filter will tell libpcap and the packet capture interface which packets we wish to capture. The first step is to compile our filter string; this is done using the `pcap_compile()` function that takes the following five arguments:

- ❏ `pcap_t *p`: This is the pcap handler that was created using the `pcap_open_live()` function.

- ❏ `struct bpf_program *fp`: This points to the `bpf_program` structure that will contain the compiled version of our filter when the `pcap_compile()` function returns.

- ❏ It will be used by the `pcap_setfilter()` function.

- ❏ `char *filter`: This contains the filter code.

- ❏ `int optimize`: This controls whether the compiled code is optimized or not. Set this to 1 to perform optimization.

- ❏ `bpf_u_int32 netmask`: This is the netmask of the interface. It was obtained by the `pcap_lookupnet()` function call.

After we compile the filter code, we need to set the filter. This is done using the `pcap_setfilter()` function that accepts the two following arguments:

- ❑ `pcap_t *p`: This is the pcap handler that was created with the `pcap_open_live()` function.

- ❑ `struct bpf_program *fp`: This is the compiled version of our filter code that was generated using the `pcap_compile()` function.

Both the `pcap_compile()` and `pcap_setfilter()` functions return 0 if they are successful and -1 if they are not. Once the filter is set by the `pcap_setfilter()` function, libpcap begins to capture the packets.

7. Now that the packet capture has begun, we need a way to see the packets:

```
pcap_loop(handle, -1, got_packet,NULL);

pcap_freecode(&filterCode);
pcap_close(handle);
```

There are two ways for us to retrieve the captured packets: we can use the `pcap_next()` function to return the next captured packet or we can use the `pcap_loop()` function that will trigger a callback for each packet that is captured. The preferable method is to use `pcap_loop()` to capture multiple packets since you set up a callback that is called when a packet is captured. The `pcap_next()` function is written for capturing single packets. We will use the `pcap_loop()` function here since we want to capture more than one packet; however, we will use the `pcap_next()` function in our *Creating a simple port scanner using libnet and libpcap together* recipe, which appears later in this chapter. The `pcap_loop()` function takes the following four arguments:

- ❑ `pcap_t *p`: This denotes the pcap handler that was created with the `pcap_open_live()` function.

- ❑ `int cnt`: This indicates the number of packets to be captured before returning. If this is set to 0 or less, the function will loop forever or until the EOF or error is encountered.

- ❑ `pcap_handler callback`: This is the function to be called for each packet that is captured. The prototype for a callback function is: `void got_packet(u_char *args, const struct pcap_pkthdr *header, const u_char *packet);`. We will see a sample callback later in this recipe.

- ❑ `u_char *args`: This is a pointer to the first argument to be passed to the callback function.

We then need to free our compiled filter and the pcap handler. This is done using the `pcap_freecode()` and `pcap_close()` functions.

8. Now, let's create our callback function in the following manner:

```
void got_packet(u_char *args, const struct pcap_pkthdr *header,
const u_char *packet) {

    if (packet != NULL) {
    NSLog(@"Got Packet");
    }
}
```

We can't arbitrarily define our callback function because then the `pcap_loop()` function will not know how to call it. The prototype for the callback looks like this: `void got_packet(u_char *args, const struct pcap_pkthdr *header, const u_char *packet);`, where it takes the following three arguments:

- `u_char *args`: This corresponds to the `u_char *args` line in the `pcap_loop()` function.
- `const struct pcap_pkthdr *header`: This is the `pcap` header that contains information about when the packet was sniffed and how large it is.
- `cont u_char *packet`: This is the packet itself. We will see how to read this packet in future recipes.

Currently, the code simply logs that we received a packet each time a packet is captured. We will be building on this callback function in the upcoming recipes of this chapter.

How it works...

To capture packets using libpcap, we followed the ensuing steps:

1. We used the `pcap_lookupdev()` function to determine the network interface.
2. We opened the interface by using the `pcap_open_live()` function.
3. We determined the network information for the interface by using the `pcap_lookupnet()` function.
4. Then, we compiled the filter code by using the `pcap_compile()` function.
5. Next, we set the filter. We used the `pcap_setfilter()` function to do so.
6. We used the `pcap_loop()` function to retrieve the captured packets and to set the callback function to be used when we retrieve a packet.
7. Lastly, we created the callback function to call when we retrieve a packet.

Decoding Ethernet headers

If we recall how the headers are layered from this chapter's introduction, the first layer we will need to peel off is the Ethernet (Link layer) header. It looks like this:

The hardware will filter out the preamble, so we will not have access to it, but we need to retrieve the following elements:

- **Destination Address**: This is the MAC address of the computer that this packet is being sent to
- **Source Address**: This is the MAC address of the computer that this packet came from
- **Type**: This is used to indicate the type of protocol that is encapsulated. Some of the common protocols are as follows:
    - 0x0800—IPv4
    - 0x0806—ARP
    - 0x8035—RARP
    - 0x86DD—IPv6
- **Data**: This indicates the payload
- **Frame Check Sequence**: This indicates the checksum that is added to the frame to detect transmission errors

We will build a PCAP_Headers.h file that contains the structures and constants needed to decode the various packet headers. The entries in the PCAP_Headers.h file for the Ethernet header are as follows:

```
//Ethernet header
#define ETHERNET_SIZE 14
#define ETHERNET_ADDRESS_LENGTH 6
struct pcap_ethernet {
    u_char ether_dhost[ETHERNET_ADDRESS_LENGTH];
    u_char ether_shost[ETHERNET_ADDRESS_LENGTH];
    u_short ether_type;
};

#define ETHERTYPE_IP      0x0800
#define ETHERTYPE_ARP     0x0806
```

We start off by defining the Ethernet header size to be 14 bytes. This is the 6 bytes for the destination address, 6 bytes for the source address, and 2 bytes for the type.

We then define the address length to be 6 bytes.

Next we define a `pcap_ethernet` structure that represents the Ethernet headers. We will use this structure to retrieve the Ethernet information from our packet that is captured by libpcap.

Finally we define two types of protocols: the IP and ARP protocols.

Getting ready

Prior to running this recipe, we need to follow the *Adding libpcap to your project* recipe explained earlier in this chapter. We also need to go through the *Capturing packets* recipe explained earlier in this chapter to begin capturing packets prior to decoding them.

How to do it...

To decode the Ethernet header we will modify the `got_packet()` callback function to decode the Ethernet headers and determine if it is an IP, ARP, or other type of packet. We will also be logging the sender and the destination MAC addresses from the Ethernet headers.

The libpcap callback function requires three arguments. These are as follows:

▸ `u_char *args`: This is the pointer to the first argument to be passed to the callback function

▸ `const struct pcap_pkthdr *header`: This is the `pcap` header that contains the information about when the packet was sniffed and how large it is

▸ `const u_char *packet`: This is the packet itself

Let's look at the code to decode the Ethernet header:

```
void got_packet(u_char *args, const struct pcap_pkthdr *header,const
u_char *packet) {

    if (packet != NULL) {
        const struct pcap_ethernet *ethernet = (struct pcap_ethernet
*)packet;

        NSString *sMac = [NSString stringWithFormat:@"%02X:%02X
:%02X:%02X:%02X:%02X",ethernet->ether_shost[0],ethernet->ether_
shost[1],ethernet->ether_shost[2],ethernet->ether_shost[3],ethernet-
>ether_shost[4],ethernet->ether_shost[5]];
```

```
        NSString *dMac = [NSString stringWithFormat:@"%02X:%02X
:%02X:%02X:%02X:%02X",ethernet->ether_dhost[0],ethernet->ether_
dhost[1],ethernet->ether_dhost[2],ethernet->ether_dhost[3],ethernet-
>ether_dhost[4],ethernet->ether_dhost[5]];

        NSLog(@"Source MAC:  %@", sMac);
        NSLog(@"Destin MAC:  %@", dMac);
        switch (ntohs(ethernet->ether_type)) {
            case ETHERTYPE_IP:
                NSLog(@"IP:  %d", ethernet->ether_type);
                // decodeIp(packet);
                break;
            case ETHERTYPE_ARP:
                NSLog(@"ARP:  %d", ethernet->ether_type);
                // decodeArp(packet);
                break;
            default:
                break;
        }
    }
}
```

Now let's look at the steps to decode the Ethernet header:

1. We start the got_packet() function by verifying that the packet itself is not NULL. If it is NULL, we simply bypass all of the code.

    If the packet is not NULL, we typecast it to the custom pcap_ethernet structure that we discussed in the introduction of this recipe. This allows us to retrieve the Ethernet header information from our packet.

2. Once we have our packet typecasted as a pcap_ethernet structure, we convert the source and destination host's MAC address from u_char arrays to NSString. This is done with the stringWithFormat method of NSString.

3. Finally we create a switch statement that switches on the type of protocol that the packet contains. We determine the type of protocol by looking at the ether_type element of the Ethernet header. In the PCAP_Headers.h file, we define two protocol types: ETHERTYPE_IP and ETHERTYPE_ARP. If the protocol is of any other type, we skip it.

You will notice that we are calling the decodeIp() and decodeArp() functions in the switch statement. We will discuss these functions in the *Decoding IP headers* and *Decoding ARP headers* recipes. Once we create these functions, we will be able to uncomment these two lines.

How it works...

To retrieve the Ethernet header information from the packet, we typecasted the packet into the custom `pcap_ethernet` structure that is defined in our `PCAP_Headers.h` file. The `pcap_ethernet` structure looks like this:

```
struct pcap_ethernet {
    u_char ether_dhost[ETHERNET_ADDRESS_LENGTH];
    u_char ether_shost[ETHERNET_ADDRESS_LENGTH];
    u_short ether_type;
};
```

After we typecast the packet, we are able to pull out the destination and source MAC addresses and the protocol type.

Decoding IP headers

In the *Decoding Ethernet headers* recipe, we created the `got_packet()` callback function that libpcap called for each packet that was captured. In this function, we showed you how to pull the Ethernet header information from the packet and created a `switch` statement that called different functions based on the protocol type. In that `switch` statement, we made a reference to a `decodeIp()` function that is used to decode the IP headers. In this recipe, we will create this `decodeIp()` function.

The IP header is a part of the second layer (Internet layer) of our header stack. Its structure is shown in the following diagram:

The components are explained as follows:

- ▶ **Version**: This is the version of the IP packet. It can either be 4 (IPv4) or 6 (IPv6). For our examples, we will only look at IPv4.

- ▶ **Header Length**: This indicates the number of the 32-bit words in the TCP header. The minimum value is 5.

- ▶ **Type of Service**: This is now known as **DSCP (Differentiated Services Code Point)**; it may indicate a particular quality of service that is needed.

- ▶ **Total Length**: This is the total length of the packet, including the header and data, in bytes. The minimum size is 20 bytes and the maximum size is 65535 bytes. Some networks set restrictions on the packet size that may cause the packet to be fragmented.

- ▶ **Identification**: This field is primarily used to uniquely identify the fragments of an original packet.

- ▶ **Flags**: This includes the following three flags as defined in the IP packet:

    - ❑ **Bit 0**: This reserved bit must be 0.

    - ❑ **Bit 1**: If the **Don't Fragment** (**DF**) flag is set and fragmentation is needed to route the packet, the packet will be dropped.

    - ❑ **Bit 2**: If a packet is fragmented, all of the fragments will have the **More Fragments** (**MF**) flag set, except for the last one. This flag is cleared for the packets that are not fragmented.

- ▶ **Fragment Offset**: This specifies the offset of a particular fragment relative to the beginning of the original unfragmented packet.

- ▶ **Time to Live**: This gives the number of hops the packet can be routed through. This number is decremented at each hop until it reaches its destination or 0.

- ▶ **Protocol**: This indicates the IP protocol ID.

- ▶ **Header Checksum**: This indicates the checksum of the IP header.

- ▶ **Source Address**: This indicates the IPv4 address of the sender.

- ▶ **Destination Address**: This indicates the IPv4 address of the destination.

- ▶ **IP Option**: This field is not normally used.

If you recall from this chapter's introduction, we need to build a PCAP_Headers.h file that contains the structures and constants that are needed to decode the various packet headers. To retrieve the IP header information, we define a pcap_ip structure that will be used to typecast the packets that are captured. The pcap_ip structure looks like this:

```
struct pcap_ip {
    u_int8_t  ip_vhl;            // header length and version
    u_int8_t  ip_tos;            // type of service
    u_int16_t ip_len;            // total length
    u_int16_t ip_id;             // identification
    u_int16_t ip_off;            // fragment offset
#define IP_RF 0x8000             // reserved fragment flag
#define IP_DF 0x4000             // don't fragment flag
#define IP_MF 0x2000             // more fragments flag
#define IP_OFFMASK 0x1fff        // mask for fragmenting bits
    u_int8_t  ip_ttl;            // time to live
```

```
    u_int8_t  ip_p;             // protocol
    u_int16_t ip_sum;           // checksum
    struct  in_addr ip_src, ip_dst;  // source and dest address
};
```

We also define the following two functions in the `PCAP_Headers.h` file:

```
#define GET_IP_VERSION(ip)     (((ip)->ip_vhl & 0xf0) >> 4)  //get
version
#define GET_IP_HEADER_LENGTH(ip)   ((ip)->ip_vhl & 0x0f)     //get
header length
```

Getting ready

Prior to running this recipe, we need to follow the *Adding libpcap to your project* recipe provided earlier in this chapter. We also need to go through the *Capturing packets* recipe (earlier in this chapter) to capture packets prior to decoding them.

You should also go through the *Decoding Ethernet headers* recipe. We will expand the code from that recipe to include a section for decoding the IP headers.

How to do it...

Let's decode the IP header. The following function is used to decode our IP packets:

```
void decodeIp(const u_char *packet) {
    const struct pcap_ip *ip = (struct pcap_ip *)(packet + ETHERNET_
SIZE);
    uint version = GET_IP_VERSION(ip);
    NSString *from = [NSString stringWithFormat:@"%s",inet_ntoa(ip-
>ip_src)];
    NSString *to = [NSString stringWithFormat:@"%s",inet_ntoa(ip->ip_
dst)];
    switch (ip->ip_p) {
        case IPPROTO_TCP:
            NSLog(@"Found TCP packet from: %@  to:  %@",from,to);
    //    decodeTCP(packet);
            break;
        case IPPROTO_UDP:
            NSLog(@"Found UDP packet from: %@  to:  %@",from,to);
        //    decodeUDP(packet);
            break;
        case IPPROTO_ICMP:
            NSLog(@"Found ICMP packet from: %@  to:  %@",from,to);
        //    decodeICMP(Packet);
```

```
            break;
        default:
            NSLog(@"Found Unknown packet from: %@  to:  %@",from,to);
            break;
    }
}
```

Let's look at the steps to decode the IP header:

1. We begin the `decodeIp()` function by typecasting the packet as a `pcap_ip` structure. Notice how we offset the packet by the size of the Ethernet header (`packet + ETHERNET_SIZE`). We do this because the Ethernet headers encapsulate the IP headers. If we had not offset the address, we would retrieve the Ethernet header information instead of the IP headers.

2. Next, we determine the IP version by using the `GET_IP_VERSION` function that we defined in the `PCAP_Headers.h` file. We use the standard `inet_ntoa()` function to convert the IP source and destination addresses from a host address in the network byte order to a C string.

3. Finally, we create a `switch` statement that switches on the IP protocol type and calls the appropriate decoding function. These functions will be discussed in the later recipes, but for now they are commented out.

How it works...

To retrieve the IP header information from the packet, we typecasted the packet to the custom `pcap_ip` structure that is defined in our `PCAP_Headers.h` file. We had to offset the address of the packet by the size of the Ethernet header to ensure that we were retrieving the IP header and not the Ethernet headers.

After we typecasted the packet, we were able to pull out the IP addresses and the protocol type using the functions defined in our `PCAP_Headers.h` file.

Decoding ARP headers

In the *Decoding Ethernet headers* recipe, we created the `got_packet()` callback function that libpcap called for each packet that was captured. In this function, we learned how to pull out the Ethernet header information from the packet and created a `switch` statement that switched on the protocol type. In that `switch` statement, we made a reference to the `decodeArp()` function that is used to decode the ARP headers. In this recipe, we will create that `decodeArp()` function.

The ARP header is a part of the second layer (Internet layer) of our header stack. Its structure is shown in the following diagram:

Let's take a look at the fields of the ARP header:

- **Hardware Type**: This specifies the network protocol type. Some of the defined values are:
    - 1 – Ethernet
    - 6 – IEEE 802 network
    - 7 – ARCNET
    - 15 – Frame Relay
    - 18 – Fibre Channel
    - 20 – Serial Line

- **Protocol Type**: This specifies the internetworking protocol type. Some of the defined values are:
    - 0x0800 – IPv4
    - 0x0806 – ARP
    - 0x8035 – RARP
    - 0x86DD – IPv6

- **Hardware Address Length**: This specifies the length of the hardware address in bytes. The Ethernet address size is 6 bytes.

- **Protocol Address Length**: This specifies the length of the protocol address in bytes. The IPv4 address size is 4 bytes.

- **OP Code**: This specifies the operation that the sender is performing. The defined values are:
    - 1 – Request
    - 2 – Reply

- **Source Hardware Address**: This denotes the hardware address of the sender.
- **Source Protocol Address**: This denotes the protocol address of the sender.
- **Destination Hardware Address**: This denotes the hardware address of the receiver.
- **Destination Protocol Address**: This denotes the protocol address of the receiver.

If you recall from the chapter introduction, we need to build a PCAP_Headers.h file that contains the structures and constants needed to decode the various packet headers. To retrieve the ARP header information, we define a pcap_arp structure that we will typecast this packet to. This is similar to what we did in the *Decoding Ethernet headers* recipe of this chapter. The pcap_arp structure looks like this:

```
struct pcap_arp {
    u_int16_t arp_htype;    // Hardware Type
    u_int16_t arp_ptype;    // Protocol Type
    u_char    arp_hlen;      // Hardware Address Length
    u_char    arp_plen;      // Protocol Address Length
    u_int16_t arp_type;     // ARP type
    u_char    arp_sha[6];    // source hardware address
    u_char    arp_spa[4];    // source IP address
    u_char    arp_dha[6];    // destination hardware address
    u_char    arp_dpa[4];    // destination IP address
};
```

We also define two constants in the PCAP_Headers.h file for the ARP headers. These are as follows:

```
#define ARP_REQUEST 1    // ARP Request
#define ARP_REPLY 2      // ARP Reply
```

Getting ready

Prior to running this recipe, we need to follow the *Adding libpcap to your project* recipe that appears earlier in this chapter. We also need to go through the *Capturing packets* recipe to begin capturing the packets prior to decoding them.

You should also go through the *Decoding Ethernet headers* recipe of this chapter because we will expand that code for this recipe to include a section for decoding the ARP headers.

How to do it...

Let's decode the ARP header. The following function decodes the ARP packets:

```
void decodeArp(const u_char *packet) {
    const struct pcap_arp *arp = (struct pcap_arp *)(packet +
ETHERNET_SIZE);
    switch (ntohs(arp->arp_type)) {
        case ARP_REQUEST:
            NSLog(@"ARP Request");
            NSLog(@"From:   %d.%d.%d.%d",arp->arp_spa[0],arp->arp_
spa[1],arp->arp_spa[2],arp->arp_spa[3]);
```

```
            NSLog(@"To:      %d.%d.%d.%d",arp->arp_dpa[0],arp->arp_
dpa[1],arp->arp_dpa[2],arp->arp_dpa[3]);
            break;

        case ARP_REPLY:
            NSLog(@"ARP Response");
            NSLog(@"From:   %02X:%02X:%02X:%02X:%02X:%02X",arp-
>arp_sha[0],arp->arp_sha[1],arp->arp_sha[2],arp->arp_sha[3],arp->arp_
sha[4],arp->arp_sha[5]);
            NSLog(@"To:      %d.%d.%d.%d",arp->arp_dpa[0],arp->arp_
dpa[1],arp->arp_dpa[2],arp->arp_dpa[3]);
            break;

        default:
            NSLog(@"ARP Type:  %d",arp->arp_type);
            break;
    }
}
```

Let's look at the steps to decode the ARP header:

1. We begin the `decodeArp()` function by typecasting the packet as a `pcap_arp` structure. Notice how we offset the packet by the size of the Ethernet header (`packet + ETHERNET_SIZE`). We do this because the Ethernet headers encapsulate the ARP headers. If we do not offset the packet, we will retrieve the Ethernet header information instead of the ARP header.

2. The remainder of the `decodeArp()` function is a `switch` statement that displays different information depending on whether the ARP type is a request, reply, or unknown. If the packet is an ARP request, we display the IP address for the sender and receiver. If the packet is an ARP response, we display the sender's MAC address and the receiver's IP address.

How it works...

To retrieve the ARP header information from the packet, we typecasted the packet to the custom `pcap_arp` structure that is defined in our `PCAP_Headers.h` file. We had to offset the address of the packet by the size of the Ethernet header to ensure that we were retrieving the ARP header and not the Ethernet header.

Once we had the `pcap_arp` structure, we could pull out the address information and tell if the packet is an ARP request or reply.

Decoding TCP headers

In the *Decoding IP headers* recipe of this chapter, we created a `decodeIp()` function that decoded the IP headers of a packet. In that function, if the protocol type was TCP, we called a `decodeTcp()` function. We will create the `decodeTcp()` function in this recipe.

The TCP header is a part of the third layer (Protocol layer) of our header stack.

The TCP header looks like this:

Let's take a look at the fields of the TCP header:

- **Source Port**: This identifies the port that the packet is being sent from on the sending device.

- **Destination Port**: This identifies the port that the packet is going to on the receiving device.

- **Sequence Number**: This is the initial sequence number for this session if the SYN flag is set. If the SYN flag is not set, this is the sequence number of the first data byte of this segment for this session.

- **Acknowledgement Number**: This value is the next sequence number that the receiver is expecting if the ACK flag is set. The first ACK packet that is sent by each end of the communication acknowledges the other end's initial sequence number.

- **Data Offset**: This is the size of the TCP header.

- **Reserved**: This is reserved for future use; it should be set to `0`.

- **Flags**: The TCP flags are as follows:

    - **NS**: This flag implements the **Explicit Congestion Notification** (**ECN**) nonce that protects against concealment.

    - **CWR**: This flag stands for Congestion Window Reduced.

    - **ECE**: This flag indicates that the TCP peer is ECN-capable if the SYN flag is also set.

    - **URG**: This flag indicates that the **Urgent Pointer** field of the header is significant.

    - **ACK**: This flag indicates that the **Acknowledgement Number** field is significant. All of the packets after the initial SYN packet sent by the client should have this flag set.

- ❑ **PSH**: This flag indicates that the data needs to be pushed up to the receiving application immediately and not wait for any additional packets to fill the buffer.

- ❑ **RST**: This flag resets the connection.

- ❑ **SYN**: This flag synchronizes the sequence numbers; it is set in the first packet that is sent from one device to another.

- ❑ **FIN**: This flag indicates that the device has finished talking.

▶ **Window**: This is the maximum size of data that the sender of this segment is willing to accept from the receiver at any point of time.

▶ **Checksum**: This is the checksum for the TCP header.

▶ **Urgent Pointer**: This is used in conjunction with the URG flag. It contains the sequence number for the last byte of urgent data.

If you recall from the chapter introduction, we need to build a PCAP_Headers.h file that contains the structures and constants that are needed to decode the various packet headers. To retrieve the TCP header information, we define a pcap_tcp structure that we will typecast the packet to. This is similar to what we did in the *Decoding Ethernet headers* recipe of this chapter. The pcap_tcp structure looks like this:

```
struct pcap_tcp {
    u_short tcp_sport;          // source port
    u_short tcp_dport;          // destination port
    u_int   tcp_seq;            // sequence number
    u_int   tcp_ack;            // acknowledgement number
    u_int tcp_x2:4,             // (unused)
          tcp_off:4;             // offset
    u_char  tcp_flags;
#define TCP_FIN   0x01
#define TCP_SYN   0x02
#define TCP_RST   0x04
#define TCP_PUSH 0x08
#define TCP_ACK   0x10
#define TCP_URG   0x20
#define TCP_ECE   0x40
#define TCP_CWR   0x80
#define TCP_FLAGS          (TH_FIN|TH_SYN|TH_RST|TH_ACK|TH_URG|TH_
ECE|TH_CWR)
    u_short tcp_win;            // window
    u_short tcp_sum;            // checksum
    u_short tcp_urp;            // urgent pointer
};
```

Getting ready

Prior to running this recipe, we need to follow the *Adding libpcap to your project* recipe explained earlier in this chapter. We also need to go through the *Capturing packets* recipe to begin capturing the packets prior to decoding them.

You should have also gone through the *Decoding Ethernet headers* and *Decoding IP headers* recipes because we will expand the code from those recipes to include a section for decoding the TCP headers.

How to do it...

Let's decode the TCP header. The `decodeTcp()` function is as follows:

```
void decodeTcp(const u_char *packet) {
    struct pcap_ip *ip = (struct pcap_ip *)(packet + ETHERNET_SIZE);
    int offset = GET_IP_HEADER_LENGTH(ip)*4;
    struct pcap_tcp *tcp = (struct pcap_tcp *)(packet + ETHERNET_SIZE
+ offset);

    int from = ntohs(tcp->tcp_sport);
    int to = ntohs(tcp->tcp_dport);
    NSString *flags = [NSString stringWithFormat:@"%s%s%s%s%s%s",(tcp-
>tcp_flags & TCP_FIN) ? "F" : "",
                (tcp->tcp_flags & TCP_SYN) ? "S" : "",
                (tcp->tcp_flags & TCP_RST) ? "R" : "",
                (tcp->tcp_flags & TCP_PUSH)? "P" : "",
                (tcp->tcp_flags & TCP_ACK) ? "A" : "",
                (tcp->tcp_flags & TCP_URG) ? "U" : ""];
    NSLog(@"TCP packet from port: %d to port: %d with flags: %@",
from, to, flags);
}
```

Let's look at the steps to decode the TCP header:

1. Since the IP packet can be of variable lengths, the first thing we need to do is obtain the size of the IP header so that we can calculate the offset needed to retrieve the TCP header. We begin our `decodeTcp()` function by typecasting the packet as `pcap_ip` (IP header) and then retrieve the size of the IP header using the `GET_IP_HEADER_LENGTH` function.

2. Once we have the size of the IP header, we can calculate the offset to the TCP header by adding the sizes of the Ethernet and IP headers. With the offset we can typecast the packet as a `pcap_tcp` structure.

3. We retrieve the source and destination ports from the header using the `ntohs()` function that converts the port information from the network byte order into the host byte order. We then create a `flags` string that lists the TCP flags that are set within the packet. Finally, we log the source port, destination port, and TCP flags.

How it works...

To retrieve the TCP header information from the packet, we first had to determine the size of the IP header, since the IP header can be of varying sizes. We do this by retrieving the IP header in the same manner that we did in the *Decoding IP headers* recipe of this chapter.

Once we had the size of the IP header, we can calculate the offset to the TCP header. With the offset, we can typecast the packet as a `pcap_tcp` structure and retrieve the information that we need from the TCP header.

Decoding UDP headers

In the *Decoding IP headers* recipe of this chapter, we created a `decodeIp()` function that decoded the IP headers of a packet. If the protocol type was UDP in that function, we called a `decodeUdp()` function. We will create the `decodeUdp()` function in this recipe.

The UDP header is a part of the third layer (Protocol layer) of our header stack. This is what the UDP header looks like:

Let's take a look at the fields of the UDP header:

- ▶ Source Port: This field identifies the port used by the sender, and it can be assumed that any reply should be sent to this port. If no reply is needed or wanted, we should set this port to `0`, indicating that we are not expecting a reply.

- ▶ Destination Port: This field identifies the port on the client to which the datagram has to be sent. The port should be a valid port number between `0` and `65535`.

- ▶ Length: This field indicates the size of the UDP header and the payload.

- ▶ Checksum: This field indicates the checksum for the UDP header.

If you recall from the chapter introduction, we need to build a `PCAP_Headers.h` file that contains the structures and constants needed for decoding the various packet headers. To retrieve the UDP header information, we define a `pcap_udp` structure that we will be typecasting the packet header to. This is similar to what we did in the *Decoding Ethernet headers* recipe of this chapter. The `pcap_udp` structure looks like this:

```
struct pcap_udp {
    unsigned short int udp_sport;    // source port
    unsigned short int udp_dport;    // destination port
    unsigned short int udp_len;      // length
    unsigned short int udp_sum;     //checksum
};
```

Getting ready

Prior to running this recipe, we need to follow the *Adding libpcap to your project* recipe explained earlier in this chapter. We also need to go through the *Capturing packets* recipe to begin capturing the packets prior to decoding them.

You should also go through the *Decoding Ethernet headers* and *Decoding IP headers* recipes of this chapter because we will expand on these recipes to include a section for decoding the UDP headers.

How to do it...

Let's decode the UDP header. The following function decodes the UDP packets:

```
void decodeUdp(const u_char *packet) {
    struct pcap_ip *ip = (struct pcap_ip *)(packet + ETHERNET_SIZE);
    int offset = GET_IP_HEADER_LENGTH(ip)*4;
    struct pcap_udp *udp = (struct pcap_udp *)(packet + ETHERNET_SIZE
+ offset);

    int from = ntohs(udp->udp_sport);
    int to = ntohs(udp->udp_dport);
    NSLog(@"UDP packet from port:  %d  to port:  %d", from, to);
}
```

Let's take a look at the steps to decode the UDP header:

1. Since the IP packet can be of variable length, the first thing that we need to do is obtain the size of the IP header so that we can calculate the offset needed to retrieve the UDP header. We begin our `decodeUdp()` function by typecasting the packet as `pcap_udp` (IP header) and then retrieve the size of the IP header using the `GET_IP_HEADER_LENGTH` function.

2. Once we have the size of the IP header, we can calculate the offset to the UDP header by adding the sizes of the Ethernet and IP headers. With the offset, we typecast the packet as a `pcap_udp` structure.

3. Finally, we retrieve the source and destination ports from the header and then log the UDP packet port information.

How it works...

To retrieve the UDP header information from the packet, we had to first determine the size of the IP header since the IP header can be of varying sizes. We do this by retrieving the IP header in the same manner that we did in the *Decoding IP headers* recipe of this chapter.

Once we have the size of the IP header, we could calculate the offset to the UDP header. With the offset, we can typecast the packet as a `pcap_udp` structure and retrieve the information that we need from the UDP header.

Decoding ICMP headers

In the *Decoding IP headers* recipe of this chapter, we created a `decodeIp()` function that decoded the IP headers of a packet. If the protocol type was ICMP in that function, we called a `decodeICMP()` function. We will create the `decodeICMP()` function in this recipe.

Even though our layer diagram shows the ICMP packet as a part of the Internet layer, from the libpcap point of view, it is a part of the third layer (Protocol layer) of our header stack; this is because the IP header encapsulates the ICMP header.

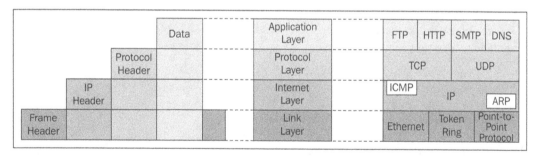

The ICMP header looks like this:

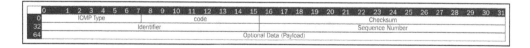

The components are explained as follows:

▶ **ICMP Type**: This field identifies the ICMP message type. The Echo request message is type 8 and the Echo reply is type 0.

▶ **Code**: This field is not used in the Echo request or reply so this is set to 0.

▶ **Checksum**: This field contains the checksum for the ICMP header.

▶ **Identifier**: This is the identification field that can be used to match the Echo request with an Echo reply.

▶ **Sequence Number**: This field contains the sequence number that can also be used to match an Echo request with an Echo reply.

▶ **Optional Data (Payload)**: This field contains the additional data sent along with the header.

If you recall from the chapter introduction, we need to build a `PCAP_Headers.h` file that contains the structures and constants needed to decode the various packet headers. To retrieve the ICMP header information, we define a `pcap_icmp` structure that we will be typecasting the packet to. This is similar to what we did in the *Decoding Ethernet headers* recipe of this chapter. The `pcap_icmp` structure looks like this:

```
struct pcap_icmp {
    u_char icmp_type;  // ICMP Type
    u_char icmp_code;  // ICMP Code
    u_short icmp_sum;    // ICMP Checksum
    u_short icmp_id;  // ID
    u_short icmp_seq;  // Sequence #
};
```

We also define six common ICMP types. This code will be used in the `u_char icmp_type` element of the `pcap_icmp` structure.

```
#define ICMP_ECHO_REPLY_TYPE 0
#define ICMP_ECHO_REQUEST_TYPE 8
#define ICMP_REDIRECT_TYPE 5
#define ICMP_DESTINATION_UNREACHABLE_TYPE 3
#define ICMP_TRACEROUTE_TYPE 30
#define ICMP_TIME_EXCEEDED_TYPE 11
```

Getting ready

Prior to running this recipe, we need to follow the *Adding libpcap to your project* recipe explained earlier in this chapter. We also need to go through the *Capturing packets* recipe in order to begin capturing the packets prior to decoding them.

You should also go through the *Decoding Ethernet headers* and *Decoding IP headers* recipes of this chapter because we will be expanding on those recipes to include a section for decoding the ICMP headers.

How to do it...

Let's decode the ICMP header. The function to decode the ICMP packets is as follows:

```
void decodeICMP(const u_char *packet) {
    struct pcap_ip *ip = (struct pcap_ip *)(packet + ETHERNET_SIZE);
    int offset = GET_IP_HEADER_LENGTH(ip)*4;
    struct pcap_icmp *icmp = (struct pcap_icmp *)(packet + ETHERNET_
SIZE + offset);

    NSString *typeStr = @"ICMP Unknown";
    int iType = icmp->icmp_type;
    switch (iType) {
        case ICMP_ECHO_REPLY_TYPE:
            typeStr=@"ICMP Reply";
            break;
        case ICMP_ECHO_REQUEST_TYPE:
            typeStr=@"ICMP Request";
            break;
        case ICMP_REDIRECT_TYPE:
            typeStr=@"ICMP Redirect";
            break;
        case ICMP_DESTINATION_UNREACHABLE_TYPE:
            typeStr=@"ICMP Unreachable";
            break;
        case ICMP_TRACEROUTE_TYPE:
            typeStr=@"ICMP Traceroute";
            break;
        case ICMP_TIME_EXCEEDED_TYPE:
            typeStr=@"ICMP Time Exceeded";
            break;

        default:
            break;
    }
    NSLog(@"ICMP packet of type:  %@", typeStr);
}
```

Let's take a look at the steps to decode the ICMP header:

1. Since the IP packet can be of variable length, the first thing that we need to do is obtain the size of the IP header so that we can calculate the offset needed to retrieve the ICMP header. We begin our `decodeICMP()` function by typecasting the packet as `pcap_ip` (IP header) and then retrieve the size of the IP header using the `GET_IP_HEADER_LENGTH` function.

2. Once we have the size of the IP header, we can calculate the offset to the ICMP header by adding the sizes of the Ethernet and IP headers. With the offset, we can typecast the packet as a `pcap_icmp` structure.

3. Finally, we create a `switch` statement that switches on the ICMP type. We use the ICMP types defined in the `PCAP_Headers.h` file to identify the ICMP type of the packet.

How it works...

To retrieve the ICMP header information from the packet, we had to first determine the size of the IP header since the IP header can be of varying sizes. We do this by retrieving the IP header in the same manner that we did in the *Decoding IP headers* recipe of this chapter.

Once we have the size of the IP header, we can calculate the offset to the ICMP header. With the offset, we can then typecast the packet as a `pcap_icmp` structure and retrieve the information that we need.

Filtering packets

In the *Capturing packets* recipe of this chapter, we showed a basic filter of `char filter[] = "arp or tcp or udp or icmp";`. In this recipe, we will take a more in-depth look at how to create a filter.

Since the libpcap library is used as the packet-capturing library for the tcpdump project, the libpcap filters take the same format as the tcpdump filter format. Any of the tcpdump filter expressions that we find on the Internet should work with libpcap. A Google search for "tcpdump filter" will return lots of results, but we will go over the basics in this recipe.

Getting ready

The filters that we will create in this recipe can be used along with the code in the *Capturing packets* recipe of this chapter. You should go through it to understand where to use these filters.

How to do it...

Let's create a filter.

When we create a filter for libpcap to use, we create it as a `char` array. We then use the `pcap_compile()` function to compile the expression to a `bpf_program`. The compiled `bpf_program` is then set using the `pcap_setfilter()` function. The following is the filter-specific code from the *Capturing packets* recipe of this chapter:

```
char filter[] = "arp or tcp or udp or icmp";
if (pcap_compile(handle, &filterCode, filter, 1, netMask) == -1) {
    pcap_close(handle);
    NSLog(@"pcap_compile failed");
    exit(2);
}

if (pcap_setfilter(handle, &filterCode) == -1) {
    pcap_close(handle);
    NSLog(@"Can't install filter");
    exit(2);
}
```

Let's take a look at some of the more useful filters:

- **Host**: The filters that work with the source and destination hosts are as follows:
    - `dst host {host}`: This matches the IPv4 or IPv6 destination fields to `{host}`
    - `src host {host}`: This matches the IPv4 or IPv6 source fields to `{host}`
    - `host {host}`: This matches the IPv4 or IPv6 fields of either the destination or the source to `{host}`
    - `ether dst {addr}`: This matches the Ethernet address of the destination host to `{addr}`
    - `ether src {addr}`: This matches the Ethernet address of the source host to `{addr}`
    - `ether host {addr}`: This matches the Ethernet address of either the destination or source host to `{addr}`

- **Network**: The filters that work with the source and destination networks are as follows:
    - `dst net {net}`: This matches the IPv4 or IPv6 destination networks to `{net}`
    - `src net {net}`: This matches the IPv4 or IPv6 source networks to `{net}`

- ❑ `net` {`net`}: This matches the IPv4 or IPv6 source or destination networks to {`net`}

▶ **Port**: The filters that work with the source and destination ports are as follows:

- ❑ `dst port` {`port`}: This matches the destination port number of the TCP or UDP packets to {`port`}

- ❑ `src port` {`port`}: This matches the source port number of the TCP or UDP packets to {`port`}

- ❑ `port` {`port`}: This matches either the destination or source port numbers of the TCP or UDP packets to {`port`}

- ❑ {`protocol`} `dst port` {`port`}: This matches the destination port number for {`protocol`} with {`port`}

- ❑ {`protocol`} `src port` {`port`}: This matches the source port number for {`protocol`} with {`port`}

- ❑ {`protocol`} `port` {`port`}: This matches either the source or destination port numbers for {`protocol`} with {`port`}

▶ **Protocol**: The filters that work with the protocol type are as follows:

- ❑ `ip proto` {`protocol`}: This matches the protocol of an IP packet to {`protocol`}

- ❑ `ip6 proto` {`protocol`}: This matches the protocol of an IP6 packet to {`protocol`}

- ❑ `ip broadcast`: This matches an IP broadcast packet

 IP protocols can be ICMP, ICMP6, IGMP, IGRP, PIM, AH, ESP, UDP, or TCP.

- ❑ `ether proto` {`protocol`}: This matches the protocol of an Ethernet packet to {`protocol`}

- ❑ `ether broadcast`: This matches an Ethernet broadcast packet

 Ethernet protocols can be IP, IP6, ARP, RARP, ATALK, AARP, DECENT, SCA, LAT, MOPDL, MOPRC, or ISO.

- ❑ {`protocol`}: This matches the protocol of the packet to {`protocol`}. This is what we used in our filter when we defined it as `arp or tcp or udp or icmp`. The protocol can be any of the IP or Ethernet protocols listed previously.

The preceding expressions can be combined using the following tokens:

- ▸ **Negation**: The tokens to be used are "!" or "not"
- ▸ **Concatenation**: The tokens to be used are "&&" or "and"
- ▸ **Alternation**: The tokens to be used are "||" or "or "

Here are some examples of `pcap` filters:

- ▸ `"tcp or udp"`: This filter captures all of the TCP and UDP packets but drops the others
- ▸ `"dst host 10.0.0.24"`: This filter captures all of the packets destined for `10.0.0.24`
- ▸ `"tcp src port 22"`: This filter captures all of the TCP packets that have a source port of `22`
- ▸ `"host 10.0.0.24 or host 10.0.026"`: This filter captures the packets that have a source or destination address of either `10.0.0.24` or `10.0.0.26`

How it works...

To create a filter for libpcap, we need to write the filter code and put it in a `char` array. We will then compile the filter code using the `pcap_compile()` function and set the filter using the `pcap_setfilter()` function.

Saving a capture file

There will be times when we want to capture packets and not view the results immediately. The libpcap library has functions to open and save the packets to a binary file. This file has the same format as a tcpdump save file.

Getting ready

Prior to running this recipe, we need to follow the *Adding libpcap to your project* recipe explained earlier in this chapter. We also need to go through the *Capturing packets* recipe. We will discuss how to modify the packet capture code in order to save the captured packets to a save file.

How to do it...

Let's save our captured packets to a file:

1. We begin by defining a `pcap_dumper_t` pointer and creating a `pcap_loop`. This will be the pointer to our save file.

    In our packet capture code from the *Capturing packets* recipe of this chapter, we want to replace the `pcap_loop` statement with the following lines:

    ```
    pcap_dumper_t *dumpfile=pcap_dump_open(handle, "~/pcapdump.
    pcap");
    if(dumpfile==NULL){
        NSLog(@"Error opening output file");
        exit(2);
    }

    pcap_loop(handle, 0, dispatcher_handler, (unsigned char *)
    dumpfile);
    pcap_dump_close(dumpfile);
    ```

    We start off by opening the packet capture dump file and write to it using the `pcap_dump_open()` function. If the `pcap_dump_open()` function is successful, it will return a `pcap_dumper_t` structure. If it fails, it will return `NULL`.

    In our `pcap_loop()` function, we pass the `pcap_dumper_t` structure as an argument to our callback function. The callback function gets called each time a packet is captured by libpcap.

    Finally, we close the dump file by using the `pcap_dump_close()` function.

2. Let's create the callback function for our `pcap_loop`. The callback function looks like this:

    ```
    void dispatcher_handler(u_char *dumpfile, const struct pcap_pkthdr
    *header, const u_char *pkt_data)
    {
        pcap_dump(dumpfile,header,pkt_data);

        //view file "tcpdump -qns 0 -A -r ~/pcapdump.pcap"
    }
    ```

    The callback function does the actual writing of the packets to the save file. This is done using the `pcap_dump()` function. This function accepts the following three arguments:

    ❏   `u_char *fp`: This argument acts as the `pcap_dumper_t` pointer for our save file. It is created using the `pcap_dump_open()` function.

- ❏ `struct pcap_pkthdr *header`: This argument acts as the pointer for the packet header data.
- ❏ `u_char *packet`: This argument acts as the pointer for the packet to be written.

How it works...

To write packets to a save file, we followed the ensuing steps:

1. We opened the file and wrote to it using the `pcap_dump_open()` function.
2. We passed the `pcap_dumper_t` structure as an argument to the callback function.
3. In the callback function, we wrote the packet to the save file using the `pcap_dump()` function.
4. When we are done writing all of our packets, we use the `pcap_dump_close()` function to close the file.

Creating a simple port scanner using libnet and libpcap together

In *Chapter 3, Using Libnet*, we discussed how to use libnet to inject packets into the network. In this chapter, we discussed how to use libpcap to capture and analyze the incoming packets. The next logical question is, "How can we use libnet and libpcap to create some really awesome network security tools?" This recipe is written to show you how we can use libnet and libpcap together.

We will build a simple port scanner that scans a range of ports on a remote device and lists whether that port is open or closed. We will implement a SYN scan. This is a scan that sends a packet with the SYN flag set, and if the port is open, the remote device will respond with a packet that has the SYN and ACK flags set. If the port is not open, the remote device will respond with a packet that has the RST flag set.

We will not go into the technical details of how libpcap and libnet work because that was covered in this chapter and in *Chapter 3, Using Libnet*. Instead, we will discuss how we can use libnet and libpcap together to create the port scanner.

Getting ready

Prior to using libnet and libpcap together, we need to follow the *Adding libpcap to your project* recipe of this chapter and the *Adding libnet to your project* recipe of *Chapter 3, Using Libnet*. The following sections will show you how to add libnet and libpcap to your project. We should be familiar with using both libnet and libpcap.

How to do it...

Let's get started:

1. We start off by defining the variables for our scanner:

```
libnet_t *lnet;
pcap_t *pcap;
char errbuf[PCAP_ERRBUF_SIZE];
bpf_u_int32 localNet, netMask;
u_int32_t source, target;
struct bpf_program filterCode;
struct pcap_pkthdr header;
const u_char *packet;
libnet_ptag_t tcp = 0, ipv4 = 0;
int reply = 0;
char *TARGETIP = "10.0.0.16";
char filter[] = "src host 10.0.0.16 && tcp";
```

Most of these will look very familiar if you have looked at the libnet and libpcap recipes in this book. The important lines to look at here are the final two lines. These define our target device's IP address; in this case, we will be scanning the device with an IP address of `10.0.0.16` and defining the filter that we will be using to capture packets with libpcap. Notice that the filter specifies the IP address of our target host and the TCP protocol. The filter line will set the filter only to capture the TCP packets from our target host.

2. Now, let's set up our libnet environment:

```
//Libnet Setup
lnet = libnet_init(LIBNET_RAW4, NULL, errbuf);
if ( lnet == NULL ) {
    NSLog(@"Error with libnet_init():  %s", errbuf);
    exit(EXIT_FAILURE);
}

target = libnet_name2addr4(lnet, TARGETIP, LIBNET_DONT_RESOLVE);
source = libnet_get_ipaddr4(lnet);
if ( source == -1 ) {
    NSLog(@"Error retrieving IP address: %s",libnet_
geterror(lnet));
    libnet_destroy(lnet);
    exit(EXIT_FAILURE);
}
```

```
libnet_seed_prand (lnet);
```

You can refer to *Chapter 3, Using Libnet*, for more details on this code.

3. Next, we will set up our libpcap environment in the following manner:

```
//PCAP Setup
char *dev = pcap_lookupdev(errbuf);
if (dev==NULL) {
    NSLog(@"Error finding default device %s", errbuf);
    exit(2);
}

pcap= pcap_open_live(dev, SNAPLEN, PROMISC, TIMEOUT, errbuf);
if (pcap == NULL) {
    NSLog(@"Can not open device %s", errbuf);
    exit(2);
}

if (pcap_lookupnet(dev, &localNet, &netMask, errbuf) == -1) {
    pcap_close(pcap);
    NSLog(@"pcap_lookupnet failed");
    exit(2);
}

if (pcap_compile(pcap, &filterCode, filter, 1, netMask) == -1) {
    pcap_close(pcap);
    NSLog(@"pcap_compile failed");
    exit(2);
}

if (pcap_setfilter(pcap, &filterCode) == -1) {
    pcap_close(pcap);
    NSLog(@"Can't install filter");
    exit(2);
}
```

We use the pcap_setFilter() function to set our filter and once the filter is set, libpcap begins capturing packets. This is fine because the filter that we set up is only looking for packets from our target host and we have not sent any packets to that host yet.

4. Now, we loop through the ports we wish to send:

```
//Looping through ports
for (int portNum=1; portNum<1024; portNum++) {
```

In this example, we loop from port `1` to port `1024` looking for any open ports.

5. We build our TCP header as follows:

```
/* Building TCP header */
if ((tcp = libnet_build_tcp (libnet_get_prand (LIBNET_PRu16),
                    portNum,
                    0,
                    0,
                    TH_SYN,
                    1024,
                    0,
                    0,
                    LIBNET_TCP_H,
                    NULL,
                    0,
                    lnet,
                    tcp)) == -1)
{
    NSLog(@"Error building TCP header: %s\n",libnet_
geterror(lnet));
    libnet_destroy(lnet);
    exit(EXIT_FAILURE);
}
```

We construct the TCP header using libnet's `libnet_build_tcp()` function, setting the port number we wish to scan.

6. We build the IPv4 header as follows:

```
/* Building IP header */
if( (ipv4 = libnet_build_ipv4(LIBNET_TCP_H + LIBNET_IPV4_H ,
                    0,
                    libnet_get_prand (LIBNET_PRu16),
                    0,
                    64,
                    IPPROTO_TCP,
                    0,
                    source,
                    target,
                    NULL,
```

```
                        0,
                        lnet,
                        ipv4)) == -1)
    {
        NSLog(@"Error building IP header: %s\n",libnet_
geterror(lnet));
        libnet_destroy(lnet);
        exit(EXIT_FAILURE);
    }
```

We build the IPv4 header using the `libnet_build_ipv4()` function; it enables us to set the source and destination IPv4 addresses.

7. Inject the packet into the network in the following manner:

```
    /* Writing packet */
    int bytes_written = libnet_write(lnet);
    if ( bytes_written == -1 )
        NSLog(@"Error writing packet: %s\n",libnet_geterror(lnet));
    else {
        reply =0;
        while (!reply) {
```

This will send our SYN packet to the target computer. If there is failure in injecting the packet, we log an error and move on.

We then start a `while` loop. This `while` loop will loop until we receive a reply from our target device for the correct port number or until the packet is `NULL` (the capture times out).

8. Now we wait for a response from the target:

```
                packet = pcap_next(pcap, &header);
                //Capture timed out
                if (packet == NULL) {
                    NSLog(@"Port %d:  No Reply (timeout)", portNum);
                    reply =1;
                } else {
                    struct pcap_ip *ip = (struct pcap_ip *)(packet +
ETHERNET_SIZE);
                    int offset = GET_IP_HEADER_LENGTH(ip)*4;
                    struct pcap_tcp *tcp = (struct pcap_tcp *)(packet +
ETHERNET_SIZE + offset);

                    int from =ntohs(tcp->tcp_sport);
                    //If port matches the packet we sent out
```

```
                    if (from == portNum) {
                        if (tcp->tcp_flags & TCP_RST) {
                            NSLog(@"Port %d: Closed", from);
                        } else if (tcp->tcp_flags & TCP_SYN) {
                            NSLog(@"Port %d:  Open", from);
                        } else {
                            NSLog(@"Port %d:  Unknown", from);
                        }
                        reply = 1;
                    }
                }
            }
        }
    }
    libnet_destroy(lnet);
    pcap_close(pcap);
```

We use the `pcap_next()` function to read the next packet that was captured. If the request times out or if there was an issue with the capture, the packet will be NULL, otherwise the function will return a u_char pointer to the data in the packet.

If the packet returns NULL, we assume that the capture timed out, log it, and set the reply to 1. This will allow us to go on to the next port. If the computer is down or behind a firewall, we may not see a reply, so we do not want to wait forever.

If the packet is not NULL, it means that we received a valid packet and need to determine the source number of the port. We compare this port number with the port that we sent the SYN packet to. If the two port numbers match, we look at the TCP flags to determine whether the port is closed (if we receive an RST packet) or opened (if we receive a SYN packet). We then set our reply to 1, which will allow us to move on to the next port to be scanned.

If the two port numbers do not match, it means that we are receiving some other communication from our target host and we need to loop back to get the next packet.

Once we have looped through all of the ports that we wish to scan, we clean up by calling the `libnet_destroy()` and `libpcap_close()` functions.

How it works...

We started off by setting up our libnet and libpcap environments. This included setting up our capture filters and capturing the packets. After we had our environments set, we started a loop that looped through the list of ports we wished to scan. In this loop, we created a TCP packet for each port with the SYN flag set and sent it to the device that we were scanning at that moment.

If you remember from our earlier examples, we used the `pcap_loop()` function that called a callback function each time a packet came in. In this example, we used the `pcap_next()` function to capture the packet from the target device because we are looking for just one packet with the correct port/address information and not at continuously capturing packets.

With our simple scanner, we are able to identify the three possible states the ports we scan can be in; they are as follows:

- ▶ If the `pcap_next()` function times out, we can assume that the port is filtered by a firewall or that the device is not reachable

- ▶ If we receive a packet with the correct port/address combination and with the RST flag set, it means that the port is closed and no application is listening on that port

- ▶ If we receive a packet with the correct port/address combination and with the SYN flag set, it means that the port is open and there is an application listening on that port

5
Apple High-level Networking

In this chapter, we will cover:

- ▶ Performing HTTP(S) synchronous GET requests
- ▶ Performing HTTP(S) synchronous POST requests
- ▶ Performing HTTP(S) asynchronous GET requests
- ▶ Performing HTTP(S) asynchronous POST requests
- ▶ Parsing an RSS feed with NSXMLParser, NSURL, and NSData
- ▶ Creating a peer-to-peer bluetooth network

Introduction

In the previous chapters, we covered a variety of libraries and APIs designed to give us low-level access to the network interfaces. These libraries and APIs are designed to give developers great flexibility in how devices communicate over the network. While this flexibility and control is nice to have, there are times when we want to communicate using standard protocols and do not want to spend time implementing the communication mechanism ourselves. This is where the higher-level libraries in the following chapters come in.

In this chapter, we will be covering some of Apple's high-level networking APIs. The APIs discussed in this chapter hide the underlying network communication mechanism from the developer and allow them to focus on implementing their business logic rather than the network code. These recipes are designed to connect to servers over the Internet or to connect multiple devices through bluetooth.

The synchronous and asynchronous HTTP(S) connection recipes are great recipes to connect to custom web services. I have used these for many projects that required me to interact with backend services to send/receive both **XML**- and **JSON**-formatted documents as well as images and PDF files.

The *Parsing an RSS feed with NSXMLParser, NSURL, and NSData* recipe is great for parsing RSS feeds (obviously), but it can also be used for other XML feeds. All you need to do is change the XML element names to match what the feed sends.

The *Creating a peer-to-peer bluetooth network* recipe uses Apple's game kit API to create a mini network between two devices. While bluetooth networks limit what you can send, they can work well while sending small amounts of information between two devices.

Performing HTTP(S) synchronous GET requests

In this recipe, we will create a `WebServiceConnectSynchronous` class that will be able to perform the HTTP `GET` requests. In the next recipe, *Performing HTTP(S) synchronous POST requests*, we will add a method to perform POST requests. If we follow the HTTP specifications to the letter, we would use the HTTP GET request to retrieve data from a server. For example, when you request a web page from a server, you submit a GET request to the server, requesting that the web page be sent to you. If you want to send information to the server, like filling out a form, you would want to submit a POST request.

For an HTTP GET request, if any parameters need to be sent to the service, they should be included in the URL. There are two primary ways to include the parameters in GET requests:

- **Path parameter**: In this method, the parameters are a part of the URL path itself. For example, in the URL `http://mytest.com/testservice/value1`, the `value1` path element is the parameter.

- **Query parameter**: In this method, the parameters are added to the URL at the end of the path as key-value pairs. For example, in the URL `http://mytest.com/testse rvice?key1=value1&key2=value2`, `key1` and `key2` are the keys, while `value1` and `value2` are the values for the keys.

The type of parameters that you use will depend on what the server expects and are usually defined by the developer who is creating the service.

Since the requests in this recipe are made synchronously, the application will freeze while it is waiting for a response from the server. This may cause usability issues if the request takes more than a second to come back. As a general rule, if you are making a synchronous request, you will want to display an activity indicator so that the user knows that the application is waiting for data to be loaded.

I normally display some sort of activity indicator over my screen and then start the synchronous HTTP request in a separate thread. Once the request from the server comes back, I send a notification to the main thread with the server response.

A synchronous request should be used only when you do not want the users interacting with your application while it is sending the HTTP request. Apple does support multiple APIs for making HTTP requests. For this recipe, we will be using `NSMutableURLRequest` and `NSURLConnection` to submit the requests.

Getting ready

This recipe is compatible with both iOS and OS X. No extra frameworks or libraries are required.

How to do it...

We will begin by creating the `WebServiceConnectSynchronous` class.

Creating the WebServiceConnectSynchronous header file

```
#import <Foundation/Foundation.h>

#define WEBSERVICESUCCESS 200

@interface WebServiceConnectSynchronous : NSObject

@property int statusCode;
@property (retain, nonatomic) NSError *error;

-(NSString *)sendGetRequest:(NSDictionary *)params toUrl:
  (NSString *)urlString;
@end
```

This `WebServiceConnectSynchronous` header file begins by defining the return code for a successful HTTP request to be `200`. This is defined within the HTTP specifications and can be used for all HTTP requests.

There are two properties that are also defined within the header file. The `statusCode` property is the code returned from the server after the request. If the request is successful, `statusCode` will contain `200`, otherwise `statusCode` will contain the HTTP error code. The `error` property will contain detailed information about any errors that occurred with the request.

The `sendGetRequest:toURL:` method will be used to send an HTTP `GET` request to the server. The return value will be the response from the server. The `parms` parameter will be an `NSDictionary` object that contains the parameters to pass to the server. If you recall from the introduction, the `GET` query parameters take the form of key-value pairs and really lend themselves to being defined in an `NSDictionary` object, which also stores information in the key-value pairs.

The `sendGetRequest:toURL:` method returns an `NSString` object with a response from the request. This is used when we are expecting text back from the server like XML, JSON, or HTML. If we wish to receive binary files, such as PDF or images, back from the server, we can change the return type to an `NSData` object instead of the `NSString` object. We will point out the change needed when we discuss the code.

Creating the sendGetRequest:toURL: method

Let us first start by creating a `sendGetRequest` method.

```objc
- (NSString *)sendGetRequest:(NSDictionary *)params toUrl:
    (NSString *)urlString {

  NSMutableString *paramString = [NSMutableString
    stringWithString:@"?"];
  NSArray *keys = [params allKeys];
  for (NSString *key in keys) {
    [paramString appendFormat:@"%@=%@&",key,
      [params valueForKey:key]];

  }
  NSString *urlRequest = [NSString stringWithFormat:@"%@%@",
    urlString,[paramString substringToIndex:
    [paramString length]-1]];

  NSMutableURLRequest *request =[NSMutableURLRequest
    requestWithURL:[NSURL URLWithString:urlRequest]];
  [request setHTTPMethod:@"GET"];

  NSURLResponse *res;
  NSData *resp = [NSURLConnection sendSynchronousRequest:request
    returningResponse:&res error:&error];

  NSHTTPURLResponse *httpResponse = (NSHTTPURLResponse *)res;
  statusCode = [httpResponse statusCode];

  return [[NSString alloc] initWithData:resp
    encoding:NSUTF8StringEncoding];
}
```

We begin the `sendGetRequest:toUrl:` method by taking the `NSDictionary` object that contains the parameters we want to pass to the server, and converting it to a formatted string. The parameter string for query parameters should be formatted as `key=value` and multiple parameters should be separated with an ampersand (`&`) symbol. A parameter string with multiple parameters will look like this: `key1=value1&key2=value2&key3=value3`.

This method can be used for both path parameters and query parameters. If the web service takes a path parameter, we can include it in the URL and leave the `parmas NSDictionary` empty.

Once we have our parameter string, we append it to the URL to create the final URL that will be used to connect to the server. We then create an `NSMutableURLRequest` object using the `NSURL` object that we create using `urlRequest`. We set the request type of the `NSMutableURLRequest` object as an HTTP `GET` request.

We then call the `sendSynchronousRequest:returningResponse:error:` method of the `NSURLConnection` class. The `NSData resp` object that is returned will contain the actual response from the server. Normally, this response will be in plaintext data (XML, JSON, or HTML), but it can also be binary data if the web service returns a binary file, such as an image or PDF. In this recipe, we will be expecting a plaintext response.

The error parameter in the `NSURLConnection` call is used to get information about any specific errors. We can set this to `nil` if we do not care about the errors, but it is very helpful for troubleshooting.

We typecast `NSURLResponse` as an `NSHTTPURLResponse` object so that we can extract HTTP-specific information from the response. We are more concerned about the status code of the response and we use it to set the `statusCode` property. You can also use the `allHeadeFields:` method of the `NSHTTPURLResponse` object to get an `NSDictionary` object containing the HTTP headers from the response.

We convert the `NSData resp` object that contains the response from the server to an `NSString` object, which is then returned. We can remove the `NSData` to `NSString` conversion and return the `NSData` object if we are expecting a binary file from our server. We kept the conversion in our sample code because this type of code is used primarily to retrieve plaintext responses, such as XML, JSON, or HTML.

How it works...

To make a synchronous `GET` request using `NSURLConnection`, follow these steps:

1. Create the URL request with the parameters in the URL string.
2. Create an `NSMutableURLRequest` with the URL created in step 1.

3. Send the request using the NSURLConnection. This request will return three separate responses as follows:

- ❏ NSData: This is an object that contains the actual response. It usually takes the form of an HTML, XML, or JSON (plaintext) document. We could use Apple's NSJSONSerialization classes to process the JSON responses.
- ❏ NSHTTPURLResponse: This is an object that contains the status code and HTTP headers.
- ❏ NSError: This contains additional error information if there is a problem with the request.

Performing HTTP(S) synchronous POST requests

In this recipe, we will be adding the sendPostRequest:toUrl: method to the WebServiceConnectSynchronous class that we created in the *Performing HTTP(S) synchronous GET requests* recipe. If we follow the HTTP specifications to the letter, we would use an HTTP POST request when we want to send data to a server for processing. For example, if you fill out an HTTP form (for instance, from a login page), you would submit a POST request that contains the form information.

To perform a POST request, we should have some data to post to the server. This data takes the form of key-value pairs. These pairs are separated by an ampersand (&) symbol and each key is separated from its value by an equal (=) sign.

The keys and values to submit are as follows:

```
firstname: Jon
lastname: Hoffman
age: 44 years
```

The post request would be encoded as follows:

```
firstname=Jon&lastname=Hoffman&age=44
```

The encoded data can then be added to the HTTP request prior to being sent to the server.

Since the requests in this recipe are made synchronously, the application will freeze while it is waiting for a response from the server. This may cause usability issues if the request takes more than a second to come back. As a general rule, if you are making a synchronous request, you will want to display an activity indicator so that the user knows that the application is waiting for data to be loaded.

I normally display some sort of activity indicator over my screen and then start the synchronous HTTP request in a separate thread. Once the request from the server comes back, I send a notification to the main thread with the server response.

A synchronous request should be used only when you do not want the users interacting with your application while it is making the HTTP request. Apple does support multiple APIs for making HTTP requests; for these recipes we will be using `NSMutableURLRequest` and `NSURLConnection` to submit our requests.

Getting ready

This recipe is compatible with both iOS and OS X. No extra frameworks or libraries are required.

How to do it...

Let's add the `POST` method to our `WebServiceConnectSynchronous` class.

Updating the WebServiceConnectSynchronous header file

This header file is the same header file that we created in the *Performing HTTP(S) synchronous GET requests* recipe, except that we are adding the `sendPostRequest:toUrl:` method. This method will be used to send an HTTP `POST` request to the server. The return value will be the response from the server as shown in the following snippet:

```
#import <Foundation/Foundation.h>

#define WEBSERVICESUCCESS 200

@interface WebServiceConnectSynchronous : NSObject

@property int statusCode;
@property (retain, nonatomic) NSError *error;

-(NSString *)sendGetRequest:(NSDictionary *)params toUrl:(NSString *)
urlString;
-(NSString *)sendPostRequest:(NSDictionary *)params toUrl:(NSString *)
urlString;
@end
```

The `parms` parameter in the `sendPostRequest:toUrl:` method is an `NSDictionary` object that contains the parameters to be passed to the server. If you recall from the introduction, the `POST` parameters take the form of key-value pairs and really lend themselves to being defined in an `NSDictionary` object that also stores information in key-value pairs. The second parameter of this method is the URL that we will be sending the request to.

The `sendPostRequest:toUrl:` method returns an `NSString` object with the response from the server. This is used when we are expecting text, such as XML, JSON, or HTML, back from the server. If we wish to receive binary files, such as PDF or images, back from the server, we would change the return type to an `NSData` object instead of an `NSString` object. We will point out the change needed when we discuss the code.

Creating the sendPostRequest:toUrl: method

The `POST` request is very similar to the `GET` request as seen in the following code snippet:

```
-(NSString *)sendPostRequest:(NSDictionary *)params toUrl:(NSString *)
urlString {

  NSMutableString *paramString =
    [NSMutableString stringWithString:@""];
  NSArray *keys = [params allKeys];
  for (NSString *key in keys) {
    [paramString appendFormat:@"%@=%@&",key,
      [params valueForKey:key]];]];
  }
  NSString *postString = @"";
  if ([paramString length] > 0)
    postString = [paramString substringToIndex:
      [paramString length]-1];

  NSMutableURLRequest *request =[NSMutableURLRequest
    requestWithURL:[NSURL URLWithString:urlString]];
  [request setHTTPMethod:@"POST"];
  [request setHTTPBody:[postString
    dataUsingEncoding:NSUTF8StringEncoding]];

  NSURLResponse *res;
  NSData *resp = [NSURLConnection sendSynchronousRequest:request
    returningResponse:&res error:
&error];

  NSHTTPURLResponse *httpResponse = (NSHTTPURLResponse *)res;
  statusCode = [httpResponse statusCode];

  return [[NSString alloc] initWithData:resp
    encoding:NSUTF8StringEncoding];
}
```

We begin the `sendPostRequest:toUrl:` method by taking the `params` parameter, which contains the parameters that we want to pass to the server, and converting it to a formatted string. The parameter string for an HTTP `POST` request should be formatted as `key=value`, and multiple parameters should be separated with an ampersand (`&`). A parameter string with multiple parameters will look like this: `key1=value1&key2=value2&key3=value3`.

We will have a trailing `&` symbol in our parameter string because the preceding code writes each parameter as `key=value&` with an `&` symbol at the end to prepare it for the next key-value pair. Therefore, after we build the `paramString`, we check to see if the length of the parameter string is greater than `0`, and if so, we remove the trailing `&` symbol.

Once we have the `paramString`, we create an `NSMutableURLRequest` using `NSURL` that we created using the `urlString` parameter. We set the request type of the `NSMutableURLRequest` object as an HTTP `POST` request.

We then call the `sendSynchronousRequest:returningResponse:error:` method of the `NSURLConnection` class. The `NSData resp` object that is returned will contain the actual response. Normally, this response will be plaintext data (such as XML, JSON, or HTML), but it can also be binary data if the web service returns a binary file such as an image or PDF. For example here, we will be expecting a plaintext response.

The `error` parameter in the `NSURLConnection` call is used to get information about any errors in the request. You can set this to `nil` if you do not care about the errors, but it is very helpful for troubleshooting purposes.

We typecast `NSURLResponse` as an `NSHTTPURLResponse` so that we can extract the HTTP-specific information from the response. We are more concerned about the status code of the response and we use it to set the `statusCode` property. You can also use the `allHeadeFields:` method of the `NSHTTPURLResponse` object to get an `NSDictionary` object that contains the headers from the response.

We convert the `NSData resp` object that contains the response from the server to an `NSString` object that will be returned. We can remove the `NSData` to `NSString` conversion if we were expecting binary files from our server; however, we kept the conversion in our sample code because this type of code is used primarily to retrieve plaintext data, such as XML, JSON, or HTML.

How it works...

To make a synchronous `POST` request using `NSURLConnection`, follow these steps:

1. Create an `NSString` object containing the parameters to pass to the server. This string will take the format of `key1=value1&key2=value2`, where each key-value pair is separated by an `&` symbol and each key is separated from the value by the `=` symbol.

2. Create an `NSMutableURLRequest` with the URL created in step 1.

3. Add the parameter string to the `NSURLMutableRequest`.

4. Send the request using the `sendSynchronousRequest:ReturningResponse :error` method from the `NSURLConnection` class. This request will return three separate responses as follows:

    ❏ `NSData`: This is an object that contains the actual response. This usually takes the form of an HTML, XML, or JSON (plaintext) document. We can use Apple's `NSJSONSerialization` classes to process the JSON responses.

    ❏ `NSHTTPURLResponse`: This is an object that contains the status code and HTTP headers.

    ❏ `NSError`: This is an object that contains additional error information if there is a problem with the request.

Performing HTTP(S) asynchronous GET requests

In this recipe, we will create a `WebServiceConnectAsynchronous` class that will be able to perform an HTTP `GET` request asynchronously. If we follow the HTTP specifications to the letter, we would be using the HTTP `GET` request to retrieve data from a server. For example, when you request a web page from a server, you submit an HTTP `GET` request.

For an HTTP `GET` request, if any parameters need to be sent to the resource, they should be included in the URL. There are two primary ways to include the parameters in a `GET` request:

▶ **Path parameter**: In this method, the parameters are part of the URL path itself. For example, in the URL `http://mytest.com/testservice/value1`, the `value1` path element is the parameter.

▶ **Query parameter**: In this method, the parameters are added to the URL at the end of the path as key-value pairs. Let's consider the URL `http://mytest.com/testser vice?key1=value1&key2=value2`. In this URL, `key1` and `key2` are the keys while `value1` and `value2` are the values.

The type of parameters that you use will depend on what the server expects.

Asynchronous requests do have a major advantage over synchronous requests shown in the synchronous recipes. When an asynchronous request is made, control is returned back to the app while it waits for a response from the server. This allows the user to continue to interact with the app while we are loading content. However, this is a double-edged sword because there are times we do not want the user to interact with our app while it is loading content.

 Some people say that synchronous requests must never be used when loading web services. However, my philosophy is to use the type of request that is right for your application. You can always make a synchronous request in a separate thread so that your user interface does not freeze when you make the web service call.

Getting ready

This recipe is compatible with both iOS and OS X. No extra frameworks or libraries are required.

How to do it...

Let's create the `WebServiceConnectAsynchronous` class.

Creating the WebServiceConnectAsynchronous header file

The header file for the `WebServiceConnectAsynchronous` class is as follows:

```
#import <Foundation/Foundation.h>

#define WEBSERVICENOTIFICATIONSUCCESS @"WebserviceConnectSuccess"
#define WEBSERVICENOTIFICATIONERROR @"WebserviceConnectError"

@interface WebServiceConnectAsynchronous : NSObject {
  NSMutableData *responseData;
}

- (void)sendGetRequest:(NSDictionary *)params toUrl:
  (NSString *)urlString;

@end
```

We define the name of the two notifications that we will use depending on if the web service request was successful or not. These notifications are `WEBSERVICENOTIFICATIONSUCCESS` and `WEBSERVICENOTIFICATIONERROR`. A successful notification will contain an `NSString` object that represents the response from the server, while an error notification will contain an `NSError` object.

We also define a method: the `sendGetRequest:toURL:` method. This method will be used to send a `GET` request to the server. The return value will be the response from the server.

Creating the sendGetRequest:toURL: method

The `sendGetRequest:toURL:` is the method that we call to send the asynchronous request to the server. The code for this method is as follows:

```
- (void)sendGetRequest:(NSDictionary *)params toUrl:
  (NSString *)urlString {

  responseData = [[NSMutableData alloc]init];
```

```
    NSMutableString *paramString = [NSMutableString
      stringWithString:@"?"];
    NSArray *keys = [params allKeys];
    for (NSString *key in keys) {
      [paramString appendFormat:@"%@=%@&",key,
        [params valueForKey:key]];
    }

    NSString *urlRequest = [NSString
      stringWithFormat:@"%@%@",urlString,[paramString
      substringToIndex:[paramString length]-1]];

    NSMutableURLRequest *request =[NSMutableURLRequest
      requestWithURL:[NSURL URLWithString:urlRequest]];
    [request setHTTPMethod:@"GET"];

    [[NSURLConnection alloc] initWithRequest:request
      delegate:self];
}
```

We begin the `sendGetRequest:toUrl:` method by taking the `params` object, which contains the parameters that we want to pass to the server, and converting it to a formatted string. The parameter string for query parameters should be formatted as `key=value` and multiple parameters should be separated by `&`. A parameter string with multiple parameters will look like this: `key1=value1&key2=value2&key3=value3`.

 This method can be used for both path parameters and query parameters. If the web service takes a path parameter, include it in the URL and do not put any parameters in the NSDictionary.

Once we have our parameter string, we append it to the URL to create the final URL that will be used to connect to the server.

We then create an `NSMutableURLRequest` object using an `NSURL` object. We create it using `urlRequest` and set the request type as an HTTP `GET` request.

Finally, we create the `NSURLConnection` object using the `initWithRequest:delegate:` method. This will create an asynchronous request to the server defined in the `NSMutableURLRequest` object and all callbacks from the asynchronous request will be sent to the delegate defined by the delegate parameter. In this code, we define the delegate as the current object.

We will need to create the six callback methods that will be used as we receive responses back from the server.

 Even though some of these methods are not required, I would recommend implementing all of them, even if the only thing you do is log from them. They will definitely help when you are troubleshooting issues.

Creating the connection:didReceiveResponse: callback method

The `connection:didReceiveResponse:` method is called when the connection has received sufficient data to construct an `NSURLResponse` object as shown in the following snippet:

```
- (void) connection: (NSURLConnection *) connection
  didReceiveResponse: (NSURLResponse *) response
{
  NSLog(@"Received Response - WebServiceConnect");
  [responseData setLength:0];
}
```

There is the rare case where we may receive multiple `connection:didReceiveResponse:` calls for the same request. In Apple's delegate reference for the `NSURLConnectionDelegate` protocol, they noted that when the content type of the load data is `multipart/x-mixed-replace`, the delegate will receive multiple `connection:didReceiveResponse:` calls.

In our code, we will set the length of the response data to 0, which will clear out the data to ensure that there is nothing in the data that would corrupt our response.

Creating the connection:didReceiveData: callback method

The `connection:didReceiveData:` method is called when data is received from our request.

```
- (void) connection: (NSURLConnection *) connection
  didReceiveData: (NSData *) data
{
  [responseData appendData:data];
  NSString*tmp = [[NSString alloc] initWithData :
    responseData encoding:NSUTF8StringEncoding];
  NSLog(@"Resonse so far:  %@", tmp);
}
```

It is very rare for all data from a response to come back through a single call to `connection:didReceiveData:`. Therefore, we need to append the data to our `responseData` variable each time this method is called.

We also log the response so that we can see what is coming back. You can safely comment out these lines, but they are helpful when trying to troubleshoot issues.

Creating the connection:didFailWithError: callback method

The `connection:didFailWithError:` method is called when the response failed to return correctly.

```
- (void) connection: (NSURLConnection *) connection
didFailWithError: (NSError *) error
{
    [[NSNotificationCenter defaultCenter] postNotificationName:WEBSERVIC
ENOTIFICATIONERROR object: error ];
}
```

In the preceding code, we post a notification that the request failed so that any code listening for the notification will know about the failure. We also send the `NSError` object containing the error with the notification so that the listening code can determine what caused the error.

Creating the connectionDidFinishLoading: callback method

The `connectionDidFinishLoading:` method is called when the entire response has been received from the server as shown in the following code snippet:

```
- (void) connectionDidFinishLoading: (NSURLConnection *)
    connection
{
    NSString *res = [[NSString alloc] initWithData:responseData
encoding:NSUTF8StringEncoding];
    NSLog(@"Results: '%@'", res);
    [[NSNotificationCenter defaultCenter]
        postNotificationName:WEBSERVICENOTIFICATIONSUCCESS
        object:res];
}
```

There should be one or more `connection:didReceiveReponse:` calls prior to calling the `connectionDidFinsihLoading:` method. Therefore, the `responseData` object will contain the entire response from the server.

The preceding code will convert the `responseData` object to an `NSString` object and then post a notification that the web service call was successful. The notification will contain the response as an `NSString` object. We could remove the `NSData` to `NSString` conversion and return the `NSData` object if we were expecting a binary file from our server. We kept the conversion in our sample code because this type of code is typically used to retrieve plaintext messages, such as XML, JSON, or HTML. We could use Apple's `NSJSONSerialization` classes to process JSON responses.

Creating the connection:willSendRedirect:redirectResponse: callback method

The `connection:willSendRequest:redirectResponse:` method is called when it is determined that the request is going to be redirected to another URL. This is done in the following manner:

```
- (NSURLRequest *)connection: (NSURLConnection *)connection
  willSendRequest: (NSURLRequest *)request redirectResponse:
  (NSURLResponse *)redirectResponse;
{
    NSLog(@"Redirecting:  %@", request.URL);
    return request;
}
```

In most instances, this would be allowed, but there are times when we may not want our request to be redirected. If we did not want our request to be redirected, we will return `nil`.

Creating the connection:willCacheResponse: callback method

Finally, the last delegate method is the `connection:willCacheResponse:` method. This method is called prior to the response being cached to allow us the opportunity to alter the response prior to caching it, as shown in the following code snippet:

```
- (NSCachedURLResponse *)connection:(NSURLConnection *)
  connection willCacheResponse:(NSCachedURLResponse*)
  cachedResponse {
    return nil;
}
```

We set the return value to `nil` to make sure the response is not cached. It is preferable to not cache the response while interacting with web services that are used as APIs because we want to make sure that each call gets sent to the server and we do not receive a cached response.

If you are making multiple connections with the same `WebServiceConnectAsynchronous` object, you will have problems with the response data from the multiple requests being combined. All the callback methods contain an `NSURLConnection` parameter that will tell you what connection the callback is for. You can use this to identify which connection is making the callback and decide how to handle it.

How it works...

When we made the synchronous requests the application froze while it waited for a response from the server. With the asynchronous `GET` request, once the request is made, control is turned back to the application while our code waits for the response. As data is received, our callback methods are called to handle the response.

The events that will trigger a callback are as follows:

> ▶ If a redirect occurs, the `connection:willSendRequest:redirectResponse:` method is called to process the redirect.

> ▶ When there is enough data received to construct an `NSURLResponse`, the `connection:didReceiveResponse:` method is called. This is where we will want to reset any objects that are needed to handle the response data as we receive it.

> ▶ If there is an error, the `connection:didFailWithError:` method is called with an `NSError` object that we can parse to determine what caused the error.

> ▶ Once our client begins to receive the response from the server, the `connection:didReceiveData:` method is called with an `NSData` object that contains the response. This method is called multiple times until all the data is received.

> ▶ When all the data has been received, the `connectionDidFinishLoading:` method is called to let us know that we have received everything from the server.

Performing HTTP(S) asynchronous POST requests

In this recipe, we will be adding the `sendPostRequest:toUrl:` method to the `WebServiceConnectAsynchronous` class that we created in the *Performing HTTP(S) asynchronous GET requests* recipe. If we follow the HTTP specifications to the letter, we would use the HTTP `POST` request when we want to send data to a server for processing. For example, if you fill out an HTTP form (for instance, from a login page), you would submit an HTTP `POST` request that contains the form information.

To perform a `POST` request, you should have some data to *post* to the server. This data takes the form of a key-value pair, just like the `GET` query request. We also submit the data in the same format as the `GET` query request, where each key-value pair is separated by & and each key is separated from its value by =. Here is an example.

If we had the following key-value pairs:

```
firstname: Jon
lastname: Hoffman
age: 44 years
```

Our POST request will be encoded as follows:

```
firstname=Jon&lastname=Hoffman&age=44
```

The encoded data can then be added to the HTTP request prior to being sent to the server.

Asynchronous requests do have a major advantage over synchronous requests described in the synchronous recipes. When an asynchronous request is made, control is returned back to the app while it waits for a response back from the server. This allows the user to continue to interact with the app while we are loading the content. However, this is a double-edged sword because there are times when we do not want the user to interact with our app while it is loading content.

> Some people say that synchronous requests must never be used while loading web services; however, my philosophy is to use the type of request that is right for your application. You can always make a synchronous request in a separate thread so that your user interface does not freeze while making the web service call.

Getting ready

This recipe is compatible with both iOS and OS X. No extra frameworks or libraries are required.

How to do it...

For this recipe, we will be updating the WebServiceConnectAsynchronous class that we created in the *Performing HTTP(S) synchronous GET requests* recipe. Let's get started.

Updating the WebServiceConnectAsynchronous header file

The new WebServiceConnectAsynchronous header file is as follows:

```
#import <Foundation/Foundation.h>

#define WEBSERVICESUCCESS 200

#define WEBSERVICENOTIFICATIONSUCCESS @"WebserviceConnectSuccess"
#define WEBSERVICENOTIFICATIONERROR @"WebserviceConnectError"

@interface WebServiceConnectAsynchronous : NSObject {
  NSMutableData *responseData;
}
```

```
- (void) sendGetRequest: (NSDictionary *) params toUrl:
  (NSString *) urlString;
- (void) sendPostRequest: (NSDictionary *) params toUrl:
  (NSString *) urlString;

@end
```

The only update to the `WebServiceConnectAsynchronous` header file is to add the `sendPostRequest:toURL:` method, which will be used to send a POST request to the server.

Creating the sendPostRequest:toURL: method

Let us take a look at how to create the `sendRequest:toURL:` method:

```
- (void) sendPostRequest: (NSDictionary *) params toUrl:
  (NSString *) urlString {

  responseData = [[NSMutableData alloc] init];
  NSMutableString *paramString = [NSMutableString
    stringWithString:@""];
  NSArray *keys = [params allKeys];
  for (NSString *key in keys) {
    [paramString appendFormat:@"%@=%@&", key,
      [params valueForKey:key]];
  }
  NSString *postString = @"";
  if ([paramString length] > 0)
    postString = [paramString substringToIndex:
      [paramString length]-1];

  NSMutableURLRequest *request =[NSMutableURLRequest
    requestWithURL:[NSURL URLWithString:urlString]];
  [request setHTTPMethod:@"POST"];
  [request setHTTPBody:[postString
    dataUsingEncoding:NSUTF8StringEncoding]];
  [[NSURLConnection alloc] initWithRequest:request delegate:self];
}
```

We begin the `sendPostRequest:toUrl:` method by taking the `params` object that contains the parameters that we want to pass to the server and converting it to a formatted string. The parameter string for query parameters should be formatted as `key=value` pairs and multiple parameters should be separated with `&`. A parameter string with multiple parameters will look like this: `key1=value1&key2=value2&key3=value3`.

Once we have our parameter string, we create an `NSMutableURLRequest` using `NSURL`, which we create using `urlString`. We then set the request method to a `POST` method and add the parameters to the request.

We create `NSURLRequest` using the `initWithRequest:delegate:` method. This will create an asynchronous request to the URL defined in the `NSMutableURLRequest` and all callbacks from the request will use the delegate defined by the delegate parameter. In the preceding code, we define the delegate as the current object.

The `POST` request will use the same callbacks that we created in the *Performing HTTP(S) asynchronous GET requests* recipe. Please refer to it for details on the callback methods.

How it works...

When we made the synchronous requests, the application *froze* while it waited for a response from the server. With the asynchronous `GET` and `POST` requests, once the request is made, control is turned back to the application. As data is received from the server, the callback methods are called to handle the response.

The events that will trigger a callback are as follows:

  ▸ If a redirect occurs, the `connection:willSendRequest:redirectResponse` method is called to process the redirect.

  ▸ When there is enough data received to construct the `NSURLResponse` object, the `connection:didReceiveResponse:` method is called. This is where we will want to reset any objects that are needed to handle the response data as we receive it.

  ▸ If there is an error, the `connection:didFailWithError:` method is called with an `NSError` object that we can parse to determine the cause of the error.

  ▸ Once our client begins to receive the response from the server, the `connection:didReceiveData:` method is called with an `NSData` object that contains the response. This method is called multiple times until all the data is received.

  ▸ When all the data has been received, the `connectionDidFinishLoading:` method is called to let us know that we have received everything from the server.

Parsing an RSS feed with NSXMLParser, NSURL, and NSData

While this recipe shows you how to parse an RSS feed using `NSXMLParser`, `NSURL`, and `NSData`, it is very easy to convert this code to parse any XML feed. All you need to do is change the tags that you are looking for.

In the previous recipes, we used `NSURLConnection` to access web services. For this recipe, we will be using the `dataWithContentsFromURL:` method of the `NSData` class to access a web service. We will assume that the response is an XML data feed and will use the `NSXmlParser` to parse the XML feed.

This recipe will load and parse the XML content synchronously. You will want to display an activity indicator to let the user know that the application did not *freeze* while the URL was loading. As in the synchronous HTTP `GET` and `POST` request recipes, it is recommended that we send the `dataWithContentsFromURL:` request in a separate thread. This allows us to display an activity indicator, letting the user know that we are loading information and that our application did not *freeze*.

An RSS feed can have several tags, but for our purpose we will be looking for the `title`, `description`, and `pubDate` tags.

Getting ready

This recipe is compatible with both iOS and OS X. No extra frameworks or libraries are required.

How to do it...

Let's parse our RSS feed.

Creating the RSSItem header file

We begin by creating a class to hold the information we are extracting from the RSS feed. This class will be called `RSSItem`. We will begin by creating the header file in the following manner:

```
#import <Foundation/Foundation.h>

@interface RSSItem : NSObject

@property (strong, nonatomic) NSString *title, *description;
@property (strong, nonatomic) NSDate *date;

@end
```

The `RSSItem` class will have the following three properties:

- `title`: It will contain the contents of the RSS `title` tag
- `description`: It will contain the contents of the RSS `description` tag
- `date`: It will contain the contents of the `pubDate` tag as an `NSDate` object

Creating the RSSItem implementation file

Now, let's look at the implementation file for the `RSSItem` class.

```
#import "RSSItem.h"
```

```
@implementation RSSItem
-(instancetype)init {
  if ( self = [super init] ) {
    self.title = @"No Title";
    self.description = @"No Description";
    self.date = [[NSDate alloc] init];
  }
  return self;
}

@end
```

The only method that we define is the default constructor to initialize our properties. This class is designed to hold the information that is coming back in the RSS feed.

Creating the ParseRSS header file

We will now create the ParseRSS class that retrieves the contents of a URL and then parses the XML. We will begin by creating the ParseRSS header file in the following manner:

```
#import <Foundation/Foundation.h>

@interface ParseRSS : NSObject<NSXMLParserDelegate> {
  NSXMLParser * rssParser;
  NSString * currentElement;
  NSMutableString *currentElementString;
  NSMutableDictionary *currentElementData;
  NSDateFormatter *formatter;
}

@property (strong, nonatomic) NSMutableArray *items;

-(id)initWithUrl:(NSString *)urlString;

@end
```

Inside the interface declaration of the ParseRSS class, we define that this class will implement the NSXMLParserDelegate protocol. This is the delegate that we use for our XML parsing.

We define several instance variables that will be used by NSXmlParser to parse the XML document. We also define an NSDateFormatter class reference that will be used to convert the date from the RSS feed to an NSDate object.

The items property will contain the results once the parser has finished parsing the XML document.

We also define one constructor that will be used to create instances of our `ParseRss` class. This constructor takes one parameter, which will be the URL containing the RSS feed that needs to be parsed.

Creating the initWithUrl: constructor

Lets begin building our `ParseRSS` implementation file and also look at the `initWtihUrl` constructor. This can be done in the following manner:

```
#import "ParseRSS.h"
#import "RSSItem.h"

#define ITEMSEPERATOR @"item"
#define ITEMTITLEKEY @"title"
#define ITEMDESCRIPTIONKEY @"description"
#define ITEMDATEKEY @"pubDate"

#define RSSDATEFORMATTER @"EEE, dd MMM yyyy HH:mm:ss Z"
@implementation ParseRSS

-(id)initWithUrl:(NSString *)url {
  if(self == [super init]) {
    currentElementData = [[NSMutableDictionary alloc] init];
    currentElementString = [[NSMutableString alloc] init];
    formatter = [[[NSDateFormatter alloc] init] retain];
    [formatter setDateFormat:RSSDATEFORMATTER];
  }

  [self parseXMLFileAtURL:url];
  return self;
}
```

We begin the `ParseRSS` implementation by defining several constants. These constants are used by the `NSXMLParser` class to identify the information we want to pull out of the RSS feed.

The `RSSDATEFORMATTER` constant is used by `NSDateFormatter` to convert the date from the RSS feed to an `NSDate` object.

The `initWithUrl:` constructor begins by initiating the `currentElementData` and `currentElementString` objects. As the `NSXMLParser` class parses the XML document, we will be using the `currentElementString` object as a temporary storage to hold the value of the current element. The `currentElementData` object will contain the information we want to pull out of each post. This will be the information that we want to store in the `RSSItem` object.

We end the `initWithUrl:` constructor by calling the `parseXmlFileAtUrl:` method, which will parse the XML document from the specified URL.

Creating the parseXMLFileAtUrl: method

The `parseXMLFileAtURL:` method retrieves the XML document from the URL, initializes the NSXMLParser, and begins parsing the document in the following manner:

```
-(void)parseXMLFileAtURL:(NSString *)URL {
  items = [[NSMutableArray alloc] init];

  NSURL *xmlURL = [NSURL URLWithString:URL];
  NSData *myData = [NSData dataWithContentsOfURL:xmlURL];

  rssParser = [[NSXMLParser alloc] initWithData:myData];
  [rssParser setDelegate:self];
  [rssParser parse];
}
```

The `parseXmlFileAtURL:` method begins by initiating the item's `NSMutableArray`. We then create an `NSURL` object from the URL parameter that was passed into this method.

The `dataWithContentsOfURL:` method from the `NSData` class makes an HTTP `GET` request to a URL and waits for the data to be returned from the server. This one-line request is a lot simpler than the `NSUrlConnection` object used in the previous recipes, but with this simplicity you lose a lot of control, namely, you are limited to making synchronous `GET` requests.

We then initiate the `NSXMLParser` class, which sets the delegate and finally begins parsing our document.

Creating the parserDidStartDocument: NSXMLParserDelegate method

The first `NSXMLParserDelegate` method we are going to create is the `parserDidStartDocument:` method, which is also the first `NSXmlParser` delegate method that is called, as shown in the following snippet:

```
-(void)parserDidStartDocument:(NSXMLParser *)parser {
  NSLog(@"found file and started parsing");
}
```

This method is called when the `NSXMLParser` class determines that it has an XML document that can be parsed and is about to begin parsing.

Creating the parser:parserErrorOccurred: NSXMLParserDelegate method

We will now look at the `parser:parserErrorOccurred:` method:

```
- (void)parser:(NSXMLParser *)parser parseErrorOccurred:
  (NSError *)parseError {
  NSString * errorString = [NSString stringWithFormat:@"Unable to
    download RSS feed from web site (Error code %i )",
    [parseError code]];
    NSLog(@"Error:  %@", errorString);


}
```

The `parser:parseErrorOccurred:` delegate method is called if there is a problem with the XML document and the parser is unable to parse it.

Creating the parser:didStartElement:namespaceURI:qualifiedName:attributes: NSXMLParserDelegate method

Let us now move on to the `parser:didStartElement:namespaceURI:qualifiedName:attributes:` method:

```
- (void)parser:(NSXMLParser *)parser didStartElement:
  (NSString *)elementName namespaceURI:(NSString *)namespaceURI
  qualifiedName:(NSString *)qName attributes:
  (NSDictionary *)attributeDict{
  currentElement = [elementName copy];
  currentElementString = [NSMutableString stringWithString:@""];
  if ([elementName isEqualToString:ITEMSEPERATOR])
    {
    [currentElementData removeAllObjects];
    }
}
```

The `parserDidStartElement:namespaceURI:qualifiedName:attributes:` delegate method is called when the parser detects that an XML tag has started. For example, if we have the XML tag pair `<xmlTag>value</xmlTag>`, the `parserDidStartElement:namespaceURI:qualifiedName:attributes:` method is called when the parser encounters the first `<xmlTag>`. This allows us to store the element name. In our example, the element name is `xmlTag`, and it resets the value stored in the `currentElementString` object.

We also check to see if the element name is equal to the `<status>` tag since the `status` tag denotes that we are about to parse a new post in the RSS feed. If it is equal to the `<status>` tag, we remove all the objects from the `currentElementData` dictionary so that the values from our previous post do not get mixed with the next post.

Creating the parser:didEndElement:namespaceURI:qualifiedNa me: NSXMLParserDelegate method

The `parser:didEndElement:namespaceURI:qualifiedName:` delegate method is called when the parser detects that an XML tag has ended. For example, if we have the XML tag pair `<xmlTag>value</xmlTag>`, the `parser:didEndElement:namespaceURI:qu alifiedName:` method is called when the parser encounters the `</xmlTag>`. This allows us to store the value of our `currentElementString` object with the appropriate key in our `currentElementData` dictionary as shown in the following code snippet:

```
- (void)parser:(NSXMLParser *)parser didEndElement:
  (NSString *)elementName namespaceURI:(NSString *)namespaceURI
  qualifiedName:(NSString *)qName{
  if ([elementName isEqualToString:ITEMSEPERATOR])
  {
    RSSItem *item = [[[RSSItem alloc] init] autorelease];
    item.description = [currentElementData
      objectForKey:ITEMDESCRIPTIONKEY];
    item.title = [currentElementData objectForKey:ITEMTITLEKEY];
    item.date = [formatter dateFromString:[currentElementData
      objectForKey:ITEMDATEKEY]];
    [items addObject:item];
  }
  NSString *string = [currentElementString
    stringByTrimmingCharactersInSet:[NSCharacterSet
    whitespaceAndNewlineCharacterSet]] ;
    if([currentElement isEqualToString:ITEMDATEKEY])
      [currentElementData setObject:[string copy]
        forKey:ITEMDATEKEY];
    if([currentElement isEqualToString:ITEMTITLEKEY])
      [currentElementData setObject:[string copy]
        forKey:ITEMTITLEKEY];
    if([currentElement isEqualToString:ITEMDESCRIPTIONKEY])
      [currentElementData setObject:[string copy]
        forKey:ITEMDESCRIPTIONKEY];
}
```

We trim `currentElementString` by calling the `stringByTrimmingCharacterInSet:` method to remove any new line or white spaces at the beginning and end of `currentElementString`.

Finally, we look to see if `currentElement` is one of the three tags that we are looking for, and if it is, we store the trimmed version of `currentElementString` in our `currentElementData` dictionary object with the appropriate key.

Creating the parser:foundCharacters: NSXMLParserDelegate method

The `parser:foundCharacters:` delegate method is called when the parser finds the value between a set of tags in the following manner:

```
- (void)parser:(NSXMLParser *)parser foundCharacters:
  (NSString *)string
{
  [currentElementString appendString:string];
}
```

In the previous method, you were probably wondering where we got the `currentElementString` object from. The `parser:foundCharacters:` delegate method is called when the parser finds the value between a set of tags. For example, if we have the XML tag pair `<xmlTag>value</xmlTag>`, the `parser:foundCharacters:` method is called when the parser gets to `value`. Since the `value` can be very long, the `parser:foundCharacters:` method may be called multiple times so that the `currentElementString` object is an `NSMutableString` that we continue to append the value `foundCharacters` value to. The `currentElementString` is reset in the `parserD idStartElement:namespaceURI:qualifiedName:attributes:` delegate method, as shown in the *Creating the parser:didStartElement:namespaceURI:qualifiedName:attributes: NSXMLParserDelegate method* section of this recipe, so that the value is cleared at the start of each new XML tag.

Creating the parserDidEndDocument: NSXMLParserDelegate method

The `parserDidEndDocument:` method is called when `NSXmlParser` reaches the end of the XML document.

```
- (void)parserDidEndDocument:(NSXMLParser *)parser
{
    NSLog(@"Items %d",[items count]);
}
```

In this example, we simply log the number of items found.

How it works...

We begin by retrieving the XML document from the URL of our service. We use the `dataWithContentsOfURL:` method of the `NSData` class to perform a synchronous `GET` request to a URL.

Once we have the XML document, we use `NSXmlParser` to parse the document. The `NSXMLParserDelegate` class specifies that we need to create six delegate methods to perform the parsing. The methods are:

- `parserDidStartDocument:` This is called when the parser begins parsing the XML document

- `parser:parseErrorOccurred:` This is called if there is an error in the XML document

- `parserDidStartElement:namespaceURI:qualifiedName:attributes:` This is called when an XML tag is opened

- `parser:didEndElement:namespaceURI:qualifiedName:` This is called when an XML tag is closed

- `parser:foundCharacters:` This is called when the parser is reading the value of an XML tag

- `parserDidEndDocument:` This method is called when the parser has completed parsing the XML document

Once the `NSXmlParser` finishes parsing the XML document, the `items` property will contain an array of `RSSItem` objects. Each `RSSItem` object will contain the information for one post.

Creating a peer-to-peer bluetooth network

In this recipe, we will create a peer-to-peer bluetooth network, which we will use to exchange text messages. To create a bluetooth peer-to-peer network, we will use Apple's **Game Kit** framework. So, we will need to add the Gamekit framework to our project.

The downloadable code for this project creates a peer-to-peer network that is used to exchange text messages. Each individual message that is sent over the bluetooth network can have a maximum size of 90 KB. If the data that we are sending is greater then 90 KB, we will need to break the data apart and send it as multiple messages.

We will be implementing the `GKPeerPickerController` and `GKSession` delegate methods. The `GKPeerPickerController` method provides a standard user interface, which allows one iOS device to connect to another iOS device. Once the two devices are connected, a `GKSession` object is returned. The `GKSession` object is used to send and receive data between the two peers.

When the peer picker that is displayed by the `GKPeerPickerController` class is looking for other devices to connect to, it looks as follows:

Once other devices are found, `GKPeerPickerController` will display the names of these other devices as shown in the following screenshot:

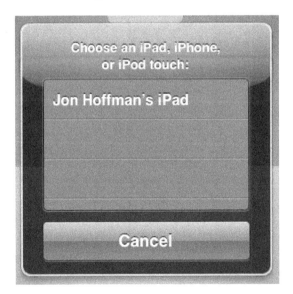

Getting ready

This recipe is compatible only with iOS. We will need to add Apple's Gamekit framework to our project.

How to do it...

Let's create the bluetooth connection.

Displaying the GKPeerPickerController

The first thing we need to do is establish the connection between our two devices. This is done with the `GKPeerPickerController` class, therefore, the first method we will implement is the method to display the GKPeerPickerController. This is done as follows:

```
-(void)sessionConnect {
  self.mPeerPicker = [[GKPeerPickerController alloc]init];
  self.mPeerPicker.delegate = self;
  self.mPeerPicker.connectionTypesMask =
    GKPeerPickerConnectionTypeNearby;
  [mPeerPicker show];
}
```

We begin by initiating our `mPeerPicker` object, which will display the peer picker. We set the `GKPeerPickerController` delegate to the current object and define the `connectionTypeMask` to be `GKPeerPickerConnectionTypeNearby`, which tells the peer picker to look for a bluetooth connection. Finally, we call the show method, which will display the peer picker.

Creating the two delegate methods for GKPeerPickerControllerDelegate

We will now need to implement two delegate methods for `GKPeerPickerControllerDelegate`. The first is the `peerPickerController: sessionForConnectionType:` method that returns a `GKSession` object for a given session type. In our case, we only defined one connection type and that is `GKPeerPickerConnectionTypeNearby` as shown in the following snippet:

```
-(GKSession *) peerPickerController:(GKPeerPickerController *)
  picker sessionForConnectionType:(GKPeerPickerConnectionType)
  type {
  self.mSession = [[GKSession alloc]initWithSessionID:
    @"PacktPubPeer" displayName:nil sessionMode:GKSessionModePeer]
  return mSession;
}
```

We create a new session using a session ID constant that uniquely identifies our service. In this example, our session ID is `PacktPubPeer`. If you have two versions of your application, like a standard and pro version, you can broadcast the same session ID in each application so that users can communicate no matter which version they have.

The other delegate method for `GKPeerPickerControllerDelegate` that we need to implement is the `peerPickerController:didConnectPeer:toSession:` method.

```
- (void)peerPickerController:(GKPeerPickerController *)picker did
  ConnectPeer:(NSString *)peerID toSession:(GKSession *)session {
  [mSession setDataReceiveHandler:self withContext:NULL];
  [mPeerPicker dismiss];
  self.mPeerPicker = nil;
}
```

The `peerPickerController:didConnectPeer:toSession:` is called when a session between two devices have been accepted by both parties. The first thing we do is set the `dataReceiveHandler` for the session to the current object. This object should implement the `GKSession` delegate methods that are called when new messages come in. We will learn about this method shortly.

After we set the `dataReceiveHandler`, we dismiss the `GKPeerPickerController` and set it to `nil`.

Disconnecting from the peer network

We now need a way to disconnect from our peer network. This is done using the following `sessionDisconnect` method:

```
- (void)sessionDisconnect {
  [self.mSession disconnectFromAllPeers];
}
```

To disconnect, we call the `disconnectFromAllPeers` method of our `GKSession` object. This will disconnect the device from the other devices on our peer-to-peer network.

Sending data to the peer

Now, let's create the `sendDataToPeer:` method to send data across our peer-to-peer network. We do it in the following manner:

```
- (void)sendDataToPeer:(NSString *)text{
    NSError *error;
    [self.mSession sendDataToAllPeers:[text dataUsingEncoding:NSSt
ringEncodingConversionAllowLossy] withDataMode:GKSendDataReliable
error:&error];
}
```

The `mSession` object was created in the `peerPickerController:sessionForConnect ionType:` method in the previous section. We call the `sendDataToAllPeers:withData Mode:error:` method to send the message to all the peers in our network.

Receiving data from the peer

When a new message is received, the `receiveData:fromPeer:inSession:context:` delegate method is called in the following manner:

```
- (void)receiveData:(NSData *)data fromPeer:(NSString *)peer
  inSession: (GKSession *)session context:(void *)context {
  NSString *receivedStr = [NSString stringWithUTF8String:
    [data bytes]];
  NSLog(@"Received >>>>>>>> %@",receivedStr);
}
```

In the preceding code, we take the `NSData` object, convert it to a string, and log it. In the downloadable code, the sample application for this recipe let's you create a peer-to-peer network and then send text messages between the two devices. The code also implements several optional delegate methods.

How it works...

To create our peer-to-peer bluetooth network between two devices, the first thing we needed to do was to establish a connection between the devices. This is done with `GKPeerPickerController`. The `GKPeerPickerController` class displays a user interface that lets the user select other devices to connect to. When a device attempts to connect to another device, the users of the other device can opt to either accept or decline the connection.

Once the connection is made, we receive a `GKSession` object that can then be used to send and receive data. We also set the `dataReceiveHandler` to our current class; therefore, we need to implement the `receiveData:fromPeer:inSession:context: GKSession` delegate method to handle incoming messages from other peers.

6
Bonjour

In this chapter, we will cover:

- ▶ Publishing a Bonjour service
- ▶ Discovering a Bonjour service
- ▶ Resolving a Bonjour service
- ▶ Creating an echo server that uses Bonjour to advertise the service
- ▶ Creating an echo client that uses Bonjour to discover the service

Introduction

Bonjour is Apple's implementation of **Zero Configuration Networking** (**Zeroconf**). Zeroconf is a methodology that automatically creates a usable computer network without manual operator intervention or the need for special configuration servers. Bonjour locates devices and services on a local network using the **multicast Domain Name System** (**mDNS**) service.

In other words, Bonjour allows for the automatic discovery and configuration of devices and services without the user having to manually configure them. A great example of Bonjour in the real world is a printer connected to the USB port of an Apple Time Capsule. Any device that has Bonjour enabled and is connected to the local network will be able to find and use the printer without the network configuration of the printer.

The Bonjour API provides a solution to publish, browse, and resolve a service or device. The main thing to be kept in mind is that Bonjour does not implement the service; it just provides a means to discover and find the service.

Bonjour was originally introduced by Apple in 2002 as Rendezvous, but was renamed to Bonjour in 2005. Apple has made the source code for the Bonjour mDNS responder available as part of the Darwin open source project.

In the final two recipes of this chapter, we will use the echo server and client that we built in *Chapter 2, Apple Low-level Networking*, and put a Bonjour wrapper around them so that our echo client can automatically find the echo server and connect to it. In those examples, we will highlight the separation between Bonjour and the implementation of the service.

Publishing a Bonjour service

Bonjour allows for the discovery of network devices and services on an IP network without a centralized server. In this recipe, we will create a class called `BonjourPublishServices` that will contain the code needed to publish a service with `NSNetService`.

The `NSNetService` class is normally used to publish information about a socket server. While it is also typical for `NSNetService` and the socket server to be running within the same application, it is not a requirement since `NSNetService` does not use, nor is it dependent on the socket server in any way.

As the publication of the service may not happen instantaneously, `NSNetService` should publish the request asynchronously. `NSNetService` uses delegate methods to handle the notifications of the service publication. Each delegate method receives an `NSNetService` object that identifies the service calling the method; therefore, one delegate can handle multiple services.

While it is possible for one delegate to manage multiple service publications, my preference is to have a one-to-one relationship between the delegate and the service that it publishes. This allows me to manage the `NSNetService` object totally within the delegate class.

How you manage multiple service publications should depend on the needs of the project you are working on.

Getting ready

This recipe is compatible with both iOS and OS X. No extra frameworks or libraries are required.

How to do it...

Let's create our `BonjourPublishServices` class:

1. We will begin by creating the header file for the `BonjourPublishServices` class:

   ```
   #import <Foundation/Foundation.h>

   typedef NS_ENUM(NSUInteger, BonjourPublishStatus) {
   ```

```
    BONJOURPUBLISHSTOPPED,
    BONJOURPUBLISHSTARTED
};
#define BONJOURNOTIFICATIONSTOP @"bonjourstopped"
#define BONJOURNOTIFICATIONSTART @"bonjourstarted"

@interface BonjourPublishServices : NSObject
<NSNetServiceDelegate>

@property int status;
@property (strong, nonatomic) NSNetService *service;
@property (retain, nonatomic) NSString *publishedName;

-(void)startServiceOfType:(NSString *)type andPort:(int)port;
-(void)stopService;

@end
```

The header file begins by defining an enum that will be used to define the state of the service. We then define two constants (BONJOURNOTIFICATIONSTOP and BONJOURNOTIFICATIONSTART) that specify the names of the notifications that our BonjourPublishServices class will be sending.

We will also define three properties within the BonjourPublishServices header file: the status property that will contain the present status of our Bonjour publication service, the service property that will contain the NSNetService object that we are publishing, and the publishedName property that will contain the name that the service is published under. Unless we specifically disable service renaming (using the publishWithOptions: method), our service can be renamed if there is a naming conflict with another service on the existing network. Therefore, when our service is initially published, it is good practice to store it under its published name.

If we wanted BonjourPublishServices to handle multiple service publications, we would want to change the service property to a NSMutableDictionary object in order to hold the multiple services. The NSMutableDictionary key could be the name that the service is published under, as the name needs to be unique.

Finally, we defined two methods: one to publish our service with a specified service type and port, and the other to stop publishing our service.

2. Now, let's build the BonjourPublishServices implementation file:

```
#import "BonjourPublishServices.h"

@implementation BonjourPublishServices
```

```
-(void)startServiceOfType:(NSString *)type andPort:(int)port {
   self.status = BONJOURPUBLISHSTOPPED;
   self.service = [[NSNetService alloc] initWithDomain:@""
   type:type name:@"" port:port];
   if (self.service) {
     [self.service setDelegate:self];
     [self.service publish];
   }
   else {
     [[NSNotificationCenter defaultCenter]
   postNotificationName:BONJOURNOTIFICATIONSTOP object:nil];
   }
}
```

The `startServiceOfType:andPort:` method is used to publish our service, and it accepts two parameters. These parameters are as follows:

- ❑ `type`: This is a service type. The service type is an `NSString` object, which represents both the application layer protocol (HTTP, FTP, and so on) and the transport protocol (TCP or UDP) in a specific format that looks like `_{protocol}._{transport}`. As an example, if we were to publish an SFTP service using TCP, the service type would be `_SFTP._tcp`.

- ❑ `port`: This is a service type that represents the port number to which the service we are publishing is bound. This number can range from 0 to 65535.

We begin the `startServiceOfType:andPort:` method by creating an instance of the `NSNetService` class using the `initWithDomain:type:name:port:` constructor. This constructor takes four arguments, which are stated as follows:

- ❑ `Domain`: This argument is used to specify the domain in which our service has to be registered. To specify the default domain, pass `@""`. We will want to use the default domain unless there is a specific reason for not using it.

- ❑ `type`: This is the service type that we pass into our method and has been described previously.

- ❑ `name`: This argument is used to specify the name that is used to advertise the service. If we pass `@""`, `NSNetService` will advertise the service under the device's name. As mentioned earlier, unless we specifically disable service renaming, the service could be renamed if there is a conflict on the local network.

- ❑ `port`: This is an argument that the service is bound to.

If we receive a valid `NSNetService` object (not nil), we set the delegate to our current object, and then call the `publish` method in order to publish the service. If we want to disable the renaming of the service, we would use the `publishWithOptions:` method and set the `NSNetServiceNoAutoRename` flag.

3. Let's create the `stopService` method:

```
-(void)stopService {
  [self.service stop];
  [[NSNotificationCenter defaultCenter]
    postNotificationName:BONJOURNOTIFICATIONSTOP
    object:nil];
}
```

The `stopService` method simply calls the `stop` method of the `NSNetService` object. Then, we have to send out a notification that the service has stopped.

4. We now need to create the four delegate methods for our `NSNetService` instance. We will start with the `netServiceWillPublish:` method:

```
-(void)netServiceWillPublish:(NSNetService *)sender {
  self.status = BONJOURPUBLISHSTOPPED;
}
```

The `netServiceWillPublish:` method is called prior to the service being published through Bonjour. In our example, we set the `status` property to `stop`. This method can be used to verify whether the service we are advertising is actually running prior to publishing it through Bonjour.

5. Now, we are going to create the `netServiceDidPublish:` delegate method:

```
-(void)netServiceDidPublish:(NSNetService *)sender {
  self.status = BONJOURPUBLISHSTARTED;
  self.publishedName = sender.name;
  [[NSNotificationCenter defaultCenter]
    postNotificationName:BONJOURNOTIFICATIONSTART
    object:nil];
}
```

The `netServiceDidPublish:` method is called once the service has been successfully published. In this method, we set the `publishedName` property to the actual name that the service was published under, and the `status` property to `start` in order to show that the service is published through Bonjour. We then send a notification that the service has been published.

6. We will now create the `netService:didNotPublish:` delegate method:

```
-(void)netService:(NSNetService *)sender
didNotPublish:(NSDictionary *)errorDict {

  self.status = BONJOURPUBLISHSTOPPED;
  [[NSNotificationCenter defaultCenter]
    postNotificationName:BONJOURNOTIFICATIONSTOP
    object:nil];

}
```

The `netService:didNotPublish:` method is called when there is an issue in publishing the service. The `errorDict` dictionary will contain the errors.

7. The last delegate method is the `netServiceDidStop:` method:

```
-(void)netServiceDidStop:(NSNetService *)sender {
    self.status = BONJOURPUBLISHSTOPPED;
    [[NSNotificationCenter defaultCenter]
        postNotificationName:BONJOURNOTIFICATIONSTOP
        object:nil];
}
```

The `netServiceDidStop:` method is called when the service is stopped.

8. To publish a service with the `BonjourPublishServices` class, we use the `startServiceOfType:andPort:` method as shown in the following lines of code:

```
pubService = [[BonjourPublishServices alloc] init]
[pubService startServiceOfType:@"_message._tcp."
    andPort:9711];
```

9. To stop the publication of a service, we would call the `stopService` method as shown in the following line of code:

```
[pubService stopService];
```

The downloadable code for this chapter contains a project that publishes a service using the `BonjourPublishServices` class but does not actually listen for any requests on the socket.

How it works...

To publish a service, we perform the following steps:

1. Initialize the `NSNetService` instance with the `name`, `type`, `Domain`, and `port` arguments.
2. Assign a delegate to the `NSNetService` instance.
3. Publish the `NSNetService` instance with the `publish` method.

Discovering a Bonjour service

In this recipe, we will use the `NSNetServiceBrowser` class to look for our published service.

The `NSNetServiceBrowser` class is used to find the services that are published by `NSNetService`. Once we initialize the `NSNetServiceBrowser` object, we need to assign a delegate, and then we can begin browsing for services. Taking into account the possibility of delays in receiving responses from the services and also because services can come online or go offline at any time, the `NSNetServiceBrowser` object performs the service discovery asynchronously. The `NSNetServiceBrowser` class relies on the delegate methods to handle the notifications of the services coming online or going offline.

Getting ready

This recipe is compatible with both iOS and OS X. No extra frameworks or libraries are required.

How to do it...

In this recipe, we will create a `BonjourBrowserService` class that will have all the code and callback methods required to discover services:

1. We will begin by creating our `BonjourBrowserService` header file:

```
#import <Foundation/Foundation.h>
typedef NS_ENUM(NSUInteger, BonjourBrowserStatus) {
    BONJOURBROWSERSTOPPED,
    BONJOURBROWSERSEARCHING
};
#define BONJOURBROWSERNOTIFICATION @"bonjourBrowserChange"
@interface BonjourBrowserService : NSObject<NSNetServiceBrowserDel
egate>

@property int status;
@property (strong, nonatomic) NSNetServiceBrowser *serviceBrowser;
@property (strong, nonatomic) NSMutableArray *services;

- (void)startBrowsingForType:(NSString *)type;
- (void)stopBrowsing;

@end
```

We begin the `BonjourBrowserService` header file by defining an `enum` that will be used to define the state of the browser. We then define a constant (`BONJOURBROWSERNOTIFICATION`), which is the name of the notification that the `BonjourBrowserService` header file uses to notify the listening objects that the state of the browser has changed.

We define three properties: a `status` property that will hold the current status of our browser, a `serviceBrowser` property that contains the instance of our `NSNetServiceBrowser` class, and an `NSMutableArray` property that will contain a list of all the active services that our browser has found.

Finally, we define two methods: one to start the browser (`startBrowsingForType:`) and the other to stop our browser (`stopBrowsing`).

2. Now, let's take a look at the implementation file for the `BonjourBrowserService` class:

```
#import "BonjourBrowserService.h"

@implementation BonjourBrowserService

-(id)init {
  self = [super init];
  if (self) {
    self.services = [[NSMutableArray alloc] init];
    self.status = BONJOURBROWSERSTOPPED;
  }
  return self;
}
```

We begin the `BonjourBrowserService` class by creating a default constructor that initiates the `services` property and sets the `status` property to BONJOURBROWSERSTOPPED in order to indicate that the browser is not active.

3. Let's create the `startBrowsingForType:` method:

```
-(void)startBrowsingForType:(NSString *)type {
    self.serviceBrowser = [[NSNetServiceBrowser alloc] init];
    [self.serviceBrowser setDelegate:self];
    [self.serviceBrowser searchForServicesOfType:type
inDomain:@""];
    self.status = BONJOURBROWSERSEARCHING;
}
```

The `startBrowsingForType:` method begins by initiating the `NSNetServiceBrowser` object. We then set the delegate for the `NSNetServiceBrowser` class to the current object as we will be implementing the delegate methods within this class. Finally, we call the `searchForServicesOfType:inDomain:` method to search for the service type defined within the local domain.

4. Let's create the `stopBrowsing` method to stop our browser:

```
-(void)stopBrowsing {
   [self.serviceBrowser stop];
   [self.services removeAllObjects];
}
```

The `stopBrowsing` method stops the `NSNetServiceBrowser` class from running and removes all of the `NSNetService` objects from the `services` property. If our application wants to retain the list of services after the `NSNetServiceBrowser` object has stopped searching, we can keep the `NSNetService` objects, but this information will become out of date very quickly.

5. The next five methods are the `NSNetServiceBrowser` delegate methods. These methods will be called at various times in the `NSNetServiceBrowser` object's life cycle. We will start with the `netServiceBrowserWillSearch:` method:

```
-(void)netServiceBrowserWillSearch:(NSNetServiceBrowser *)
aNetServiceBrowser {
   self.status = BONJOURBROWSERSEARCHING;
   [self changeNotification];
}
```

The `netServiceBrowserWillSearch:` method is called prior to the `NSNetServiceBrowser` object starting the search.

6. Let's create the `netServiceBrowserDidStopSearch:` delegate method:

```
-(void)netServiceBrowserDidStopSearch:(NSNetServiceBrowser *)
aNetServiceBrowser {
   self.status = BONJOURBROWSERSTOPPED;
   [self changeNotification];
}
```

The `netServiceBrowserDidStopSearch:` method is called when the `NSNetServiceBrowser` object has stopped searching.

7. Now let's create the `netServiceBrowser:didNotSearch:` method:

```
-(void)netServiceBrowser:(NSNetServiceBrowser *)aNetServiceBrowser
didNotSearch:(NSDictionary *)errorDict {
   self.status = BONJOURBROWSERSTOPPED;
   [self changeNotification];
}
```

The `netServiceBrowser:didNotSearch:` method is called if an error occurs while searching for services. The `errorDict` dictionary will contain all the errors.

8. Now, let's look at the `netServiceBrowser:didFindService:moreComing:` method:

```
-(void)netServiceBrowser:(NSNetServiceBrowser *)aNetServiceBrowser
didFindService:(NSNetService *)aNetService moreComing:(BOOL)
moreComing {
    [self.services addObject:aNetService];
    if (!moreComing)
    [self changeNotification];
}
```

The `netServiceBrowser:didFindService:moreComing:` method is called each time the browser finds a new service. The `moreComing` variable indicates whether the browser has found additional services that it will be sending notifications for. Even if `moreComing` is `false`, we could still receive additional `netServiceBrowser:didFind:moreComing:` calls as additional services are found. The `moreComing` flag only indicates if the browser is currently aware of additional services.

In this method, we add the `NSNetService` object to our `NSMutableArray` service. We then send out a change notification only if we know that there are no additional services coming in. If there are 20 services queued up in the browser, we do not want to update our user interface 20 times; instead, we will wait until we have all of the services identified, and then send the change notification to update our user interface.

9. Next, we look at the `netServiceBrowser:didRemoveService:moreComing:` method:

```
-(void)netServiceBrowser:(NSNetServiceBrowser *)aNetServiceBrowser
didRemoveService:(NSNetService *)aNetService moreComing:(BOOL)
moreComing {
    [self.services removeObject:aNetService];
    if (!moreComing)
    [self changeNotification];
}
```

The `netServiceBrowser:didRemoveService:moreComing:` method is called each time a service disappears from the network. This occurs if the service is no longer being published and does not indicate that the service itself is down.

In this method, we remove the service from the `services` property, and then send out a change notification only if there are no additional services that need to be removed.

10. Finally, we look at the `changeNotification` method:

```
-(void)changeNotification {
  [[NSNotificationCenter defaultCenter]
    postNotificationName:BONJOURBROWSERNOTIFICATION
    object:nil];
}
```

The `changeNotification` method sends a notification to any listening object that something has changed within our browser service, that is, a service was added, a service was removed, the browser stopped, or the browser started. It is up to the listening code to determine what changed and what to do with it.

How it works...

To discover published services using the `NSNetServiceBrowser` class, perform the following steps:

1. Initiate an `NSNetServiceBrowser` object.
2. Set a delegate to receive notifications from the `NSNetServiceBrowser` object.
3. Set the service type and domain to browse.
4. Respond to messages sent to the `NSNetServiceBrowser` delegate.

Resolving a Bonjour service

Now that we are able to publish and find the services, we need to be able to resolve the service so that we can connect to it. By resolving the service, we mean that we need to get the information required to establish a network connection with the actual service. This information will be the port number and either the hostname or the IP address information to connect to.

If you are going to save the connection information to connect at a later stage, you will want to save the hostname and port combination. If you are going to connect right away, you can get the `sockaddr` structure from the `NSNetService` object and use this to connect. It is recommended that you do not store the address information for future connections because the IP address can change, especially on a network that uses DHCH.

For the example code, we will be using the `sockaddr` structure to connect because it fits nicely in our BSD and CFNetwork examples. We will also show you how to pull out the hostname and port number of the `NSNetService` object.

As the service may not resolve instantaneously, `NSNetService` resolves the service asynchronously and will call one of the delegate methods depending on whether it was able to resolve the service or not.

Getting ready

This recipe is compatible with both iOS and OS X. No extra frameworks or libraries are required.

How to do it...

Let's create a `BonjourResolverService` class to resolve our service:

1. We will begin by looking at the `BonjourResolverService` header file:

    ```
    #import <Foundation/Foundation.h>

    #define BONJOURRESOLVERNOTIFICATION @"resolverComplete"

    @interface BonjourResolverService : NSObject
    <NSNetServiceDelegate>

    -(void)resolveService:(NSNetService *)service;
    @end
    ```

    We begin the header file by defining one constant. This constant (`BONJOURRESOLVERNOTIFICATION`) is the name of the notification that we will send once the service has been resolved. If there is an issue in resolving the service, we will send the same notification, but the object returned with the notification will be nil.

    We also define one method for our `BonjourResolverService` class: the `resolveService:` method. We will send the `NSNetService` class which we wish to resolve to the `resolveService:` method.

2. Let's look at the implementation file for the `BonjourResolverService` class. We will begin by looking at the `resolveService:` method:

    ```
    #import "BonjourResolverService.h"

    @implementation BonjourResolverService

    -(void)resolveService:(NSNetService *)service {
      [service setDelegate:self];
      [service resolveWithTimeout:5.0];
    }
    ```

    The `resolveService:` method takes the `NSNetService` object, sets the delegate to the current object, and then calls the `resolveWithTimeout:` method to resolve our service. Timeout is the number of seconds for which we have to wait for the service to resolve before it gives up.

3. We now need to create the two delegate methods that will be called by the `NSNetService` instance as the service gets resolved. The first method that we will look at is the `netServiceDidResolveAddress:` method:

```
-(void)netServiceDidResolveAddress:(NSNetService *)sender {
  NSArray *addresses = sender.addresses;
// Use hostname and port combination if you are saving the
connection information
//   NSString *hostname = sender.hostName;
//     int port = sender.port;
  [[NSNotificationCenter defaultCenter]
    postNotificationName:BONJOURRESOLVERNOTIFICATION
    object:addresses];
}
```

The `netServiceDidResolveAddress:` method will be called if the service was successfully resolved. We can use the `addresses` property of the `NSNetService` object if we are looking for an array of the `sockaddr` structures. If we want to store the connection information for later use, we will use the `hostName` and `port` properties to retrieve the hostname and port information from the service.

We will then send the notification that the service was resolved with the `addresses` object, which contains the `sockaddr` structures. If we were returning the hostname and port number, we would want to create an `NSDictionary` object that will contain the hostname / port combination.

4. Now, let's create the `netService:didNotResolve:` delegate method:

```
-(void)netService:(NSNetService *)sender
didNotResolve:(NSDictionary *)errorDict {
    [[NSNotificationCenter defaultCenter] postNotificationName:BON
JOURRESOLVERNOTIFICATION object:nil];
}
```

The `netService:didNotResolve:` method is called if we are unable to resolve the service information within the timeout. If this happens, we still send a notification but the object returned is nil.

How it works...

To resolve the connection information of the `NSNetService` object, we will perform the following steps:

1. Set the delegate of the `NSNetService` object.

2. Call the `resolveWithTimeout:` method.

3. Then respond to messages sent by the `NSNetService` instance to its delegate.

Creating an echo server that uses Bonjour to advertise the service

Now that we know how to publish, find, and resolve a service, let's put it all together with an actual service to connect to. In this recipe, we will take the echo server that we created in *Chapter 2, Apple Low-level Networking*, and add the code to publish the service with Bonjour.

The downloadable code for this chapter contains an iOS application that uses both the CFSocketServer class (from *Chapter 2, Apple Low-level Networking*) and the BonjourPublishServices class (from this chapter). The application, once the user clicks on the **Start** button, will attempt to publish the service; however, the echo server will start when the application first starts up. Keep in mind that publishing the service and implementing the service are two separate processes and do not actually depend on each other. When the application first starts up, the screen looks like the following screenshot:

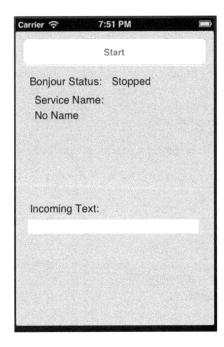

The **Bonjour Status** label shows that the service has stopped and does not have a service name. When the user clicks on the **Start** button, the application attempts to publish the service, and if successful, the screen will look like the following screenshot:

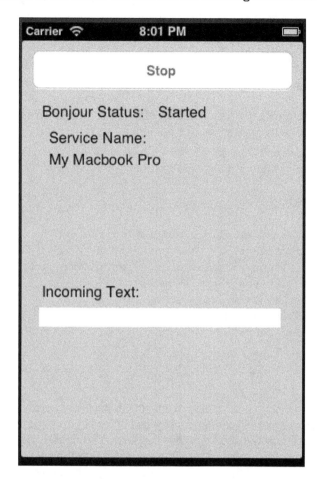

Note that the **Bonjour Status** label now shows that the service has started, and the service name it is published under is **My Macbook Pro**. Once a client connects to the service and sends some text, the **Incoming Text** line will show what the client has sent.

There are no modifications to the CFSocketServer or BonjourPublishServer classes, so we will not be going into the details of these classes in this recipe. Instead, we will show you how to use them together to create an echo server and then publish information about the server. Therefore, we will be looking at the code for the view controller of the BonjourEchoServer sample project included in the downloadable code for this chapter.

Getting ready

The view controller that we are working with is for iOS; however, the code required to publish the service is compatible with both iOS and OS X. No extra frameworks or libraries are required.

How to do it...

Let's look at the view controller code:

1. We begin by creating the header file for our view controller. This is the view controller that will manage the screen we saw earlier:

```
#import <UIKit/UIKit.h>
#import "BonjourPublishServices.h"

#define PORT 2007

@interface ViewController : UIViewController{
  UILabel *echoText;
  IBOutlet UILabel *statusLabel, *serviceNameLabel;
  IBOutlet UIButton *serviceButton;
  BonjourPublishServices *pubService;
  bool serviceStarted;
  CFSocketRef sRef;
}

@end
```

We begin by defining three `UILabel` objects that will be tied to our user interface. The `echoText` label will change as new text comes in from the client. The `statusLabel` label will show whether the service is published by Bonjour or not. The `serviceNameLabel` label will contain the name that the service is published under, or will show no name if the service is not currently published.

Next, we define the `UIButton` that will be used to start or stop the publication of the service. The label on this button will change depending on whether it can be used to start or stop the publication.

The `BonjourPublishServices pubService` object is used to start/stop the publication of our service. `CFSocketRef sRef` will be used to identify our socket that the echo server is using. Finally, the `serviceStarted` boolean will be true if the service has started, or false if it has not.

2. Now, let's look at the implementation of our view controller. We start off with the `viewDidLoad` method, so we can set up our notification listeners and also start the echo server itself. One thing to note here is that the echo server will start on startup, but the service will not be published until the user clicks on the button to publish the service. This is to demonstrate that these are two separate processes and do not rely on each other, but it is advisable to verify that the server is running prior to publishing it. It is recommended that when the server stops, we also stop publishing it through Bonjour

```
-  (void)viewDidLoad
{
   [super viewDidLoad];
   [[NSNotificationCenter defaultCenter] addObserver:self
      selector:@selector(newTextRecieved:) name:@"posttext"
      object:nil ] ;
   [[NSNotificationCenter defaultCenter] addObserver:self
      selector:@selector(bonjourStarted:)
      name:BONJOURNOTIFICATIONSTART object:nil ] ;
   [[NSNotificationCenter defaultCenter] addObserver:self
      selector:@selector(bonjourStopped:)
      name:BONJOURNOTIFICATIONSTOP object:nil ] ;
   pubService = [[BonjourPublishServices alloc] init];
   serviceStarted = NO;

   [NSThread detachNewThreadSelector:@selector(threadStart)
      toTarget:self withObject:nil];
}
```

After the view loads, we set up three notification listeners. These listeners listen for new text being received, as well as for the start/stop of the service being published.

After we set up our notification listeners, we initialize the `BonjourPublishServices` object that we will use to publish the service. We also set the `serviceStarted` boolean to `false`, indicating that we have not published our service. Finally, we create a new thread that will start up our echo server. The new thread will execute the `threadStart` method.

3. Let's look at the `threadStart` method:

```
-(void)threadStart {
   CFSocketServer *cf = [[CFSocketServer alloc]
      initOnPort:2007];

   if (cf.errorCode != NOERROR) {
      NSString *str = [NSString stringWithFormat:@"Error
         starting server.  Error code: %d",cf.errorCode];
```

```
    [self
      performSelectorOnMainThread:@selector(setLabelText:)
      withObject:str waitUntilDone:NO ];
  }
}
```

The `threadStart` method is called when we want to start the echo server. We use the `initOnPort:` constructor of the `CFSocketServer` class to start the server.

If there is an error in starting the echo server, the error message will be displayed within the `echoText` label of `UILabel`.

4. Now, let's look at the `setLabelText:` method:

```
-(void) setLabelText:(NSString *)str {
  [echoText setText:str];
}
```

The `setLabelText:` method sets the text for the `echoText` label to the text that was passed to it.

5. When a user clicks on the button named **serviceButton**, it calls the `registerService:` method. Let's take a look at this method:

```
-(IBAction) registerService:(id) sender {
  if (!serviceStarted){
    [pubService startServiceOfType:@"_echo._tcp."
      andPort:PORT];
  } else {
    [pubService stopService];
  }

}
```

The `registerService:` method checks whether the service is currently published. If the service has not been published, it calls the `startServiceOfType:andPort:` method of the `pubService` object of the `BonjourPublishServices` class to start the service. We set the `type` argument to `_echo._tcp.` to signify that this is an echo server running over TCP. We also set the `port` argument to 2007. If the service has already started, we call the `stopService` method of the `pubService` object of `BonjourPublishServices`.

6. Finally, we need to set up the three methods: `bonjourStarted:`, `bonjourStopped:`, and `newTextReceived:`, which our notification listeners will call, as follows:

```
-(void)bonjourStarted:(NSNotification *)notification {
  serviceNameLabel.text = pubService.publishedName;
  statusLabel.text = @"Started";
```

```
    serviceStarted = YES;
    serviceButton.titleLabel.text = @"Stop";
}


-(void)bonjourStopped:(NSNotification *)notification {
    serviceNameLabel.text = @"";
    statusLabel.text = @"Stopped";
    serviceStarted = NO;
    serviceButton.titleLabel.text = @"Start";
}
```

The `bonjourStarted:` and `bonjourStopped:` methods are called when the publication of our service is started or stopped, respectively. These two methods update the labels to let the user know whether the service is published or not.

The `newTextReceived:` method is called when the echo server receives new text from the client.

```
-(void)newTextRecieved:(NSNotification *)notification {
    [self
      performSelectorOnMainThread:@selector(setLabelText:)
      withObject:[notification object] waitUntilDone:NO ];
}
```

Here, we echo the text to the screen so that the user can see the incoming text.

How it works...

The key thing to be kept in mind is that the publication of the service and the service itself are totally independent of each other. It is up to the developer to make sure that the service he/she is publishing is actually running.

In our example, we start the echo server after the application has started. If there is an error in starting the echo server, an error is displayed.

When the user clicks on the **Start** button to start the service, we call the `startServiceOfType:andPort:` method of our `BonjourPublishServices` class. This method will attempt to publish the service.

After the service is published, we rely on our notification methods to handle the events. The users can enable/disable the publication of the service by clicking on the start/stop button.

Creating an echo client that uses Bonjour to discover the service

In the previous recipe, we used the CFSocketServer and BonjourPublishServices classes to create an echo server and to publish it. In this recipe, we will be using CFSocketClient, BonjourBrowserService, and BonjourResolverService to find the echo server and to connect to it.

The downloadable code for this chapter contains a BonjourEchoClient project that will search for servers published by the BonjourEchoServer project, which was covered in the *Creating an echo server that uses Bonjour to advertise the service* recipe, and then we will send a text string to the server. The server should respond back with the same string that we sent.

If the client is unable to find any published echo servers, the app would look like the following screenshot:

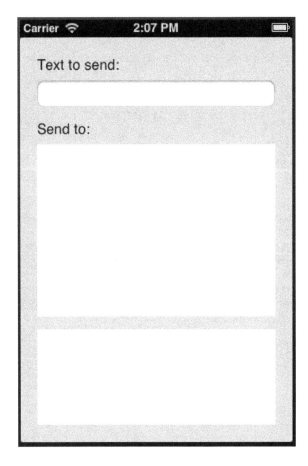

Since our client is set up to continuously pool, once a server is published, the client will detect it and list the server in the **Send to** box. The screen will look like the following screenshot:

Once a server is detected, we can then type something in the **Text to send** box, and then select the server to send the text. Once the server echoes back the response, the client will display what was sent and received in the bottom box.

For this recipe, we will be using the `CFSocketClient` class that we created in *Chapter 2, Apple Low-level Networking*, as well as the `BonjourBrowserService` and `BonjourResolverService` classes that we created earlier in this chapter.

Unlike the Bonjour echo server where we used the classes as they were originally written, we did make one modification to the `CFSocketClient` class. In the original `CFSocketClient` class, the `initWithAddress:andPort:` constructor creates the `sockaddr` structure for us using the address and port number parameters. The `BonjourResolverService` class returns an array of `sockaddr` structures, so it seems counterproductive to pull the address and port information out of the `sockaddr` structure just to rebuild it later. Hence, we add a `initWithSockAddr:` constructor to the `CFSocketClient` class.

This recipe is compatible with both iOS and OS X. No extra frameworks or libraries are required.

How to do it...

Let's create the Bonjour client application:

1. Following is the code for the `initWithSockAddr:` constructor, which we are adding to the `CFSocketClient` class:

```
-(id)initWithSockAddr:(struct sockaddr)sockaddr {
  self.sockfd = CFSocketCreate(NULL, AF_INET, SOCK_STREAM,
    IPPROTO_TCP,0, NULL,NULL);
  if (self.sockfd == NULL)
    errorcde = SOCKETERROR;
  else {
    [self logSockAddr:&sockaddr];
    CFDataRef connectAddr = CFDataCreate(NULL, (unsigned
      char *)&sockaddr, sizeof(sockaddr));
    if (connectAddr == NULL)
      errorcde = CONNECTERROR;
    else {
      CFSocketConnectToAddress(self.sockfd, connectAddr,
        30);
    }
  }
  return self;
}
```

We begin the `initWithSockAddr:` constructor by creating a `CFSocket` instance using the `CFSocketCreate()` function. The `CFSocketCreate()` function accepts several parameters in the following order:

- ❏ `CFAllocatorRef allocator`: This allocator is used to allocate memory for the new object. Generally, this is set to `NULL` or `kCFAllocatorDefault` in order to use the current default.

- ❏ `SInt32 protocolFamily`: This is the protocol family for the socket. In our example, we are using `AF_INET`, but we could also use `AF_INET6` if we wanted to use IPv6.

- ❏ `SInt32 socketType`: This is the socket type for the socket. In our example, we use `SOCK_STREAM` to create a socket stream (TCP). If we wanted to use UDP, we would set it to `SOCK_DGRAM`.

- ❏ `SINT32 protocol`: This is the protocol that we use. In our example, we set it to `IPPROTO_TCP`, but it could also be `IPPROTO_UDP`.

- ❏ `CFOptionFlags callBackTypes`: This is the callback type which is a bitwise OR combination of socket activities that should cause a callback to be called. Following are the callback types:

    - ❏ `kCFSocketNoCallBack`
    - ❏ `kCFSocketReadCallBack`
    - ❏ `kCFSocketAcceptCallBack`
    - ❏ `kCFSocketDataCallBack`
    - ❏ `kCFSocketConnectCallBack`
    - ❏ `kCFSocketWriteCallBack`

- ❏ `CFSocketCallBack callout`: This is a C function to be called when a callback type is triggered.

- ❏ `CFSocketContext *context`: This is a structure holding contextual information for the `CFSocket` instance. In our example, we set it to `NULL`.

The `sockaddr` structure will need to be converted to `CFData` in order for it to be used by the `CFSocketConnectToAddress()` function. This is done with the `CFDataCreate()` function, which returns `CFDataRef`. The `CFSocketConnectToAddress()` function is called to open up a connection to the remote server.

2. Now, let's start creating the view controller for our `BonjourEchoClient` project. Like the `BonjourEchoServer` project in this chapter, this is what we will be focusing on to show you how Bonjour works with the echo client. We start by looking at the view controller header file:

```
#import <UIKit/UIKit.h>
#import "BonjourBrowserService.h"
#import "BonjourResolverService.h"

@interface ViewController : UIViewController {
    IBOutlet UITextField *textToSend;
    IBOutlet UITextView *resultsView;
    IBOutlet UITableView *tableView;

    BonjourBrowserService *browser;
    BonjourResolverService *resolver;
}

@end
```

We begin by defining the `UITextField`, `UITextView`, and `UITableView` instances that we use in our user interface. We then define the `BonjourBrowserService` and the `BonjourResolverService` objects that we will be using.

3. Now, let's look at the implementation of our view controller:

```
- (void)viewDidLoad
{
  super viewDidLoad];
  [[NSNotificationCenter defaultCenter] addObserver:self
    selector:@selector(bonjourBrowserNotification:)
    name:BONJOURBROWSERNOTIFICATION object:nil ] ;
  [[NSNotificationCenter defaultCenter] addObserver:self
    selector:@selector(bonjourResolverNotification:)
    name:BONJOURRESOLVERNOTIFICATION object:nil ] ;

  browser = [[BonjourBrowserService alloc] init];
  resolver = [[BonjourResolverService alloc] init];
  [browser startBrowsingForType:@"_echo._tcp."];
}
```

We start off with the `viewDidLoad` method so that we can set up our notification listeners and also initiate the `BonjourBrowserService` and the `BonjourResolverService` objects. We then call the `startBrowsingForType:` method of the `BonjourBrowserService` class. This method will start browsing for published servers with the `_echo._tcp.` service type. This is the service type that we defined in the `BonjourEchoServer` project.

4. Let's look at the `bonjourBrowserNotification:` method:

```
-(void)bonjourBrowserNotification:(NSNotification
  *)notification {
  [tableView reloadData];
}
```

When we receive a notification that something has changed with our `BonjourBrowserService` object, the `bonjourBrowserNotification:` method is called. This includes the instances of when a new service is found, a server is removed, or the browser has stopped. When any of these events happen, we would want to reload our table view to update the list of services that our browser knows about.

5. We now need to implement our `UITableView` delegate methods that will be used by the table view:

```
- (CGFloat)tableView:(UITableView *)tableView
  heightForRowAtIndexPath:(NSIndexPath *)indexPath
{
  return 35;
}
```

The `tableView:heightForRowAtIndexPath:` method just tells the table view about the height of the row.

```
- (NSInteger)tableView:(UITableView *)tableView
  numberOfRowsInSection:(NSInteger)section {
  return [browser.services count];
}
```

The `tableView numberOfRowsInSection:` method tells the table view how many rows are needed. For this method, we return the number of objects in the `service` property of `BonjourBrowserService`. If you recall, the `service` property contains the list of services that the browser has found.

```
- (UITableViewCell *)tableView:(UITableView *)tableView
  cellForRowAtIndexPath:(NSIndexPath *)indexPath {

  static NSString *CellIdentifier = @"Cell";

  UITableViewCell *cell = [tableView
    dequeueReusableCellWithIdentifier:CellIdentifier];
  if (cell == nil) {
    cell = [[[UITableViewCell alloc]
      initWithStyle:UITableViewCellStyleDefault
      reuseIdentifier:CellIdentifier] autorelease];
  }

  NSNetService *service = [browser.services
    objectAtIndex:indexPath.row];
  cell.textLabel.text = service.name;
  cell.textLabel.font = [UIFont systemFontOfSize:14];
  return cell;
}
```

The `tableView cellForRowAtIndexPath:` method returns the cell for the table view and the index specified. The import part of this method is where we get the `NSNetService` object from the `services` array. We get the service name from the `NSNetService` object to display in our table view.

```
- (void)tableView:(UITableView *)tableView
  didSelectRowAtIndexPath:(NSIndexPath *)indexPath {
  [self.view endEditing:YES];
  NSNetService *service = [browser.services
    objectAtIndex:indexPath.row];
  [resolver resolveService:service];
}
```

The `tableView didSelectRowAtIndexPath:` method is called if we select one of the rows in the table view. We get the `NSNetService` object from the `service` array and pass it to our `BonjourResolverService` object.

6. Once the `BonjourResolverService` class has resolved the `NSNetService` object, it sends back a notification, which is handled by our `bonjourResolverNotification:` method:

```
- (void)bonjourResolverNotification:(NSNotification
  *)notification {
  NSArray *addresses = (NSArray *)notification.object;
  bool sent = NO;
  if (addresses != nil) {
    NSMutableString *results = [NSMutableString
      stringWithFormat:@"sent: %@\n", textToSend.text];
    for (NSData *data in addresses) {
      struct sockaddr *addr = (struct sockaddr *)[data
        bytes];
      if (!sent && addr->sa_family == AF_INET) {
        NSString *str = textToSend.text;
        CFSocketClient *cf = [[CFSocketClient alloc]
          initWithSockAddr:*addr];
        if (cf.errorCode == NOERROR) {
          NSString *recv = [cf writtenToSocket:cf.sockfd
            withChar:str];
          [results appendFormat:@"received: %@", recv];
          resultsView.text = results;
          sent = YES;
          textToSend.text = @"";
        } else {
          NSLog(@"%@", [NSString stringWithFormat:@"Error
            code %d recieved.  Server was not started",
            cf.errorCode]);
        }
      }
    }
  }
}
```

We begin the `bonjourResolverNotification:` method by retrieving the `addresses` array from the `notification` object and verifying that the array is not nil. If it is nil, this means that there was an issue in resolving `NSNetService`. We also set `sent` to `NO` to indicate that we have not sent the message to the server yet. As a service may have multiple valid addresses, we want to make sure that we only send it once.

We then start looping through the `addresses` array to get the individual `sockaddr` address structure. For each `sockaddr` structure, we look to see whether the family of address is IPv4, and whether we have sent the message yet. If we match these criteria, we will send the message to the address.

To send the message, we attempt to create an instance of the `CFSocketClient` class using the `sockaddr` structure. If the creation of the `CFSocketClient` class was successful, we call the `writtenToSocket:withChars:` method to send the message to the server. The `writtenToSocket:withChars:` method returns the server response if the message was successfully sent. We then append the message that was received to our `results` string and update our user interface.

How it works...

When the application first starts, we initiate our `BonjourBrowserService` object to begin searching for published services with the `_echo._tcp.` service type. As we continuously listen for published services, you will see them being added or removed from the table view as the servers are started and stopped.

Once a service has been found, the user can then send a message to it by typing a message in the **Text to Echo** box and selecting the server we wish to send it to.

When the user selects the server to which the message has to be sent, the first thing that we need to do is to retrieve the `NSNetService` object from the list of services. Once we have the `NSNetService` object, we then need to resolve it using our `BonjourResolverService` object.

The resolver service returns an array of `sockaddr` structures, which are the addresses of the server. Once we have the address information, we use our `CFSocketClient` class to write the message to the server and get the response. Finally, we update the user interface and wait for the next request.

7
AFNetworking 2.0 Library

In this chapter, we will cover:

- ▸ Checking the network connection type and changes
- ▸ Creating a web client using AFHTTPSessionManager
- ▸ Creating a custom response serializer
- ▸ Using the UIImageView+AFNetworking category
- ▸ Downloading files with a progress bar

Introduction

AFNetworking is an amazing network library for iOS and OS X and is incredibly easy to use. It is also very lightweight, modular, and superfast. You can download the AFNetworking library and sample code from the AFNetworking website at `https://github.com/AFNetworking/AFNetworking`.

In November 2013, the AFNetworking framework was updated to Version 2.0. This was a major update and drastically changed the way we used the library within our applications. This chapter will only cover Version 2.0 of the AFNetworking library.

For this chapter, we will be focusing on `AFHTTPSessionManager` whose class hierarchy goes back up to the `NSURLSession` class; therefore, the code in this chapter requires a minimum iOS version of 7.0 or a minimum Mac OS X version of 10.9. If your app targets iOS 6.0 or Mac OS X 10.8, you will want to use `AFHTTPRequestOperationManager` instead of `AFHTTPSessionManager`. For this chapter, we really needed to choose one of the two methods to focus on, and `AFHTTPSessionManager` has been chosen as the preferred method.

AFNetworking does require **Automatic Reference Counting** (**ARC**), so you will need to enable ARC support in your application prior to adding AFNetworking to your project. AFNetworking is distributed under a license that allows us to freely distribute our apps. The licensing terms are as follows:

> *Copyright (c) 2013 AFNetworking (http://afnetworking.com/)*
>
> *Permission is hereby granted, free of charge, to any person obtaining a copy of this software and associated documentation files (the "Software"), to deal in the Software without restriction, including without limitation the rights to use, copy, modify, merge, publish, distribute, sublicense, and/or sell copies of the Software, and to permit persons to whom the Software is furnished to do so, subject to the following conditions:*
>
> *The above copyright notice and this permission notice shall be included in all copies or substantial portions of the Software.*
>
> *THE SOFTWARE IS PROVIDED "AS IS", WITHOUT WARRANTY OF ANY KIND, EXPRESS OR IMPLIED, INCLUDING BUT NOT LIMITED TO THE WARRANTIES OF MERCHANTABILITY, FITNESS FOR A PARTICULAR PURPOSE AND NONINFRINGEMENT. IN NO EVENT SHALL THE AUTHORS OR COPYRIGHT HOLDERS BE LIABLE FOR ANY CLAIM, DAMAGES OR OTHER LIABILITY, WHETHER IN AN ACTION OF CONTRACT, TORT OR OTHERWISE, ARISING FROM, OUT OF OR IN CONNECTION WITH THE SOFTWARE OR THE USE OR OTHER DEALINGS IN THE SOFTWARE.*

Before you begin any recipe in this chapter, you will need to download the AFNetworking library at `https://github.com/AFNetworking/AFNetworking`. The class files in the AFNetworking library are divided into two directories. These directories are as follows:

- `AFNetworking`: This contains all of the networking, serialization, and session classes
- `UIKit+AFNetworking`: This contains all of the category classes that add functionality to the various views

Once you have the library, add the required classes to your project.

Checking the network connection type and changes

AFNetworking comes with the `AFNetworkReachabilityManager` class that makes it very easy to detect the network connection type of the device our application is running on and also notifies us if the connection type changes. This can come in handy if we are creating an application that is heavily reliant on the Internet or has large downloads/uploads that we want to run only when connected to Wi-Fi.

Getting ready

You will need to download and add AFNetworking to your project.

How to do it...

Let's create our reachability client by using the following code:

```
AFNetworkReachabilityManager *reachability =
[AFNetworkReachabilityManager sharedManager];

[reachability
  setReachabilityStatusChangeBlock:^(AFNetworkReachabilityStatus
    status) {
        switch (status) {
            case AFNetworkReachabilityStatusReachableViaWWAN:
                NSLog(@"----Connection WWAN");
                break;
            case AFNetworkReachabilityStatusReachableViaWiFi:
                NSLog(@"----WIFI");
                break;
            case AFNetworkReachabilityStatusNotReachable:
                NSLog(@"----Not Reachable");
                break;
            default:
                break;
        }
    }];
```

Since the AFNetworkReachabilityManager class implements the singleton design pattern, we begin by referencing the AFNetworkReachabilityManager instance using the sharedManager method. We then use the setReachabilityStatusChangeBlock: method to set a block of code to call whenever the network status changes. That's it! AFNetworking makes it that easy to monitor for any network status changes.

The sample code simply logs the network connection type. Normally, we would put some logic for each case type, but for our simple example, logging the connection type is enough.

The AFNetworkReachabilityManager class has some other useful methods and properties as well. These are as follows:

▶ managerForDomain: This method allows us to specify a specific domain that needs to be monitored

▶ networkReachabilityStatus: This property returns the current reachability status

- ▶ `reachable`: This property returns a `BOOL` variable, specifying whether the network is available or not

- ▶ `reachableViaWWAN`: This property returns a `BOOL` variable, specifying whether the network is available through WWAN

- ▶ `reachableViaWiFi`: This property returns a `BOOL` variable, specifying if the network is available through Wi-Fi

How it works...

Since `AFNetworkReachabilityManager` implements the singleton design pattern, we used the `shardManager` method to obtain the `AFNetworkReachabilityManager` instance. We then used the `setReachabilityStatusChangeBlock:` method to set up the block of code that will be called whenever the status of our network connection changes.

Creating a web client using AFHTTPSessionManager

In this recipe, we will be subclassing `AFHTTPSessionManger` to create a class that can be used to access the iTunes Search API. This class will be reliant on Apple's `NSURLSessionConfiguration` and `NSURLSessionDataTask` classes to implement the network functionality. Therefore, the minimum system requirements for this recipe will be iOS 7 or Mac OS X 10.9.

The `AFHTTPSessionManager` class is a subclass of `AFURLSessionManager` that contains methods for making standard HTTP requests, such as `GET`, `POST`, and `DELETE`. When we set the `baseURL` property, these HTTP requests will be made using relative paths. In this recipe, we will be setting the `baseURL` property to `https://itunes.apple.com/`; therefore, all HTTP requests will be made to `https://itunes.apple.com/` with any additional path elements appended at the end.

Getting ready

You will need to download and add AFNetworking to your project. This recipe requires a minimum iOS version of 7.0 or a minimum Mac OS X version of 10.9 to run.

How to do it...

Let's create the `ITunesClient` class. This class will be used to retrieve album information from the iTunes Search API.

Creating the ITunesClient header file

The ITunesClient is a subclass of AFHTTPSessionManager and is defined as follows:

```
#import "AFHTTPSessionManager.h"

@interface ITunesClient : AFHTTPSessionManager

+ (ITunesClient *)sharedClient;
- (NSURLSessionDataTask *)searchType:(NSString *)type
  withTerm:(NSString *)term completion:( void (^)(NSDictionary
    *results, NSError *error) )completion;


@end
```

Within the header file, we are defining two methods. The ITunesClient class will implement the singleton design pattern, so we will use the static sharedClient method to reference the ITunesClient instance. We will then use the searchType:withTerm:completion: method to search the iTunes library.

Creating the sharedClient method

The sharedClient method will be used to reference the ITunesClient instance:

```
+ (ITunesClient *)sharedClient {
    static ITunesClient *sharedClient = nil;
    static dispatch_once_t onceToken;
    dispatch_once(&onceToken, ^{
        NSURL *baseURL = [NSURL
            URLWithString:@"https://itunes.apple.com/"];

        NSURLSessionConfiguration *config =
            [NSURLSessionConfiguration defaultSessionConfiguration];

        sharedClient = [[ITunesClient alloc]
            initWithBaseURL:baseURL sessionConfiguration:config];
        sharedClient.responseSerializer =
            [AFJSONResponseSerializer serializer];
    });
    return sharedClient;
}
```

Within the sharedClient method, we define a static variable called sharedClient that is initialized once and only once. We ensure it is initialized only once by using the dispatch_once method from **Grand Central Dispatch** (**GCD**). This is the recommended way for implementing the singleton design pattern within Objective-C.

Within the `dispatch_once` block, we define a `baseURL` variable and set it to `https://itunes.apple.com`. This is not the full URL to the iTunes Search API but is the base URL for iTunes. We will add the rest of the URL when we call the `searchType:withTerm:completion:failure:` method. We then create `NSURLSessionConfiguratin` using `defaultSessionConfiguration`. We could customize the `NSURLSessionConfiguration`, but for this example we will simply take the defaults.

We now initiate the shared `ITunesClient` by calling the `initWithBaseURL:sesionConfiguration:` constructor. Once the `sharedClient` is initiated, we set a `responseSerializer` (we will be discussing response serializer in the *Creating a custom response serializer* recipe of this chapter). For our example, we will use the standard `AFJSONResponseSerializer` that comes with the AFNetworking library since the iTunes Search API response, by default, is in the JSON format. The response serializer will be used to parse the response.

Creating the searchType:withTerm:completion: method

The `searchType:withTerm:completion:` method is used to make a search request to the iTunes Search API in the following manner:

```objc
- (NSURLSessionDataTask *)searchType:(NSString *)type
  withTerm:(NSString *)term completion:( void (^)(NSDictionary
    *results,NSError *error) )completion {

    NSDictionary *params = [[NSDictionary alloc]
      initWithObjectsAndKeys:type,@"entity",term,@"term", nil];

    NSURLSessionDataTask *task = [self GET:@"/search"
      parameters:params success:^(NSURLSessionDataTask *task, id
        responseObject) {

            NSHTTPURLResponse *httpResponse = (NSHTTPURLResponse
              *)task.response;
            if (httpResponse.statusCode == 200) {
                dispatch_async(dispatch_get_main_queue(), ^{
                    completion(responseObject, nil);
                });
            } else {
                dispatch_async(dispatch_get_main_queue(), ^{
                    completion(nil, nil);
                });
            }

        } failure:^(NSURLSessionDataTask *task, NSError *error) {
            dispatch_async(dispatch_get_main_queue(), ^{
```

```
            completion(nil, error);
        });
    }];
    return task;
}
```

We use the `type` parameter to specify the type of search (album, music, software, and so on), and the `term` parameter is the search term. We begin this method by creating a `NSDictionary` object that contains the search term and type. The search type is set with a key of entity and the search term is set with a key of term. This `NSDictionary` will be used as the parameter for our HTTP request.

We then call the `GET:parameters:success:failure:` method that is defined in the `AFHTTPSessionManager` super class. This method makes an HTTP `GET` request to a URL that is built with the base URL, the path defined in the `GET` method, and the parameters passed in. If we pass in a type of `Album` and a term of `Jimmy+Buffett`, the iTunes API will return a list of albums by the artist Jimmy Buffett. If you would like to learn more about the iTunes Search API, you can find more information at `http://www.apple.com/itunes/affiliates/resources/documentation/itunes-store-web-service-search-api.html`.

The HTTP `POST` request is made the same way as the `GET` request in our example. All we need to do is replace the `GET:parameters:success:failure:` method with the `POST:parameters:success:failure:` method. The `POST` request puts the parameters in the request body, while the `GET` request puts the parameters in the URL.

In the `GET:parameters:success:failure:` method, we pass two blocks of code. The success block is called if the request is successful. Keep in mind that a successful call occurs when we receive a valid HTTP response back from the server. This does not mean that the request itself was successful, so, within the success block, we verify that our response code is `200`, which signifies that the call itself was successful. If the response code is `200`, we return our `responseObject` to our completion block. If the response code was not `200`, we return `nil` to our completion block.

Prior to our success block being called, `AFHTTPSessionManager` passes the response to a response serializer. If you recall from the `sharedClient` method, we defined the response serializer for this class to be `AFJSONResponseSerializer`, which parses a JSON response and returns an `NSDictionary` object that contains the results.

AFNetworking contains several standard response serializers that we can use, including `AFJSONResponseSerializer`, `AFXMLResponseSerializer`, `AFXMLDocumentResponseSerializer`, `AFPropertyListResponseSerializer`, and `AFImageResponseSerializer`. In the *Creating a custom response serializer* recipe of this chapter, we will learn how to subclass a response serializer to customize how it parses the response.

Using the ITunesClient class

The following code shows the use of `ITunesClient` with the `sharedClient` method:

```
NSString *type=@"album";
NSString *term=@"jimmy+buffett";

ITunesClient *itunesClient = [ITunesClient sharedClient];
[itunesClient searchType:type withTerm:term
  completion:^(NSDictionary *results, NSError *error) {
          if (results) {
                  NSLog(@"%@",results);
      } else {

                  NSLog(@"ERROR: %@", error);

          }
      }];
```

To use the `ITunesClient` class, we begin by referencing the `ITunesClient` instance by using the `sharedClient` method. We then call the `searchType:withTerm:completion:` method to perform the search. In this simple example, if the results are not `nil` (no errors), we log the results, otherwise we log the error from the response. By creating a client class, such as `ITunesClient`, it makes it easy to call the web API from anywhere in our code.

How it works...

In this recipe, we created the `ITunesClient` by subclassing the `AFHTTPSessionManager` class. This class implements the singleton design pattern; therefore, we started off by creating a static `sharedClient` method that is used to reference the instance. Within the `sharedClient` method, we defined the base URL that our client will be connecting to, the `NSURLSessionConfiguration` for the client, and the response serializer to be used for serializing the response that is returned.

We then created the `searchType:withTerm:completion:` method to call the iTunes Search API. This method accepts the following three parameters:

- ▶ `type`: This denotes the type of search to be performed
- ▶ `term`: This indicates the term to be searched
- ▶ `completion`: This represents the block of code that is to be performed once the search is complete

If we were creating a client class for a web API that required more than two or three parameters, we would want to create a `NSDictionary` object with the parameters needed for our HTTP request rather than passing the individual parameters into this method.

Within the `searchType:withTerm:completion:` method, we called the
`AFHTTPSessionManager` class' `GET:parameters:success:failure:` method to
perform the actual `GET` request. If we received a valid HTTP response from the web service,
AFNetworking would call the response serializer defined in our `sharedClient` method to
serialize the response and then pass the response to the success block of code. If we did not
receive a valid HTTP response, the failure block would be called.

Creating a custom response serializer

In the *Creating a web client using AFHTTPSessionManager* recipe of this chapter, we used
`AFJSONResponseSerializer`, which comes with AFNetworking, to serialize the response
that is returned from the iTunes Search API. The standard AFNetworking response serializers
work well for simple responses, but what if we want to create a custom serializer that would
parse the response for us rather than just send back an `NSDictionary` object? We can
subclass any of the response serializers provided by AFNetworking to accomplish that.

In this recipe, we will be subclassing `AFJSONResponseSerializer` so that our
`ITunesClient` class returns an `NSArray` object that contains an array of objects that in
turn contains the information from the iTunes Search API response.

Getting ready

You will need to download and add the AFNetworking to your project. You should also
complete the *Creating a web client using AFHTTPSessionManager* recipe of this chapter
since we will be elaborating on it further in this recipe.

How to do it...

Let's start by creating an `AlbumInformaiton` class.

Creating the AlbumInformation header file

The `AlbumInformation` class will be used to store information about the individual albums
returned from our iTunes Search in the following manner:

```
#import <Foundation/Foundation.h>

@interface AlbumInformation : NSObject

@property (strong, nonatomic) NSString *artistName, *albumName,
  *imgUrl, *trackCount;

-(instancetype)initWithDictionary:(NSDictionary *)dict;

@end
```

In the header file, we define four properties to store the artist name, album name, image URL, and the number of tracks in the album. There is a lot more information returned in the iTunes Search API, but for our simple example, we will pull out just these four items. If you are interested in learning more about the iTunes Search API and the data returned, you can refer to Apple's API page at http://www.apple.com/itunes/affiliates/resources/documentation/itunes-store-web-service-search-api.html.

We also define a single constructor that accepts an NSDictionary object as its only parameter. This NSDictionary object will contain the information returned from the iTunes Search API and parsed by AFJSONResponseParser.

Creating the AlbumInformation implementation file

Now, let's look at the implementation file for our AlbumInformation class:

```
#import "AlbumInformation.h"

@implementation AlbumInformation

-(instancetype)initWithDictionary:(NSDictionary *)dict {
    if (self = [super init])
    {
        self.artistName = [dict objectForKey:@"artistName"];
        self.albumName = [dict
          objectForKey:@"collectionCensoredName"];
        self.imgUrl = [dict objectForKey:@"artworkUrl100"];
        self.trackCount = [dict objectForKey:@"trackCount"];
    }
    return self;
}

@end
```

The only method that is implemented here is our custom constructor. This constructor parses the NSDictionary object and pulls out the information for our four properties.

Creating the ITunesResponseSerializer header file

Now, let's create our custom response serializer. The ITunesResponseSerializer header file looks as follows:

```
#import "AFURLResponseSerialization.h"
#import "AlbumInformation.h"

@interface ITunesResponseSerializer :AFJSONResponseSerializer

@end
```

We know by looking at the iTunes Search API that the default return type is JSON; therefore, our ITunesReponseSerializer class is going to subclass the AFJSONResponseSerializer class because it already contains the JSON parser. Essentially, we do not want to rewrite the JSON parser; we just want to parse the results from the JSON parser and return only the information that we need in an array of the AlbumInformation classes.

Our header file contains two imports: the AlbumInformation header file, which we created in step one, and the AFURLResponseSerialization header file. The AFURLResponseSerialization header file contains the header information for all of AFNetworking's built-in response serializers; therefore, anytime we use one of these, we will need to import this header file.

Creating the ITunesResponseSerializer implementation file

We will be overriding the resonseObjectFromResponse:data:error: method from the AFJSONResponseserializer method in the following manner:

```
- (id) responseObjectForResponse: (NSURLResponse *) response
  data: (NSData *) data error: (NSError *__autoreleasing *) error
{
    NSMutableArray *retArray = [[NSMutableArray alloc] init];
    NSDictionary *json = [super responseObjectForResponse:response
      data:data error:error];
    NSArray *results = [json objectForKey:@"results"];
    for (NSDictionary *result in results) {
        [retArray addObject:[[AlbumInformation alloc]
initWithDictionary:result]];
    }
    return retArray;
}
```

This method is responsible for parsing our response. Within our responseObjectForResp onse:data:error: method, we call the AFJSONResponseSerializer class' response ObjectForResponse:data:error: method to do the initial parsing of the JSON response and to return an NSDictionary object that contains the results.

We can then extract the results from the NSDictionary object and create AlbumInformation objects for each of the albums returned from the iTunes Search API. We then put the AlbumInformation objects in an NSArray object that is returned.

The responseObjectForResponse:data:error: method is also good for validating the response to ensure that we received the expected data/format back.

Adding ITunesResponseSerializer to our ITunesClient

Now, let's look at how we would use `ITunesResponseSerializer` with our `ITunesClient`:

```objc
+ (ITunesClient *)sharedClient {
    static ITunesClient *sharedClient = nil;
    static dispatch_once_t onceToken;
    dispatch_once(&onceToken, ^{
        NSURL *baseURL = [NSURL
          URLWithString:@"https://itunes.apple.com/"];

        NSURLSessionConfiguration *config =
          [NSURLSessionConfiguration defaultSessionConfiguration];

        sharedClient = [[ITunesClient alloc]
          initWithBaseURL:baseURL sessionConfiguration:config];
//      sharedClient.responseSerializer =
//          [AFJSONResponseSerializer serializer];
        sharedClient.responseSerializer =
          [ITunesResponseSerializer serializer];
    });

    return sharedClient;
}
```

Originally, the `sharedClient` method set `responseSerializer` to an
`AFJSONResponseSerializer` serializer. To use our new `ITunesResponseSerializer`,
we simply comment out the original line and then set `responseSerializer` to our new
`ITunesResponseSerializer`.

Using the new ITunesClient class

Finally, let's look at how we would use the new `ITunesClient` in our code:

```objc
NSString *type=@"album";
NSString *term=@"jimmy+buffett";
ITunesClient *itunesClient = [ITunesClient sharedClient];
[itunesClient searchType:type withTerm:term
        completion:^(NSArray *results, NSError *error) {
            if (results) {

                for(AlbumInformation *album in results) {
                    NSLog(@"--------Artist Name:  %@",
                      album.artistName);
                    NSLog(@"          Album:  %@", album.albumName);
                    NSLog(@"          img URL:  %@", album.imgUrl);
```

```
        NSLog(@"          Track Count:   %@",
            album.trackCount);
    }

    } else {
        NSLog(@"ERROR: %@", error);
    }
}];
```

This is essentially the same method from the *Creating a web client using AFHTTPSessionManager* recipe of this chapter, except that we are receiving an `NSArray` in the completion block of the `searchType:withTerm:completion:` method rather than an `NSDictionary` object. In this example, we loop through the results and log the information. In the *Using the UIImageView+AFNetworking category* recipe of this chapter, we expand on this recipe to display the information, and the album image, in an `UITableView`.

How it works...

To create our custom response serializer, we subclassed AFNetworking's `AFJSONResponseSerializer` class. We did this so that we could use the existing parser within `AFJSONResponseSerializer` rather than write our own JSON parser. AFNetworking has several built-in response parsers that you can subclass or use as is, like we did in this recipe.

We overrode the `responseObjectForResponse:data:error:` method of the `AFJSONResponseSerializer` class. This is the method that is called by AFNetworking once the response has been received and is ready to be parsed. In this method, we called the `AFJSONResponseSerializer` class' `responseObjectForResponse:data:error:` method to do the initial parsing and to return an `NSDictionary` object. We then wrote our code to extract only the data we were interested in and return the results in an `NSArray` object.

By creating a custom-response serializer, we are able to put the parsing logic in our custom-response serializer rather than having it spread across various places throughout our code.

Using the UIImageView+AFNetworking category

AFNetworking makes downloading images incredibly easy and provides a category for the `UIImageView` class that adds a method to download images asynchronously from the Internet and display them. The method added to the `UIImageView` class is `setImageWithURL:placeholder:`, which places a temporary image in the `UIImageView` class while it downloads the final image asynchronously from the URL provided. As you will see in this recipe, this method is really useful when building a `UITableView`, where each cell contains an image that needs to be downloaded from the Internet.

In the *Creating a web client using AFHTTPSessionManager* recipe, we created our `ITunesClient` class to call the iTunes Search API. Then, in the *Creating a custom response serializer* recipe, we added a custom-response serializer to extract the information that was returned from the iTunesSearch API. In this recipe, we will display this information, including the images, in the `UITableView` class. These images will be loaded on demand using the `setImageWithURL:placeholder:` method from the `UIImageView+AFNetworking` category.

For this recipe, we will be looking strictly at the view controller class that displays the `UITableView`. We will not need to change the code of the `ITunesClient`, `ITunesResponseSerializer`, or `AlbumInformation` classes from the earlier recipes.

Getting ready

You will need to download and add the AFNetworking to your project. You should have also completed the *Creating a web client using AFHTTPSessionManager* and *Creating a custom response serializer* recipes, since we will be building on the code from these two recipes to retrieve our album information from the iTunes Search API.

You will also need to include the `UIImageView+AFNetworking` class from the `UIKit+AFNetworking` directory in your project. The `UIKit+AFNetworking` files are included when you download AFNetworking.

How to do it...

Let's take a look at how we would use the `UIImageView_AFNetworking` category in our project.

Updating the ViewController header file

Let's start by adding a couple of properties in the view controller's header file. These properties are as follows:

```
@property (strong, nonatomic) IBOutlet UITableView *tableView;
@property (strong, nonatomic) NSArray *albums;
```

The `tableView` property will be `UITableView`, which we will be using to display our results, and the `albums` property, which will contain the results of the iTunes Search.

Updating the viewDidLoad method of the ViewController

Now, let's look at the implementation. We start off by updating the `viewDidLoad` method that is called when the view is displayed. Let's look at the following code snippet:

```
- (void)viewDidLoad
{
    [super viewDidLoad];
```

```
        NSString *type=@"album";
        NSString *term=@"jimmy+buffett";
        ITunesClient *itunesClient = [ITunesClient sharedClient];
        [itunesClient searchType:type withTerm:term
            completion:^(NSArray *results, NSError *error) {
                if (results) {
                    self.albums = results;
                    [self.tableView reloadData];
                } else {
                    NSLog(@"ERROR: %@", error);
                }
            }];
    }
```

In the `viewDidLoad` method, we call the `ITunesClient`, just like we did in the *Creating a custom response serializer* recipe. The only difference is that we point the `albums` property to the results returned from `ITunesClient` and then reload the `UITableView` property.

Creating the UITableView delegate methods

We now need to add the delegate methods for our `UITableView` in the following manner:

```
- (NSInteger)tableView:(UITableView *)tableView
  numberOfRowsInSection:(NSInteger)section {
    return [self.albums count];
}


- (CGFloat)tableView:(UITableView *)tableView
  heightForRowAtIndexPath:(NSIndexPath *)indexPath
{
    return 75.0;
}


- (UITableViewCell *)tableView:(UITableView *)lTableView
  cellForRowAtIndexPath:(NSIndexPath *)indexPath {
    static NSString *cellID = @"Cell";
    UITableViewCell *cell = [lTableView
      dequeueReusableCellWithIdentifier:cellID];
    if (!cell) {
        cell = [[UITableViewCell alloc]
          initWithStyle:UITableViewCellStyleSubtitle
            reuseIdentifier:cellID];
    }
    AlbumInformation *album = [self.albums
      objectAtIndex:indexPath.row];
```

```
        cell.textLabel.numberOfLines = 3;
        cell.textLabel.font = [UIFont systemFontOfSize:14];
        cell.textLabel.text = album.albumName;

        cell.detailTextLabel.font = [UIFont boldSystemFontOfSize:16];
        cell.detailTextLabel.text = [NSString
          stringWithFormat:@"Tracks:  %@",album.trackCount];

        NSURL *url = [[NSURL alloc] initWithString:album.imgUrl];
        [cell.imageView setImageWithURL:url placeholderImage:[UIImage
          imageNamed:@"loading"]];
        return cell;
}
```

These three methods are all standard `UITableView` delegate methods. The `tableView:n umbersOfRowsInSection:` method returns the number of albums in our `albums` property. The `tableView:heightForRowAtIndexPath:` method sets the height of rows in our `UITableView`. In the `tableView:cellForRowAtIndexPath:` method, we define the style of the cell as `UITableViewCellStyleSubtitle`, which contains a `titleLabel`, `detailTextLabel`, and an `imageView`.

The `indexPath` parameter that was passed into the `tableView:cellForRowAtInd exPath:` method is used to retrieve the `AlbumInformation` object from our albums `NSArray`. This is the album information that we will be displaying in this cell. We set the cell's `textLabel` to the album's `albumName` property and the cell's `detailTextLable` to the album's `trackCount` property.

Now, we come to the image that we wish to display in the cell. We have the image URL from the search results in our `AlbumInformation` object, so the first thing we need to do is to turn that into an NSURL object using NSURL's `initWithString` constructor. Once we have the NSURL object, we use the `setImageURL:placeholderImage:` method that was added to `UIImageView` by AFNetworking's `UIImageView+AFNetworking` category.

The `setImageURL:placeholderImage:` method loads the `UIImage` specified in the `placeholderImage` parameter into the `UIImageView`. It then asynchronously loads the image specified from the URL, and when the image finishes loading, it replaces the placeholder image with the image from the URL. That is really all there is to loading the `UIImageView` asynchronously and to have a placeholder image displayed while the image is loading.

Another advantage of using the `UIImageView+AFNetworking` category is that it uses `AFImageCache` (a subclass of `NSCache`) internally to optimize performance for scroll views.

How it works...

AFNetworking has a category that adds the `setImageURL:placeholderImage:` method to the `UIImageView` class. This method will display `UIImage` defined by the `placeholderImage` parameter in `UIImageView` and then load the image from the URL asynchronously. Once the image finishes loading the placeholder, the image will be replaced with the image from the URL.

AFNetworking has a `UIButton+AFNetworking` category that has a similar method. This method is known as `setImageForState:withURL:placeholderImage:`. This method functions in the same way as the `UIImageView+AFNetworking` category but loads the image into `UIButton`.

Downloading files with a progress bar

AFNetworking includes a `UIProgressView+AFNetworking` category that makes it easy to add a progress bar to either an upload or download session task. In this recipe, we will create the `NSURLSessionDownloadTask` using AFNetworking and then add a progress bar to show the progress of the download.

Getting ready

You will need to download and add AFNetworking to your project. You will also need to include the `UIProgressView+AFNetworking` class from the `UIKit+AFNetworking` directory into your project. The `UIKit+AFNetworking` files are included when you download AFNetworking.

How to do it...

Let's look at how we would add a progress bar to our projects.

Creating the download task

The download task will simply download a large file from the Internet:

```
NSURLSessionConfiguration *configuration =
  [NSURLSessionConfiguration defaultSessionConfiguration];
    AFURLSessionManager *sessionManager = [[AFURLSessionManager
      alloc] initWithSessionConfiguration:configuration];
    NSURLRequest *request = [NSURLRequest requestWithURL:[NSURL
URLWithString:@"http://ipv4.download.thinkbroadband.com/20MB.zip"]
    ];

    NSURLSessionDownloadTask *task = [sessionManager
      downloadTaskWithRequest:request progress:nil
```

```
        destination:^NSURL *(NSURL *targetPath, NSURLResponse
          *response) {
        NSURL *documentsDirectoryPath = [NSURL
   fileURLWithPath:[NSSearchPathForDirectoriesInDomains(NSDocumentDir
   ectory, NSUserDomainMask, YES) firstObject]];

        return [documentsDirectoryPath
          URLByAppendingPathComponent:@"20MB.zip"];
    } completionHandler:^(NSURLResponse *response, NSURL
      *filePath, NSError *error) {
        NSLog(@"File downloaded to: %@", filePath);

    }];
```

We begin by defining NSURLSessionConfiguration using the default session configuration, which is usually a good place to start. Once we have the default configuration, we can customize it, but for this example we will leave the default as is.

We create an instance of AFURLSessionManager and pass the NSURLSessionConfiguration that we just created. We also send an NSURLRequest with the URL of the file that we wish to download.

Next, we create an instance of the NSURLSessionDownloadTask class by using the AFURLSessionManager class' downloadTaskWithRequest:progress:destination: completionHandler: method. The four parameters for this method are as follows:

► request: This is the NSURLRequest that points to the file we want to download. We set this to the NSURLRequest that we created.

► progress: This is a progress object to monitor the download. We will be using AFNetworking's UIProgessView+AFNetworking category to handle our progress bar, so we will set this to nil in our example.

► destination: This is a block of code to be executed for determining the destination of the file being downloaded. In our example, we are saving the file to the documents directory by the name 20MB.zip.

► completionHandler: This is a block of code to be executed once the download is complete. In our example, we just log the path of the file.

If you run this code, nothing will actually happen because it is waiting for us to call the resume method for the task, but before we do that, we need to add our progressView.

Adding the progressView

Let's add our progress view and resume our download task by using the following code:

```
[self.progressView setProgressWithDownloadProgressOfTask:task
  animated:YES];
[task resume];
```

We assume that we have a property called `progressView` and that it ties back to the progress bar that we are displaying. We use the `setProgressWithDownloadProg ressOfTask:animated:` method, which is added to our `UIProgressView` by the `UIProgressView+AFNetworking` category, to tie our `NSURLSessionDownloadTask` to the progress bar. That is all we need to do; AFNetworking takes care of the rest for us.

We then start the download by calling the `resume` method of the `NSURLSessionDownloadTask`.

How it works...

In this recipe, we used the `AFURLSessionManager` class' `downloadTaskWithRe quest:progress:destination:completionHandler:` method to create the `NSURLSessionDownloadTask`. This task was used to download our file and to save it to the app's documents directory. We then added the download task to `UIProgressView` by using the `setProgressWithDownloadProgressOfTask:animated:` method, which was added to the `UIProgressView` class by the `UIProgressView+AFNetworking` category. Once the progress view was added, we called the `resume` method on `NSURLSessionDownloadTask` to start the download.

If we wished to add a progress view to an upload task, we would follow the same steps as the download task, but we would create `NSURLSessionUploadTask` (instead of `NSURLSessionDownloadTask`) and pass it to the `setProgressWithUploadProgressOf Task:animated:` method.

8
MKNetworkKit

In this chapter, we will cover:

- ▶ Creating and using the MKNetworkKit engine
- ▶ Uploading a file using MKNetworkKit
- ▶ Downloading a file using MKNetworkKit
- ▶ Using the UIImageView+MKNetworkKitAdditions.h category and caching the images
- ▶ Adding a progress bar to upload or download

Introduction

MKNetworkKit is an awesome networking framework written in Objective-C. This framework uses blocks and is ARC-ready. Although you have to write more code with MKNetworkKit over other networking frameworks such as AFNetworking, you gain more control on the working of the framework. You can download the framework from `https://github.com/MugunthKumar/MKNetworkKit`.

The MKNetworkKit framework consists of two main classes and a number of categories. The classes are as follows:

- ▶ `MKNetworkEngine`: `MKNetworkEngine` manages the connections to a host. Some of the items that `MKNetworkEngine` manages are reachability, queues, hostname, and caching. To really take advantage of `MKNetworkEngine` you should subclass it for each unique host that you are connecting to.

- ▶ `MKNetworkOperation`: This is a subclass of `NSOperation`; it wraps both the request and response classes. We can create a `MKNetworkOperation` class for each network operation that our application needs.

To use MKNetworkKit in our projects, we need to add the MKNetworkKit classes and the following Apple frameworks:

- `ImageIO.framework`
- `Security.framework`
- `SystemConfiguration.framework`
- `CFNetwork.framework`

MKNetworkKit can be used for free by attributing the author on the product's about page. If you would prefer not to attribute the author of this framework or if you wish to help support the development, you can purchase licenses on the website.

The license for the code is the same as AFNetworking:

Created by Mugunth Kumar (@mugunthkumar) on 11/11/11.

Copyright (C) 2011-2020 by Steinlogic Consulting and Training Pte Ltd

Permission is hereby granted, free of charge, to any person obtaining a copy of this software and associated documentation files (the "Software"), to deal in the Software without restriction, including without limitation the rights to use, copy, modify, merge, publish, distribute, sublicense, and/or sell copies of the Software, and to permit persons to whom the Software is furnished to do so, subject to the following conditions:

The above copyright notice and this permission notice shall be included in all copies or substantial portions of the Software.

THE SOFTWARE IS PROVIDED "AS IS", WITHOUT WARRANTY OF ANY KIND, EXPRESS OR IMPLIED, INCLUDING BUT NOT LIMITED TO THE WARRANTIES OF MERCHANTABILITY, FITNESS FOR A PARTICULAR PURPOSE AND NONINFRINGEMENT. IN NO EVENT SHALL THE AUTHORS OR COPYRIGHT HOLDERS BE LIABLE FOR ANY CLAIM, DAMAGES OR OTHER LIABILITY, WHETHER IN AN ACTION OF CONTRACT, TORT OR OTHERWISE, ARISING FROM, OUT OF OR IN CONNECTION WITH THE SOFTWARE OR THE USE OR OTHER DEALINGS IN THE SOFTWARE.

Creating and using the MKNetworkKit engine

In this recipe we will be creating a subclass of MKNetworkEngine; this creates an iTunes engine to perform a search using the iTunes Web API. While it is not necessary to create a subclass of MKNetworkEngine for each host that you are connecting to, it is recommended.

There are three main advantages to subclassing MKNetworkEngine. They are as follows:

> ▸ Each subclass of MKNetworkEngine contains its own Reachability object. This Reachability object will notify our class if there are changes in its availability or how we connect to the server.

> ▸ Each subclass also contains its own set of queues for MKNetworkOperation.

> ▸ You can customize an engine to the needs of a specific server.

For best practice, we want to set up a separate MKNetworkEngine subclass for each host that we connect to. As an example, if our application was connecting to Yahoo and iTunes, we would want to have two MKNetworkEngine subclasses; one for Yahoo and one for iTunes. We can set up our own library of engines of those engines that we want to use in multiple applications.

Everything in MKNetworkKit depends on the MKNetworkEngine and the MKNetworkOperation classes, so basic knowledge of how to set them up and use them is essential to understanding the use of the framework.

Getting ready

This recipe is compatible with both iOS and OS X. We need to download the framework from https://github.com/MugunthKumar/MKNetworkKit and add it to our project. Additionally, we will need to add the following four frameworks:

> ▸ ImageIO.framework

> ▸ Security.framework

> ▸ SystemConfiguration.framework

> ▸ CFNetwork.framework

How to do it...

Let's create the ITunesEngine header file.

Creating the ITunesEngine header file

The `ITunesEngine` class is a subclass of `MKNetworkEngine`. It is defined as follows:

```
#import "MKNetworkEngine.h"

#define ITUNESSERVER @"itunes.apple.com"
#define ITUNESSEARCHPATH @"/search"

@interface ITunesEngine : MKNetworkEngine

-(MKNetworkOperation *)searchITunesWithParams:(NSDictionary *)
parameters;
-(MKNetworkOperation *)connectToITunesWithPath:(NSString *)path
andParms:(NSDictionary *)parameters;

@end
```

We begin by defining the following two constants:

- `ITUNESERVER`: This is the hostname that we are connecting to
- `ITUNESSEARCHPATH`: This is the path to the search services

We also define the following two methods:

- `-(MKNetworkOperation *)connectToITunesWithPath:andParms:` This is the generic method that can connect to any service; we need to provide the path to the service and the parameters.

- `-(MKNetworkOperation *)searchITunesWithParams:` This is the method that will call the iTunes search service with the parameters provided. This method will call the preceding generic service and supply the path to the search service. This is a convenience method, so the client does not need to know the path to the service.

Creating the ITunesEngine implementation file

Let's take a look at how we can implement the `ITunesEngine` with the following code:

```
#import "ITunesEngine.h"

@implementation ITunesEngine

-(id)init {
    if (self = [super initWithHostName:ITUNESSERVER]) {
        return self;
    } else {
        return nil;
    }
}
```

We begin by overriding the standard `init` constructor and calling `initWithHostName:` method of the `MKNetworkEngine` class to initiate our engine. This will initiate the engine with the hostname for Apple's iTunes API, and our `MKNetworkOperation` instance will prepend this hostname to all of the requests. We can override this hostname by calling MKNetworkOperation's `initWithHost:` constructor and pass in the name of the host that we wish to connect to.

The requestor could use `initWithHostname:` to set the hostname; however, if we override the `init` method to set it, the client does not need to know the connection information.

Let's look at the `searchITunesWithParams:` method:

```
- (MKNetworkOperation *)searchITunesWithParams:(NSDictionary *)
parameters {
    return [self connectToITunesWithPath:ITUNESSEARCHPATH
andParms:parameters];
}
```

The `searchITunesWithParams:` method is a convenience method that will call the `connectToITunesWithPath:andParams:` method and set the path for the requestor. When we combine this method with the `init` method defined earlier, the requestor does not need to know anything about the connection information for the iTunes Search API. Granted, the requestor needs to know which parameters to set, but at least MKNetworkKit can hide the connection information.

Now let's look at the `connectToITunesWithPath:andParams:` method:

```
- (MKNetworkOperation *)connectToITunesWithPath:(NSString *)path
andParms:(NSDictionary *)parameters {
    MKNetworkOperation *operation = [self operationWithPath:path
params:parameters httpMethod:@"GET" ssl:NO];
    return operation;
}
```

The `connectToITunesWithPath:andParams:` method calls the `operationWithPath:params:httpMethod:ssl:` method of the `MKNetworkEngine` class to create a `MKNetworkOperation` object, which we will then return to the requestor. The `MKNetworkOperation` class is a subclass of `NSOperation` and encapsulates the request and response operations.

Using the ITunesEngine class

Now that we have our `ITunesEngine` class, let's take a look at how we can use it in our code:

```
NSDictionary *parameters = @{@"term":@"jimmy+buffett",@"entity":@"alb
um"};
ITunesEngine itunes = [[ITunesEngine alloc] init];
```

```
    MKNetworkOperation *operation = [itunes searchITunesWithParams:parame
    ters];

    [operation addCompletionHandler:^(MKNetworkOperation
    *completedOperation)
      {
         NSData *responseData = [completedOperation responseData];
         NSError *error;
         NSDictionary *dict = [NSJSONSerialization
    JSONObjectWithData:responseData options:0 error:&error];
         NSArray *results = dict[@"results"];
         UIAlertView *av = [[UIAlertView alloc] initWithTitle:@"Success"
    message:[NSString stringWithFormat:@"Found %d Albums",[results count]]
    delegate:nil cancelButtonTitle:@"OK" otherButtonTitles:nil];
            [av show];
      }errorHandler:^(MKNetworkOperation *errorOp, NSError* error) {

         UIAlertView *av = [[UIAlertView alloc] initWithTitle:@"Network
    Error" message:[NSString stringWithFormat:@"%@",error] delegate:nil
    cancelButtonTitle:@"OK" otherButtonTitles:nil];
            [av show];
    }];
    [itunes enqueueOperation:operation];
```

We begin by creating the parameters that MKNetworkEngine will use to create our request. Since the iTunes Search API uses the HTTP GET method, these parameters will be added to the URL (for example, ?term=jimmy+buffett&entity=album). If we use the HTTP POST method, MKNetworkKit will use these parameters to construct the POST request.

We initiate our ITunesEngine class by using the init constructor that we created. This will initiate the ITunesEngine using itunes.apple.com as the hostname. We do not want to create a new ITunesEngine class for each request that we make to itunes.apple.com. Remember that one of the advantages of subclassing MKNetworkEngine is that each engine has its own set of queues. By creating a global queue for your object or a global application instance (in the application delegate), you can take complete advantage of the queues for multiple network requests.

We then create MKNetworkOperation by using the searchITunesWithParams: method and passing it the parameters that we created. Now that we have an instance of MKNetworkOperation, we can add callbacks such as a completion handler or progress alerts.

In this recipe, we just need to be alerted when a request is completed so that we can process the response or display an error if something goes wrong. To add a completion handler, we need to call the addCompletionHandler:errorHandler: method.

The `CompletionHandler` section is the block of code that is to be run upon the successful completion of our request. It starts off by retrieving the response data that came back using the `responseData` property of the `completedOperation` object. We then use Apple's `NSJSONSerialization` class to parse the JSON object that was returned and write it to an `NSDictionary` object. We then retrieve the `results` array from the `NSDictionary` object and display an `alertView` that shows the number of results we received.

The `ErrorHandler`, which is called if there is an issue with the request, displays an alert with the error.

Finally, we call the `MKNetworkEngine` class's `enqueueOperation:` method to queue up our `Operation` object.

How it works...

We began by creating the `ITunesEngine` instance, which is a subclass of `MKNetworkEngine`. The `ITunesEngine` class contains the connection information for connecting to the iTunes APIs. In this example, we only connected to the iTunes Search API, but we can add additional iTunes APIs to this class if need be. To take complete advantage of the queuing capability of the engine, you need to make it a pseudo singleton and create one instance of your object for your application.

Among other things, the `ITunesEngine` class manages the reachability, queues, and caching of the requests to the host. When we created the `ITunesEngine` class we added two methods to assist in creating `MKNetworkOperation` objects from the engine. The `MKNetworkOperation` class wraps up the individual request/response into one operation.

In our code we initiated the `ITunes` engine with the `init` constructor that we created to set the hostname for the iTunes host, and then created the `MKNetworkOperation` objects with their parameters. Once we had the `MKNetworkOperation` object, we added the completion and error handlers along with the block of code to verify whether the operation was successful or had an error. At this point our operation was set to run, so we added it to the `ITunesEngine` queue by calling the `enqueueOperation:` method.

In the *Using the UIImageView+MKNetworkKitAdditions.h category and caching the images* recipe of this chapter, we will be adding image loading and caching.

Uploading a file using MKNetworkKit

In this recipe we will show you how to use MKNetworkKit to upload a file to a server by attaching it as part of a multipart form `POST` request. Since all of MKNetworkKit's functionality is encapsulated within `MKNetworkEngine` and `MKNetworkOperation`, we need to create an engine for our upload.

We will be using the `addData:forKey:mimeType:filename:` method to upload an image. The `MKNetworkOperation` class also has an `addFile:forKey:mimeType:filename:` method that allows us to attach a file directly.

Getting ready

This recipe is compatible with both iOS and OS X. We need to download the framework from `https://github.com/MugunthKumar/MKNetworkKit` and add it to our project. We also need to add the following four frameworks:

- `ImageIO.framework`
- `Security.framework`
- `SystemConfiguration.framework`
- `CFNetwork.framework`

How to do it...

Let's create the `FileUploadEngine` class.

Creating the FileUploadEngine header file

The `FileUploadEngine` class is a subclass of `MKNetworkEngine`. This class will be used when we want to upload the data to a service. If you walked though the *Creating and using the MKNetworkKit engine* recipe of this chapter, the code to create the engine will look very familiar.

The header file code for the `FileUploadEngine` class is as follows:

```
#import "MKNetworkEngine.h"

#define FILEUPLOADSERVER @"localhost:8080"
#define FILEUPLOADPATH @"/fileupload"

@interface FileUploadEngine : MKNetworkEngine

-(MKNetworkOperation *)postFileToServerWithParameters:(NSDictionary *)
params;
-(MKNetworkOperation *)postFileToServerWithParameters:(NSDictionary *)
params Path:(NSString *)path andSSL:(bool)ssl;

@end
```

We begin by defining the following two constants:

- `FILEUPLOADSERVER`: This is the hostname that we are connecting to
- `FILEUPLOADPATH`: This is the path to the search services

We also define the two methods that follow:

- `postFileToServerWithPath:Parameters:andSSL::` This is the generic method that can connect to any service on the given host. We need to provide the path to the service and the parameters.

- `postFileToServerWithParameters::` This is a method that will call the specific `FILEUPLOADSERVER` with the parameters provided. This method will call the preceding generic service and supply the path to the upload service. This is a convenience method, so the client does not need to know the path to the service.

Creating the FileUploadEngine implementation file

Now let's implement the `FileUploadEngine` class as follows:

```
#import "FileUploadEngine.h"

@implementation FileUploadEngine

-(id)init {
    if (self = [super initWithHostName:FILEUPLOADSERVER]) {
        return self;
    } else {
        return nil;
    }
}
```

We begin by overriding the standard `init` constructor and calling the `MKNetworkEngine` class's `initWithHostName:` method to initiate our engine. This will initiate the engine with the service's hostname. The `MKNetworkOperation` class will prepend this hostname to all of the requests.

The requestor could use the `initWithHostname:` method to set the hostname; however, if we use the new `init` constructor, the client does not need to know what the hostname is.

Let's look at the `postFileToServerWithParameters:` method:

```
-(MKNetworkOperation *)postFileToServerWithParameters:(NSDictionary *)
params {
    return [self postFileToServerWithParameters:params
Path:FILEUPLOADPATH andSSL:NO];
}
```

The `postFileToServerWithParams:` method is a convenience method that will call the `postFileToServerWithPath:andParams:andSSL:` method and set the path for the requestor. When we combine this method with the `init` constructor defined earlier, the requestor method does not need to know any of the connection information for the file upload server. Granted, they do need to know which parameters to set, but MKNetworkKit makes connecting to a service easy.

Now let's look at the `postFileToServerWithParameters:Path:andSSL:` method:

```
- (MKNetworkOperation *)postFileToServerWithParameters:(NSDictionary
*)params Path:(NSString *)path andSSL:(bool)ssl {
    MKNetworkOperation *operation = [self operationWithPath:path
params:params httpMethod:@"POST" ssl:ssl];
    return operation;
}
```

The `postFileToServerWithPath:andParams:` method calls the `MKNetworkEngine` class's `operationWithPath:params:httpMethod:ssl:` method to create a `MKNetworkOperation` object, which we will then return to the requestor. The `MKNetworkOperation` class is a subclass of `NSOperation` and encapsulates the request and response operations.

Using the FileUploadEngine class

Now that we have created the `FileUploadEngine` class, let's look at how we can use it:

```
NSData *imageData = UIImageJPEGRepresentation([UIImage
imageNamed:@"IMG_1168.jpg"], 1.0);

FileUploadEngine *fue = [[FileUploadEngine alloc] init];
MKNetworkOperation *operation = [fue postFileToServerWithParameters:
nil];

[operation addData:imageData forKey:@"image" mimeType:@"image/jpeg"
fileName:@"IMG_1168.jpg"];

[operation addCompletionHandler:^(MKNetworkOperation
*completedOperation)
{
    NSLog(@"Complete");
}errorHandler:^(MKNetworkOperation *errorOp, NSError* error) {

    UIAlertView *av = [[UIAlertView alloc] initWithTitle:@"Error"
message:[NSString stringWithFormat:@"%@",error] delegate:nil
cancelButtonTitle:@"OK" otherButtonTitles:nil];
    [av show];
}];
[fue enqueueOperation:operation];
```

We begin by converting our image to an `NSData` object using the `UIImageJPEGRepresentation` function. This function will read an `UIImage` object and return an `NSData` object representing the image.

We then initiate our `FileUploadEngine` object using the `init` constructor that we created. This will set the hostname of the server for us. We could use MKNetworkOperation's constructor `initWithHostname:` to set the hostname ourselves, if we needed to.

Once we have our `FileUploadEngine` object, we call the `postFileToServerWithParameters:` method to create the `MKNetworkOperation` object. We set the parameters to `nil` because we do not need to add additional parameters in our example here. If we did have additional parameters to set, we could add them.

We then add the `NSData` object to our multipart form-data. To do this we call the `addData:forKey:mimeType:filename:` method of the `MKNetworkOperation` class. That is it; MKNetworkKit takes care of the rest for us.

We add the completion and error handlers to `MKNetworkOperation`. The completion handler just logs that the operation is complete and the error handler displays an alert if we had an issue.

Finally, we call `enqueueOperation:` method of the `MKNetworkEngine` class to queue up our `operation` object.

How it works...

We began by creating the `FileUploadEngine` class that is a subclass of `MKNetworkEngine`. The `FileUploadEngine` class encapsulates the connection information for connecting to the file upload service. To take complete advantage of the queuing capability of the engine, you need to make it a pseudo singleton and create one instance of your object for your application.

In our code we initiated the `FileUploadEngine` class with the `init` constructor that we created to set the hostname and then created the `MKNetworkOperation` class. Once we had `MKNetworkOperation`, we added an `NSData` object to the operation by using the `addData:forKey:mimeType:filename:` method of the `MKNetworkOperation` class. We then added the completion and error handlers to our operation. At that point our operation was set to run, so we added it to the `FileUploadEngine` queue by calling the `enqueueOperation:` method.

In the *Adding a progress bar to upload or download* recipe ahead, we will be adding a progress bar to this operation.

Downloading a file using MKNetworkKit

In the previous recipe, we saw how to upload a file using MKNetworkKit. In this recipe we will be downloading a file from the Internet. Since all of MKNetworkKit's functionality is encapsulated within the `MKNetworkEngine` and `MKNetworkOperation` classes, we need to create an engine first.

We will be using the `downloadFileAtPath:` method of the `MKNetworkOperation` class to download the file at the specified path. We will then add the `addDownloadStream:` callback to our `MKNetworkOperation` object. This callback will write the file to a stream.

While this recipe downloads an image, we can use the same methods to download any type of file.

Getting ready

This recipe is compatible with both iOS and OS X. We need to download the framework from `https://github.com/MugunthKumar/MKNetworkKit` and add it to our project. We also need to add the following four frameworks:

- `ImageIO.framework`
- `Security.framework`
- `SystemConfiguration.framework`
- `CFNetwork.framework`

How to do it...

Let's create the `ImageDownloadEngine` class.

Creating the ImageDownloadEngine header file

The `ImageDownloadEngine` can be used to queue up multiple download requests; it is defined as follows:

```
#import "MKNetworkEngine.h"

#define FILEDOWNLOADSERVER @"a2.mzstatic.com"

@interface ImageDownloadEngine : MKNetworkEngine

-(MKNetworkOperation *)downloadFileAtPath:(NSString *)path;

@end
```

We begin the header file by defining the FILEDOWNLOADSERVER constant to point to the host that contains the files we wish to download. We then define the downloadFileAtPath: method that will create the MKNetworkOperation object.

Creating the ImageDownloadEngine implementation file

Now let's create the implementation file for ImageDownloadEngine as follows:

```
#import "ImageDownloadEngine.h"

@implementation ImageDownloadEngine

-(id)init {
    if (self = [super initWithHostName:FILEDOWNLOADSERVER]) {
        return self;
    } else {
        return nil;
    }
}
```

We begin by overriding the standard init constructor and calling the MKNetworkEngine class's initWithHostName: method to initiate our engine. This will initiate the engine with the service's hostname. The MKNetworkOperation class will prepend this hostname to all of the requests.

The requestor could use the initWithHostname: method to set the hostname; however, if we use the new init constructor, the client does not need to know what the hostname is.

Let's look at the downloadFileAtPath: method:

```
-(MKNetworkOperation *)downloadFileAtPath:(NSString *)path {
    MKNetworkOperation *operation = [self operationWithPath:path
params:nil httpMethod:@"GET" ssl:NO];
    return operation;
}
```

The downloadFileAtPath: method calls the operationWithPath:params: httpMethod:ssl: method to create the MKNetworkOperation class.

Now let's see how we can use this engine to download a file. The following code will use the ImageDownloadEngine class to download a file and save it onto the disk:

```
ImageDownloadEngine ide = [[ImageDownloadEngine alloc] init];
MKNetworkOperation *operation = [ide downloadFileAtPath:@"/us/
r1000/107/Features/22/58/71/dj.xdzqqclr.100x100-75.jpg"];
```

```
    NSArray *paths = NSSearchPathForDirectoriesInDomains(NSDocumentDirect
ory, NSUserDomainMask, YES);
    NSString *documentsDirectory = [paths objectAtIndex:0];
    NSString *appFile = [documentsDirectory stringByAppendingPathCompone
nt:@"jb.jpg"];

    [operation addDownloadStream:[NSOutputStream outputStreamToFileAtPath
:appFile append:YES]];
    [operation addCompletionHandler:^(MKNetworkOperation
*completedOperation)
      {
        NSLog(@"completed");
    }errorHandler:^(MKNetworkOperation *errorOp, NSError* error) {

        UIAlertView *av = [[UIAlertView alloc] initWithTitle:@"Error
Retrieving Weather" message:[NSString stringWithFormat:@"%@",error]
delegate:nil cancelButtonTitle:@"OK" otherButtonTitles:nil];
        [av show];
    }];
    [ide enqueueOperation:operation];
```

We begin by initiating our `ImageDownloadEngine` object using the `init` constructor that we created. This will set the hostname of the server for us. We could use MKNetworkOperation's constructor `initWithHostname:` to set the hostname ourselves, if need be.

We then call the `downloadFileAtPath:` method to create the `MKNetworkOperation` object. We then save the file to the application's document directory by getting the path to the document directory, creating a download stream using the path, and then adding that stream to our `MKNetworkOperation` object. The `MKNetworkOperation` instance will write the file that we are downloading to the stream.

We create the completion and error handlers for our `MKNetworkOperation` object. The completion handler just logs that the operation is complete and the error handler displays an alert if we had an issue.

Finally, we add our `MKNetworkOperation` object to the `ImageDownloadEngine` queue so that it runs.

How it works...

We begin by creating the `ImageDownloadObject` class that is a subclass of `MKNetworkEngine`. The `ImageDownloadEngine` class encapsulates the connection information for connecting to the image we wish to download. To take complete advantage of the queuing capability of the engine, you need to make it a pseudo singleton and create one instance of your object for your application.

In our code we initiated the `ImageDownloadEngine` class with the `init` constructor that we created to set the hostname and then called the `downloadFileAtPath:` method to create an instance of `MKNetworkOperation`. Once we had `MKNetworkOperation`, we added an `NSOutputStream` object to the `MKNetworkOperation` object using the `addDownloadStream:` method. The file was downloaded to this stream. We then added the completion and error handlers to our operation. At that point our operation was set to run, so we added it to the `FileUploadEngine` queue by calling the `enqueueOperation:` method.

In the *Adding a progress bar to upload or download* recipe ahead, we will be adding a progress bar to this operation.

Using the UIImageView+MKNetworkKitAddi tions.h category and caching the images

In this recipe we will expand on the `ITunesEngine` header file created in the *Creating and using the MKNetworkKit engine* recipe of this chapter by adjusting the caching settings of `MKNetworkEngine`. We will also use the `UIImageView+MKNetworkKitAdditions` category to download images and display them once the download is complete.

This recipe will introduce two concepts: the MKNetworkKit caching capability and using the categories that come with MKNetworkKit. We will also get a better understanding of why we subclass `MKNetworkEngine`.

Getting ready

This recipe is compatible with both iOS and OS X. We will need to download the framework from `https://github.com/MugunthKumar/MKNetworkKit` and add it to our project. Additionally, we need to add the following four frameworks:

- `ImageIO.framework`
- `Security.framework`
- `SystemConfiguration.framework`
- `CFNetwork.framework`

How to do it...

We will begin by defining the `ITunesEngine` class, just like we did in the *Creating and using the MKNetworkKit engine* recipe. This class is a subclass of the `MKNetworkEngine` class.

Creating the ITunesEngine header file

The `ITunesEngine` class is a subclass of `MKNetworkEngine`. It is defined as follows:

```
#import "MKNetworkEngine.h"

#define ITUNESSERVER @"itunes.apple.com"
#define ITUNESSEARCHPATH @"/search"

@interface ITunesEngine : MKNetworkEngine

-(MKNetworkOperation *)searchITunesWithParams:(NSDictionary *)
parameters;
-(MKNetworkOperation *)connectToITunesWithPath:(NSString *)path
andParms:(NSDictionary *)parameters;

@end
```

We begin by defining the following two constants:

- ▶ `ITUNESERVER`: This is the hostname that we are connecting to
- ▶ `TUNESSEARCHPATH`: This is the path to the search services

We also define two methods as follows:

- ▶ `connectToITunesWithPath:Params::` This is the generic method that can connect to any service; we need to provide the path to the service and the parameters.
- ▶ `searchITunesWithParams::` This is the method that will call the iTunes search service with the parameters provided. This method will call the preceding generic service and supply the path to the search service. It is a convenience method, so the client does not need to know the path to the service.

Creating the ITunesEngine implementation file

Now let's create the implementation file for `ITunesEngine` as follows:

```
#import "ITunesEngine.h"

@implementation ITunesEngine

-(id)init {
    if (self = [super initWithHostName:ITUNESSERVER]) {
        [self useCache];
        return self;
    } else {
```

```
        return nil;
    }
}
```

We begin by overriding the standard `init` constructor that calls the `MKNetworkEngine` class's `initWithHostName:` method. This will initiate the engine with the hostname for Apple's iTunes API. The `MKNetworkOperation` class will prepend this hostname to all of the requests.

By default, `MKNetworkEngine` does not cache our requests; we enable caching and set up our cache directory by calling the `useCache` method.

The requestor could use `initWithHostname:` method to set the hostname; however, if we override the `init` constructor to set it, the client does not need to know what the hostname is. We also use this constructor to set up our cache.

Let's look at the `searchITunesWithParams:` method:

```
- (MKNetworkOperation *) searchITunesWithParams: (NSDictionary *)
parameters {
    return [self connectToITunesWithPath:ITUNESSEARCHPATH
andParms:parameters];
}
```

The `searchItunesWithParams:` method is a convenience method that will call the `connectToITunesWithPath:andParams:` method and set the path for the requestor. When we combine this method with the `init` method defined earlier, the requestor does not need to know any of the connection information for the iTunes Search API. Granted they do need to know which parameters to set, but they do not need to know anything about the host or path.

Now let's look at the `connectToITunesWithPath:andParams:` method:

```
- (MKNetworkOperation *) connectToITunesWithPath: (NSString *)path
andParms: (NSDictionary *)parameters {
    MKNetworkOperation *operation = [self operationWithPath:path
params:parameters httpMethod:@"GET" ssl:NO];
    return operation;
}
```

The `connectToITunesWithPath:andParams:` method calls the `MKNetworkEngine` class's `operationWithPath:params:httpMethod:ssl:` method to create a `MKNetworkOperation` object, which we will then return to the requestor. The `MKNetworkOperation` class is a subclass of `NSOperation` and encapsulates the request and response operations.

Adjusting the cache settings

In order to adjust the cache settings to meet our needs, we will be overriding two of the `MKNetworkEngine` methods. The first is the `cacheDirectoryName` method that defines the directory our cached images will be saved to, and the second is the `cacheMemoryCost` method that defines how much of the cache will be saved to memory and how much of it will be saved onto the disk:

```
//for image cache
-(NSString *)cacheDirectoryName {
    NSArray *paths = NSSearchPathForDirectoriesInDomains(NSCachesDirec
tory, NSUserDomainMask, YES);
    NSString *documentsDirectory = [paths objectAtIndex:0];
    NSString *cacheDirectoryName = [documentsDirectory stringByAppendi
ngPathComponent:@"Hoffman.Jon.ItunesCache"];
    return cacheDirectoryName;
}
```

The `cacheDirectoryName` method allows us to define the directory that we will use for our image cache. This directory will contain the cache files of everything we download. It is a good idea to create a separate cache directory above the normal application cache so that we can clean it out using the `MKNetworkEngine` class's `emptyCache` method.

Our version of `cacheDirectoryName` retrieves the path to the application's cache directory and then appends a directory name of "`Hoffman.jon.ItunesCache`". If this directory does not exist, `MKNetworkEngine` will create it:

```
-(int)cacheMemoryCost {
    return 0;
}
```

The `cacheMemoryCost` method defines how much cache we wish to keep in memory and how much we want to write onto the disk. The `cacheMemoryCache` method returns an `integer` value. The larger the number, the more MKNetworkKit caches to memory. In our example, we will return zero, which tells MKNetworkKit to cache everything onto the disk. Normally, you would not want to do this because in-memory cache is much quicker, but we want to see the disk cache in action. You can adjust this setting depending on how much memory your application can reserve for the memory cache. If your application sends a `UIApplicationDidReceiveMemoryWarningNotification`, MKNetworkKit will dump the in-memory cache onto the disk.

Using the new ITunesEngine class

Now that we have our cache set up, let's load in some images to see it in action. The sample project for this recipe (and the *Creating and using the MKNetworkKit engine* recipe) displays a list of *Jimmy Buffett* albums in a `UITableView`.

Let's modify the `tableView:cellForRowAtIndexPath:` method to download and display the album cover:

```
- (UITableViewCell *)tableView:(UITableView *)lTableView cellForRowAtI
ndexPath:(NSIndexPath *)indexPath {
    static NSString *cellID = @"Cell";
    UITableViewCell *cell = [lTableView dequeueReusableCellWithIdenti
fier:cellID];
    if (!cell) {
        cell = [[UITableViewCell alloc] initWithStyle:UITableViewCellS
tyleSubtitle reuseIdentifier:cellID];
    }

    NSDictionary *album = [self.albums objectAtIndex:indexPath.row];

    cell.textLabel.numberOfLines = 3;
    cell.textLabel.font = [UIFont systemFontOfSize:14];
    cell.textLabel.text = [album objectForKey:@"collectionName"];

    cell.detailTextLabel.font = [UIFont boldSystemFontOfSize:16];

    cell.detailTextLabel.text = [NSString stringWithFormat:@"Tracks:
%@",[album objectForKey:@"trackCount"]];

    NSURL *url = [[NSURL alloc] initWithString:[album
objectForKey:@"artworkUrl60"]];

    [cell.imageView setImageFromURL:url placeHolderImage:[UIImage
imageNamed:@"loading"] usingEngine:self.itunes animation:NO ];

    return cell;
}
```

We begin by setting up the `UITableViewCell`. We will be using the `UITableViewCellStyleSubtitle` cell style that includes a `UIImageView` to display our album cover.

We then retrieve an `NSDictionary` object that contains the album information for this cell and displays the album title and the number of tracks in the album. Then we retrieve the URL of the album cover image and convert it into an NSURL object.

We use the `setImageFromURL:placeHolderImage:usingEngine:animation:` method that was added to the `UIImageview` class by the `UIImageView+MKNetworkKit Additions` category. This method will load the image from the URL and, while it is loading, put the `placeHolderImage` in place. It will use the queues and cache settings from the provided `MKNetworkEngine` object. In our case we will use the `ITunesEngine` class to load the images. Finally, we can add the animation when the image is displayed.

How it works...

By default, MKNetworkKit does not cache responses. This means that each time you request a file from the Internet, MKNetworkKit will retrieve it. This is usually the behavior we want because when you make a request to a Web API, you expect to get the latest results. `MKNetworkOpertion` also has a method `isCachedResponse` that can be used to check whether the response is a cached response or not.

To enable the cache with MKNetworkKit, the first thing we did was set the cache directory overriding the `MKNetworkEngine` class's `cacheDirectoryName` method. We want to make sure that we create a separate cache directory for each engine's cache so that we can use the `clearCache` method to clear out the cached files only for our engine.

The next thing we did was overrode the `cacheMemoryCost` value to adjust the in-memory cache setting. By default, this method returns `10`; we tell MKNetworkKit to cache the last 10 requests in memory. Depending on the memory footprint of your application, you may adjust this by increasing or decreasing it. Our sample project set the in-memory cost to `0` so that all of the requests were cached onto the disk. We did this so you could see what was cached, but this is probably not what we would do for a production application.

Finally, we called the `MKNetworkEngine` class's `useCache` method to set up the cache directory and enabled caching for this engine. We would only want to enable cache for the engines that specifically need it. It would also be acceptable to have two engines for the same host, one that enables caching and one that doesn't.

Adding a progress bar to upload or download

When we have a large upload or download, we generally want to have a progress indicator that we can show to the users so that they have an idea of how much longer the upload or download will take. The MKNetworkKit makes showing a progress indicator incredibly easy.

In this recipe we will be adding a progress indicator that will show the progress of downloading a large file. We will be using the `onDownloadProgressChanged:` callback of the `MKNetworkOperation` class to track the progress of our download. If we want the progress indicator to work for an upload, we need to use the `onUploadProgressChanged:` callback.

This recipe is compatible with both iOS and OS X. We need to download the framework from `https://github.com/MugunthKumar/MKNetworkKit` and add it to our project. Additionally, we need to add the following four frameworks:

- `ImageIO.framework`
- `Security.framework`
- `SystemConfiguration.framework`
- `CFNetwork.framework`

How to do it...

Let's create the `FileDownloadEngine` header file.

Creating the FileDownloadEngine header file

The header file for the `FileDownloadEngine` looks like this:

```
#import "MKNetworkEngine.h"

#define DOWNLOADHOST @"download.aptana.com"

@interface FileDownloadEngine : MKNetworkEngine

-(MKNetworkOperation *)downloadFileAtURL:(NSString *)urlString
andSSL:(bool)ssl;

@end
```

We begin by defining a constant that will contain the host that we will be connecting to by default. We also define the `downloadFileAtURL:andSSL:` method that returns an instance of the `MKNetworkOperation` class.

Creating the FileDownloadEngine implementation file

Now let's create the implementation file for the `FileDownloadEngine` class:

```
#import "FileDownloadEngine.h"

@implementation FileDownloadEngine

-(id)init {
    if (self = [super initWithHostName:DOWNLOADHOST]) {
```

```
        return self;
    } else {
        return nil;
    }
}
```

We begin by overriding the standard `init` constructor which calls the `MKNetworkEngine` class's `initWithHostName:` method to initiate our object. This will initiate the engine with the hostname defined by the `DOWNLOADHOST` constant. The `MKNetworkOperation` class will prepend this hostname to all of the requests.

We can override this hostname by calling MKNetworkOperation's `initWithHost:` constructor and passing in the name of the host we wish to connect to.

Let's look at the `downloadFileAtURL:andSSL:` method:

```
-(MKNetworkOperation *)downloadFileAtURL:(NSString *)urlString
andSSL:(bool)ssl {
    MKNetworkOperation *operation = [self operationWithPath:urlString
params:nil httpMethod:@"GET" ssl:ssl];
    return operation;
}
```

The `downloadFileAtURL:` method calls the `operationWithPath:params:httpMethod:ssl:` method to create a `MKNetworkOperation` class.

Now let's look at how we can use this engine and add a progress indicator to `MKNetworkOperation`:

```
FileDownloadEngine fde = [[FileDownloadEngine alloc]init];
 MKNetworkOperation *operation = [fde downloadFileAtURL:DOWNLOADPATH
andSSL:NO];

 NSArray *paths = NSSearchPathForDirectoriesInDomains(NSDocumentDirect
ory, NSUserDomainMask, YES);
 NSString *documentsDirectory = [paths objectAtIndex:0];];
 NSString *filePath = [documentsDirectory stringByAppendingPathCompone
nt:@"myFile.dmg"];

 [operation addDownloadStream:[NSOutputStream outputStreamToFileAtPath
:filePath append:YES]];
 [operation onDownloadProgressChanged:^(double progress) {
    progressView.progress = progress;
    progressLabel.text = [NSString stringWithFormat:@"%0.2f",(progre
ss*100)];
 }];
 [fde enqueueOperation:operation];
```

We begin by initiating our `FileDownloadEngine` object by using the custom `init` constructor that we created. Once the object is initiated, we use the `downloadFileAtURL:andSSL:` method to create an instance of the `MKNetworkOperation` class.

We want to save the file to the application's document directory, so we retrieve the path to the documents directory and then append the name of the file to the path. We then create a download stream using the previously created path and add it to our `MKNetworkOperation` object. The MKNetworkKit will write the file that we are downloading to the stream.

The `onDownloadProgressChanged` block is called at various times during the download process. The value of the `double` parameter ranges from 0 to 1 depending on the progress of the download. We have to update `UIProgressView` and `progressLabel` as the download progresses.

The `onUploadProgressChanged:` function operates exactly like the `onDownloadProgressChanged:` function. The only difference is that the `onUploadProgressChanged:` callback monitors uploads while the `onDownloadProgressChanged:` callback monitors downloads.

We finally add the operation to the `FileDownloadEngine` queue by calling the `enqueueOperation:` method. We can add a completion and error handler to notify us when the download or upload is complete, but it is not required as our progress bar will show us when the download is complete.

How it works...

If we want to add a progress indicator to `MKNetworkOperation` we will have to add the `onDownloadProgressChanged:` or `onUploadProgressChanged:` callback. These callbacks are called at various times when a file is being downloaded or uploaded.

The callback has one parameter, `double`. This double ranges from 0 (when nothing has been downloaded) to 1 (when the download is complete). Inside the callback we update our progress indicator using the `double` parameter that is passed in.

Index

N

name argument, service type 202
nameWithSockaddr: method 17, 19
net {net} 156
netService:didNotResolve: method 211
netServiceBrowser:didFindService:
    moreComing: method 208
netServiceBrowser:didNotSearch: method
    207
netServiceBrowser:didRemoveService:
    moreComing: method 208
netServiceBrowserWillSearch: method 207
netServiceDidPublish: method 203
netServiceDidResolveAddress: method 211
netServiceDidStop: method 204
netServiceWillPublish: method 203
network
    about 155
    dst net {net} 155
    net {net} 156
    src net {net} 155
network address information
    retrieving 12-16, 46, 47
network address resolution
    AddrInfo class used 20-22
    AddrInfo header file, creating 17
    AddrInfo implementation file, creating 17-20
    CFNetworkUtilities header file, creating 48
    CFNetworkUtilities implementation file,
        creating 49-55
    performing 16, 48
NetworkAddressStore class 12
network connection type
    checking 228-230
networkConnectionType: method 80
NetworkDetect header file
    about 79
    creating 79
NetworkDetect implementation file
    creating 79, 80
network device information
    retrieving 128-130
networkReachabilityStatus property 229
network status
    checking 78, 79

NetworkDetect header file, creating 79
NetworkDetect implementation file, creating
    79, 80
newDataReceived: method 41
newTextReceived: method 217
NOERROR 23
NS 146
NSData 172
NSData resp object 171, 175
NSDictionary object 233
NSError 172
NSHost class 46
NSHost object 47
NSHTTPURLResponse object 172, 175
NSMutableArray property 206
NSMutableData object 41, 42
NSMutableDictionary key 201
NSMutableDictionary object 201
NSMutableURLRequest object 178
NSNetServiceBrowser class 204, 206, 209
NSNetServiceBrowser object 205-207
NSNetService class 200
NSNetService object 200, 209, 211, 225
NSURLConnection object 178
NSURLSession class 227

O

onDownloadProgressChanged block 269
onUploadProgressChanged: callback 266
onUploadProgressChanged: function 269
OP Code field 143
operationWithPath:params:httpMethod:ssl:
    method 251, 256, 259
Optional Data (payload) 101, 152

P

packet
    about 84
    building 85
    capturing 130-135
    construction 85
    control information (header) 84
    filtering 154, 155, 157
    IP header 86

Thank you for buying
iOS and OS X Network Programming Cookbook

About Packt Publishing

Packt, pronounced 'packed', published its first book "*Mastering phpMyAdmin for Effective MySQL Management*" in April 2004 and subsequently continued to specialize in publishing highly focused books on specific technologies and solutions.

Our books and publications share the experiences of your fellow IT professionals in adapting and customizing today's systems, applications, and frameworks. Our solution based books give you the knowledge and power to customize the software and technologies you're using to get the job done. Packt books are more specific and less general than the IT books you have seen in the past. Our unique business model allows us to bring you more focused information, giving you more of what you need to know, and less of what you don't.

Packt is a modern, yet unique publishing company, which focuses on producing quality, cutting-edge books for communities of developers, administrators, and newbies alike. For more information, please visit our website: www.packtpub.com.

Writing for Packt

We welcome all inquiries from people who are interested in authoring. Book proposals should be sent to author@packtpub.com. If your book idea is still at an early stage and you would like to discuss it first before writing a formal book proposal, contact us; one of our commissioning editors will get in touch with you.

We're not just looking for published authors; if you have strong technical skills but no writing experience, our experienced editors can help you develop a writing career, or simply get some additional reward for your expertise.

iOS Development Using MonoTouch Cookbook

ISBN: 978-1-84969-146-8   Paperback: 384 pages

109 simple but incredibly effective recipies for developing and deploying applications for iOS using C# and .NET

1. Detailed examples covering every aspect of iOS development using MonoTouch and C#/.NET

2. Create fully working MonoTouch projects using step-by-step instructions

3. Recipes for creating iOS applications meeting Apple's guidelines

RubyMotion iOS Development Essentials

ISBN: 978-1-84969-522-0   Paperback: 262 pages

Create apps that utilize iOS device capabilities without learning Objective-C

1. Get your iOS apps ready faster with RubyMotion

2. Use iOS device capabilities such as GPS, camera, multitouch, and many more in your apps

3. Learn how to test your apps and launch them on the AppStore

4. Use Xcode with RubyMotion and extend your RubyMotion apps with Gems

Please check **www.PacktPub.com** for information on our titles

Xcode 4 Cookbook

ISBN: 978-1-84969-334-9   Paperback: 402 pages

Over 100 recipes to build your own fun and exciting iOS applications

1. Learn how to go about developing some simple, yet powerful applications with ease using recipes and example code

2. Teaches how to use the features of iOS 6 to integrate Facebook, Twitter, iCloud, and Airplay into your applications

3. Lots of step-by-step recipe examples with ample screenshots right through to application deployment to the Apple App Store to get you up to speed in no time, with helpful hints along the way

Flash iOS Apps Cookbook

ISBN: 978-1-84969-138-3   Paperback: 420 pages

100 practical recipes for developing iOS apps with Flash Professional and Adobe AIR

1. Build your own apps, port existing projects, and learn the best practices for targeting iOS devices using Flash

2. How to compile a native iOS app directly from Flash and deploy it to the iPhone, iPad or iPod touch

3. Full of practical recipes and step-by-step instructions for developing iOS apps with Flash Professional

Please check **www.PacktPub.com** for information on our titles

www.ingramcontent.com/pod-product-compliance
Lightning Source LLC
LaVergne TN
LVHW062308060326
832902LV00013B/2098